Doctoral Student Skills

Doctoral Student Skills offers a comprehensive overview of the key skills doctoral students need to succeed in their studies and prepare for academic and non-academic jobs. Revealing the often-hidden rules of graduate school success, it guides students through challenges like selecting a research topic, choosing an advisor, preparing for conferences, publishing their work, and entering the job market.

The book begins by explaining how to survey the job market and identify "signifiers" that will signal to future employers the student's suitability for a job. It then guides students to reflect on their own experiences and abilities to identify their areas of comparative advantage. Providing detailed instructions on how to acquire key signifiers – including conference presentations, publications, grants, awards, and teaching experience – the volume prepares students for future professional success, while teaching them how to leverage these activities to enhance their progress in their present studies. The book is designed to be used as a course text or for self-study. Each chapter features reflective exercises that can be used individually or in small groups, along with recommended readings and additional resources to enhance student learning.

Christopher L. Pallas is Associate Professor of Conflict Management at Kennesaw State University, USA. He has been training and mentoring doctoral students in research methods and professional skills for over ten years. He is winner of the European Consortium for Political Research's European Political Science Prize.

Doctoral Student Skills: Using Your Comparative Advantage to Succeed in Grad School and Prepare for the Job Market is an absolute must-read for doctoral students. Not only does it succinctly communicate the essential professional skills doctoral students need in order to be competitive on the job market, the book also lays out an easy-to-follow, thorough plan for students to gain these skills and produce the outputs that signal marketability. From developing a research agenda, to publishing, to attending conferences and securing funding, this book provides doctoral students with a clear roadmap for success.

– Kelly Ann Krawczyk, MPA, PhD, *Associate Professor and PhD Program Director, Auburn University Department of Political Science, USA*

As PhD study and the academic job market have changed, much of the advice to research students has remained the same. This valuable book changes that, providing relevant and practical advice about both completing your doctorate and developing your career beyond your viva.

– Dr. Neil McLean, *Director Academic and Professional Development Division, London School of Economics, UK*

In *Doctoral Student Skills*, Pallas will show you how to develop professional skills for success, understand your job environment to find your comparative advantage, and create a roadmap for an early academic career.

– Helen K. Liu, *Professor of Political Science and The Graduate Institute of Public Affairs, National Taiwan University*

Doctoral Student Skills

Using Your Comparative Advantage to
Succeed in Grad School and Prepare
for the Job Market

CHRISTOPHER L. PALLAS

Routledge
Taylor & Francis Group

NEW YORK AND LONDON

Cover image: Tempura / Getty Images

First published 2023
by Routledge
605 Third Avenue, New York, NY 10158

and by Routledge
4 Park Square, Milton Park, Abingdon, Oxon, OX14 4RN

Routledge is an imprint of the Taylor & Francis Group, an informa business

© 2023 Christopher L. Pallas

Library of Congress Cataloging-in-Publication Data
Names: Pallas, Chris, 1977-author.
Title: Doctoral student skills: using your comparative advantage to succeed in
grad school and prepare for the job market/Christopher L. Pallas.
Description: New York, NY: Routledge, 2022. | Includes bibliographical
references and index.
Identifiers: LCCN 2022003788 (print) | LCCN 2022003789 (ebook) |
ISBN 9781032202426 (paperback) | ISBN 9781032202433 (hardback) |
ISBN 9781003262831 (ebook)
Subjects: LCSH: Doctoral students–Handbooks, manuals, etc. | Doctoral
students–Vocational guidance–Handbooks, manuals, etc. | Universities and
colleges–Graduate work–Handbooks, manuals, etc.
Classification: LCC LB2386 .P35 2022 (print) | LCC LB2386 (ebook) |
DDC 378.2–dc23/eng/20220425
LC record available at https://lccn.loc.gov/2022003788
LC ebook record available at https://lccn.loc.gov/2022003789

ISBN: 978-1-032-20243-3 (hbk)
ISBN: 978-1-032-20242-6 (pbk)
ISBN: 978-1-003-26283-1 (ebk)

DOI: 10.4324/9781003262831

Typeset in Avenir and Dante
by Deanta Global Publishing Services, Chennai, India

Contents

Acknowledgments

I am grateful to the doctoral students at Kennesaw State who participated in my PhD student mentorship group and whose encouragement to write a book along these lines helped launch this project. I am also grateful for the support of Joseph Bock, former Director of Kennesaw State University's School of Conflict Management, Peacebuilding and Development, and of Cortney Stewart, who served as research assistant, sounding board, and preliminary reader for much of this volume. Lastly, I thank my wife and children for their love, patience, and practical support during the writing process.

The Need to Develop Professional Skills

1

The start of a PhD can be overwhelming. The PhD requires a set of skills and a mindset that are different from what most students have needed in their previous academic or professional careers. You have probably discovered this already. Doctoral students are expected to not just learn new material, but also to generate new inquiries that expand human knowledge. Doing this requires generating research questions and coupling them with appropriate research methods to achieve robust answers. Yet at the beginning of your doctoral studies, you may have no idea what a good research question is or what techniques you will need to do your research.

At the same time, you may be hearing fellow students talk about their conference presentations, grant applications, student teaching, and publications. You may not be familiar with what all these things are or how to do them, but you will quickly glean that they are part of your professional development and will impact your marketability for future jobs, whether as an academic or in another research-related field.

You may also be feeling overwhelmed, overworked, and isolated. Especially if you are the first person in your family, community, or circle of friends to attempt a PhD, you may be worried that there is some sort of secret strategy or inside knowledge that allows people to win their advisor's favor and land top professional positions. You may be afflicted by "imposter syndrome" as you compare yourself to your classmates. You may also be struggling to hold together your personal life or manage

DOI: 10.4324/9781003262831-1

family obligations as you wade through your PhD coursework and write your doctoral dissertation or thesis. [1]

In principle, your advisor (i.e., the chair of your PhD committee)[2] will help you navigate writing the dissertation, doing professional development, and perhaps even overcoming your personal challenges, as part of what is called an apprenticeship model of education. In practice, most advisors focus on dissertation completion. Your advisor is short on time, and many figure that writing conference papers, doing student teaching, and managing your schedule are things you can learn on your own. After all, they somehow figured it out themselves when they were students.

Even if your advisor is willing to help, you may not know what help you need to request. Most advisors engage advisees responsively, rather than proactively. The PhD signals an ability to conduct independent research, and you cannot demonstrate that ability if your advisor leads you through the whole process. Self-direction and self-teaching are fundamental skills for future success, and your advisor's benign neglect forces you to learn them. As a result, your advisor meets with you when you request it and discusses the items on your agenda. Most advisors do not reach out to you and say, "Let's have a meeting Thursday and discuss your options for conference presentations."

This book aims to address these shortcomings in the apprenticeship model. It will introduce you to the skills you need to master, but it also goes a good bit further. There are plenty of books available on how to complete your dissertation, and academic advice columns, like those published in the *Chronicle of Higher Education* or *Times Higher Education*, often discuss professional development. What makes this book different is that it does not treat professional development as a series of discrete tasks that exist outside of your dissertation writing. Instead, this book frames professional development and dissertation completion as part of an integrated whole.

The purpose of this book is to help you think about your doctoral studies, particularly the dissertation-writing process, as a preparatory environment for future professional success. To be marketable as a PhD holder, you must acquire key skills (such as the ability to do research), write and defend your dissertation,

---

1 The final output of doctoral study is known as the dissertation in the US and as the thesis in the UK. I completed my doctorate in the UK, but since I am writing from the US, the default term I use in this book is dissertation.

2 Some universities assign students a separate advisor to guide them early in the program, until a chair is chosen. However, I use the terms "advisor" and "chair" interchangeably because the mentorship function of the roles is usually the same and because, once a chair is chosen, the chair typically takes over the advising role.

and develop professional outputs (such as publications) that signal your competency to external audiences. This is true regardless of what you want to do with your PhD. Academia is not the only professional outcome of doctoral study. Obviously, hard science PhDs are employed throughout industry and government, but social science and humanities PhDs also have many options. Numerous jobs at think tanks, government agencies, and nongovernmental organizations (NGOs) require a PhD. Marketability for all these jobs requires some ability to signal key competencies beyond having completed your dissertation.

If you view writing the dissertation and developing marketability as discrete tasks, their demands compete with one another. The result is a zero-sum game: either you apply yourself toward completing the dissertation but find yourself unmarketable because you did not develop professional outputs, or you spend time teaching and publishing but take a very long time to earn your degree.

What this book will teach you to do is integrate these pieces strategically so that progress on your PhD facilitates developing your marketability and the activities you undertake to develop your marketability enhance your PhD. You will do this in two main ways. First, you will identify an area of comparative advantage that grounds your PhD and helps you stand out in the job market. Second, you will plan your professional development activities so that they coincide with related dissertation-writing work and facilitate external feedback on the dissertation itself.

Before digging further into those processes, however, it is important to reflect more on why it is necessary to have a systematic, strategic approach to preparing for the job market. In this chapter, we will begin by discussing what employers are seeking when they hire a PhD and why preparing early is the key to being competitive. We will then reflect on your goals for the PhD and how a lack of tacit knowledge forms a barrier to marketability. Finally, we will discuss in more detail exactly what this book contains and how to use it.

Preparing Early for the Job Market

Holding a PhD is not enough to get you a job. That fact may surprise you and, if so, you are not alone. I have been teaching professional skills to PhD students for a decade and I regularly have students who are shocked and discouraged when they learn about the state of the job market. For years, a shift has been taking place in higher education making the job market for PhD holders more crowded, but knowledge of that shift has not yet filtered down to the general public, including most prospective PhD students. Not so long ago, PhD programs were found mostly at elite institutions, like top national universities in

Europe and Ivy League institutions and flagship state universities in the US. The number of PhD graduates was likewise fairly small (National Center for Science and Engineering Statistics 2019). A PhD in hand, a good dissertation, and perhaps some networking assistance from one's advisors were enough to land a tenure-track position if one wanted an academic career. Similarly, until fairly recently it was rare for practitioner positions to require a research degree. A master's degree or extensive field experience was enough and holding a PhD made someone exceptional. Most people assume that this is still the case.

Unfortunately for you, it is not. The 2018 Survey of Earned Doctorates found that 31% of doctoral graduates in the US had no definitive commitment for employment or postdoctoral study (National Center for Science and Engineering Statistics 2019). PhD programs have proliferated over the last several decades; the number has increased more than 60% since the 1970s (National Center for Science and Engineering Statistics 2019). They are present at more schools, and they have multiplied within schools. Some of these new programs justify their existence by having a narrow and specialized focus, but the job market is not always as specialized as the programs are. You can hold a PhD in Computational and Applied Mathematics, but you will still be competing against the many candidates with PhDs in Computer Science or Math. And you will be competing, especially if you want an academic job: while more and more PhDs are being generated, tenure-track hiring has not kept pace. Particularly in the US, universities are using an increasing number of term-limited and part-time instructors to reduce costs and while managing ever-higher student enrollment (AAUP 2010). Graduates who fail to land tenure-track jobs and take temporary or part-time positions continue to apply and compete for tenure-track positions in future years. Thus, the tenure-track academic job market is marked by anemic demand for new hires and an ever-growing supply of applicants (Huerta n.d.).

The bottom line is that the job market is more competitive than ever. When I look at postings for entry-level academic positions and participate in hiring processes, it is evident that to be considered for many positions, new candidates must now hold achievements that were previously only expected of junior professors with several years of job experience. These include conference presentations, multiple journal articles, and prospects for external funding (Larson 2020). Practitioners face their own expectations. PhD-level posts are often relatively senior. Candidates may be required to have previous professional experience, specific research skills, and an ability to communicate research to policymakers. Overseas positions may also require experience working in a certain geographic region and related language skills.

To be marketable, you must acquire the qualifications necessary to make yourself a successful job candidate while you are still a PhD student. This requires re-envisioning the PhD: moving from seeing it as a process of acquiring a degree to a process of preparing for the job market. In this new vision, preparing for the job market is no longer something you do during the last one or two semesters of your studies; it is something that you do from the first day in your program and that shapes your conduct throughout your time there. Using your whole time of study for job market preparation requires careful planning and an ability to strategically integrate the acquisition of professional "signifiers" – signals to future employers of your qualifications as a job candidate – into the PhD process.

Why Do You Want a PhD?

With that in mind, it is useful to reflect on why you are completing the PhD. A strategic process of professional development begins by outlining clear goals. In spite of the challenges and cautions I have just shared, the start of your PhD program is also a time to dream. Many of your dreams will be tempered by the challenges of the PhD process and the constraints of the job market, but if you do not start out with high hopes and big goals, there is little chance that you will achieve the best possible outcomes. Exercise 1.1 will facilitate the process of outlining your goals.

EXERCISE 1.1: REFLECTING ON CAREER GOALS

Get started in planning your professional development by reflecting on the following questions:

1. Do you have a lifetime career goal, such as a job you hope to hold before retirement?
2. What is the job you hope to hold one year after earning your PhD? Be as specific as possible.
3. What is the job you hope to hold five to ten years after earning your PhD? Again, be as specific as possible.
4. Are there other jobs you would be content with if your preferred jobs were not available? If so, what are they?
5. Looking at your answers for 1–4, what are the characteristics of a job (salary, location, type of work, pace of life, etc.) that would make you content with it?
6. Which characteristics are most important to you? Which are non-negotiable and which are flexible?

The objective of the exercise is to help you reflect on your ambitions, but also on your values. Especially if you are attending a prestigious institution, you can easily get caught up in the idea that teaching at a similarly prestigious, research-focused university is the best possible career option (Cassuto 2011). Indeed, your professors may treat taking a tenure-track position at a less prestigious university or a job outside academia as a kind of career failure. Adopting such an attitude yourself, however, can undermine your job search by limiting the options you consider or by alienating hiring committees who sense your disdain for their institution or organization (Potter 2009; Perlmutter 2012).

Even more importantly, focusing on the wrong goals can undermine your own happiness. For example, if you pursue money or status, you may find yourself with little time to devote to family or other relationships. If you insist on living only in a certain city, you may have to take a job you dislike to achieve your goal. With that in mind, you may want to do the exercise two or three times. In particular, if you get to questions 5 and 6 and the common characteristics of your jobs are prestige, name recognition, or high salary, consider revising your answers to reflect your deeper and more enduring values.

Uncovering Tacit Knowledge

Once you have some idea of where you want to go, you can begin developing a strategy for getting there. However, you may not know what steps are needed to effectively pursue your objectives. This requires learning the many tacit, or unspoken, lessons of doctoral training.

Whether your goal is to become a professor or to work outside of academia, your success as a PhD student and your future marketability as a professional researcher are dependent on a wealth of tacit knowledge (Calarco 2020). Certain skills, tips, and practices are not taught in any regular class, yet they play a key role in determining whether you complete your PhD in a timely fashion and with a quality product, and whether potential employers see you as a good fit for their organization. These include things like how to write a conference paper, publish an academic article, win awards, or obtain grants – key signifiers to prospective employers of your credibility as a researcher. They also include skills like organizing your time, maintaining your motivation, and managing your relationship with your advisor – things that will help you complete your degree and get into the job market.

A few schools (including the LSE, where I studied for my PhD) have classes or workshops where some of these skills are taught to students. More commonly, it is expected that students will learn them from their advisors in the one-on-one mentoring relationship that is at the heart of the PhD. Yet expectation does not always match with reality. The truth is that the quality of advising is very uneven and even the best advisors are busy and short on time (Brabazon 2013). Unless you are coauthoring work with them on one of their projects, they may not have time to read multiple drafts of your first academic article, advise you on journal submission strategies, or preview the PowerPoint deck for your first conference presentation. Not all advisors are able to get deep enough into your personal life to coach you on how to stay motivated or balance your studies with your family commitments. Earning a PhD also requires that the student demonstrate her or his ability to function as an independent researcher – to self-motivate, self-manage, and self-teach. Therefore, some advisors may also feel that forcing you to "figure it out your-self" is an appropriate test of your suitability for the degree.

The bottom line is that much of this tacit knowledge is not transmitted consistently between advisors and students. I had excellent (albeit quite busy) advisors, yet in my own progression from PhD student to PhD candidate to junior professor I still had to piece this knowledge together through a combination of trainings, conference panels on professional development, academic advice columns, conversations with senior colleagues, and a lot of trial and error.

This book is intended to help you avoid as much of that struggle as possible by making explicit that heretofore tacit knowledge. It provides an organized discussion of the key skills most students in the social sciences and other fields need to make it from new PhD student to successfully employed researcher.

My objectives here are twofold. My first objective is to offer a service to students and advisors by making the skills learning process less dependent on advisor input. My hope is that advisors will recommend this book to their students, that students will recommend this book to each other, and that more universities will provide students with formal training in professional skills.

My second objective is to improve fairness and access in the profession. As I have noted, the students who are most successful on the job market – whether for academic or non-academic posts – are usually those who have acquired the most or best signifiers of their research competence and potential for future performance.[3] The result is that the job market can

---

3 PhD-granting institutions manifest an additional bias toward hiring graduates of a small num-ber of elite universities (Clauset, Arbesman, and Larremore 2015), but the job market – even for academic jobs – is much broader than PhD-granting schools.

become tilted in favor of those students with the best knowledge of how to play the academic game. Understanding the game may come more easily to students who have family members who have themselves earned advanced degrees or occupy high-level professional positions, and students who have attended elite research institutions as undergraduates. Unscrupulous advisors may further tilt the playing field by doling out knowledge to the students they most favor, while withholding it from others (Miranda 2021). Yet if the ranks of future professors and professional researchers are filled only by students from privileged or elite backgrounds to the exclusion of other well-qualified candidates, it does a disservice to both society and the research professions (Swidler 2019). By making the rules of the game and the strategies for success more transparent, I hope that this book helps level the playing field between students from different backgrounds and expands the opportunities of under-represented or marginalized communities.

How to Use This Book

This book lays bare the tacit knowledge you need to build an effective strategy for success in your doctoral studies and future job search. I have organized this book to present the advice I think you are most likely to need in your research student career in a sequence that follows your likely career progression. Because of my own education and experience, my advice is skewed toward students in the social sciences and humanities. Some points may be less relevant to students in the hard sciences, although I believe that most of the advice is universally applicable. I strongly encourage you to read or at least skim the entire book as early as possible in your student career (preferably your first year in the program) and then return to it later to review the guidance on specific tasks. Many of the most important research signifiers, especially conference presentations and journal publications, have significant lag times. It can be almost a year between when you submit an abstract and when you get to present at a major conference, and journal articles can take one or two years to appear in print, even in an "online first," prepublication version. Teaching experience, which is crucial if you plan an academic career, can take at least a semester to arrange and another one or two terms to complete.

Far too often, I see students waiting to begin acquiring signifiers: waiting until their coursework is done, waiting until they have passed comprehensive exams, waiting until they have defended their dissertation proposal, waiting until their data are collected, even waiting until they have a complete first draft of their dissertation. The result is that many students complete the PhD with few of the signifiers necessary for them to compete well on the job market. They then struggle to write articles or conference papers while teaching as adjunct instructors or working a non-research job. Reading the whole book now will help you think about your career and your aspirations and plan for success.

The next two chapters of this book are designed help you develop a plan for maximizing your future marketability. As you read Chapter 2, you will learn to survey the job market and identify what your future employers are seeking in a successful job applicant. Then, in Chapter 3, you will translate these general expectations into a list of specific signifiers and develop a roadmap for acquiring them during your progress through your doctoral studies.

Chapters 4, 5, and 6 are designed to help you launch your research agenda and lay the foundations for your progress through the PhD. In Chapter 4 you will work on identifying areas of comparative advantage: places where your previous experience, personal inclinations, and prior studies give you a head start over other scholars in developing quality research. In Chapter 5 you will begin translating these comparative advantages into a research agenda and even a specific research question. This process is best aided by dialogue with your dissertation advisor, so Chapter 6 discusses how to select your advisor and manage your working relationship with her or him.

Once you have a research agenda, it is time to begin acquiring signifiers. Even prior to beginning your fieldwork, your dissertation proposal can form the basis for conference papers, publications, and grant applications. The number of opportunities only increases as your research progresses, and the process of inviting external feedback on your work by presenting it, submitting it for publication, or using it as the basis of grant applications will enhance your dissertation.

Chapter 7 will teach you how to select which conferences to apply to attend and provides detailed instructions on how to write the paper abstract that is at the heart of most conference applications. Once your work is accepted, you will need to attend, present, and network with other scholars; Chapter 8 covers these topics. Chapter 9 will teach you how to publish your work (ideally every conference paper should evolve into a publication), including how to select appropriate journals, manage the submission process, and handle reviewer feedback. Chapter 10 will discuss winning funding. You will learn about the various types of funding available, how to identify those opportunities for which you are most competitive, and how to apply. Finally, for those students interested in an academic career, Chapter 11 will help you get started in teaching without losing momentum on your dissertation completion.

Even with an excellent road map and a good relationship with your advisor, the PhD is mentally and emotionally draining. Most students experience moments of frustration, discouragement, and hopelessness in which their work bogs down and they wonder if they will ever complete their studies. With that in mind, Chapter 12 discusses managing your time and motivation to maintain steady progress on your signifiers and the dissertation itself.

Finally, the light at the end of the tunnel! If all goes well, in three to five years you will be entering the job market. Even if you have done an excellent job acquiring signifiers, you will still need to find job openings and showcase your qualifications to others, both in your written applications and in-person interviews. Chapter 13 will show you how.

Recommended Readings

Davis, L. (2011). What I tell my graduate students. *The Chronicle of Higher Education*, 6 March 2011.

Miranda, E. (2021). The leaky pipeline playbook. *Insider Higher Ed*, 13 August 2021.

Van Bavel, J., Lewis, N., & Cunningham, W. (2019). In the tough academic job market, two principles can help you maximize your chances. *Science*, 10 July 2019.

Additional Resources

Cassuto, L. (2011). Changing the way we socialize doctoral students. *The Chronicle of Higher Education*, 10 January 2011.

Castellanos, J., Gloria, A., & Kamimura, M. (2006). *The Latina/o Pathway to the Ph.D.* Sterling, VA: Stylus Publishing, Inc.

Green, A., & Scott, L. (2003). *Journey to the PhD: How to Navigate the Process as African Americans*. Sterling, VA: Stylus Publishing, Inc.

Wyck, J. (2017). Needed: A new graduate adviser-advisee relationship. *Inside Higher Ed*, 27 November 2017.

Responding to the Job Market

2

Presumably, you are pursuing the PhD because you are seeking a job that requires a research credential – either an academic posting or another professional position in which you will be responsible for conducting, commissioning, or evaluating research. As stated in Chapter 1, holding a PhD is no guarantee of landing such a job. Instead, prospective employers will be looking for additional indicators of your research competency and related abilities. In this chapter, we will discuss how to identify the specific signifiers that are most appealing to different employers and how to develop a plan for acquiring these during your doctoral studies.

To begin the process, it is useful to reflect on what a PhD signifies. Taught degrees, like most undergraduate and master's degrees and certain other doctorates like the Juris Doctor (JD), focus primarily on imparting subject matter expertise, often in a broad area, along with some measure of critical thinking, writing ability, and research skill. In the PhD, this balance is reversed: you are a researcher first and a subject matter expert second. The PhD primarily signals your ability to act as an independent researcher. You will gain some subject matter expertise along the way, but it will tend to focus on the narrow, niche area of your dissertation research. (Because I am writing from the US, I will use the term dissertation to describe the primary output of the PhD; I trust that students and colleagues in the UK will understand that in their context I mean the thesis.) Most future employers will not be particularly interested in your extensive knowledge of World Trade Organization policymaking or Ogaden pastoralist culture. They will hire you because your research in these niche areas has demonstrated your capacity to design research, collect and analyze data, and produce credible findings.

DOI: 10.4324/9781003262831-2

To be a researcher means that you are no longer simply expert in the knowledge others have generated or collected; you yourself are generating new knowledge. While students pursuing other degrees may be required to learn how to do research and even undertake research projects, the PhD is exceptional for requiring that what the student creates is *novel* – i.e., a new and unique contribution to human knowledge. Moreover, it is tacitly understood in most fields that the student's contribution will be achieved independently. Dissertations are single-authored works and, even if doctoral advisors sometimes appear as coauthors on articles based on the student's dissertation (a practice to which I generally object – see Chapter 6), the student is always the first author.

Employers seek out PhD holders (hereafter "PhDs") for their research expertise. PhDs may be expected to design research projects and collect and analyze data. In some roles, they are expected to evaluate grant proposals or design research projects to be carried out by others. PhDs may also be expected to evaluate the quality of others' research in order to identify the most important and credible findings and devise data-driven policies and plans. In all of these cases, employers are looking for employees who can work independently, with minimal supervision or assistance.

In short, if your goal is to land a PhD job, you will need to signal as strongly as possible to potential employers that you can fulfill such roles. In addition, you need to recognize the other qualifications employers may be seeking, such as an ability to teach students or win grants. Once you understand the qualifications you require for maximum marketability, you can then begin to devise a strategy to acquire those while also completing your dissertation. This chapter will help you identify those qualifications. We will begin by discussing where to find job advertisements and how to read them to identify employer interests. We will then discuss how to examine the career trajectories of recent hires to determine what it may really take to be competitive for a given position. We will conclude by reflecting more on your personal desires and reviewing the values and interests that drive your career choices.

What the Market Demands

While most employers seeking out a PhD are expecting research expertise, they may be interested in different applications of that expertise. An academic employer, for instance, may be interested in your ability to do research that yields published articles and enhances the reputation and prestige of the university. A government agency or nonprofit may be more interested in your ability to analyze data in an existing dataset to yield policy-relevant conclusions or synthesize others' research into a briefing on recent developments in the field. Most employers also have additional, non-research skills they are seeking, such as the ability to teach a core course in the department curriculum or to liaise with foreign counterparts in their native language.

In essence, each employer has their own set of boxes that they want candidates to check. However, these boxes will be similar across employers in the same field or at the same type of institution. For instance, many development NGOs will be looking for project management experience or language abilities. Most universities will be looking for a record of publication and an ability to teach certain courses. Therefore, it is useful to begin looking at job advertisements now, so that you can get a sense for what your preferred employers are seeking. This will allow you to establish a tentative end goal for your professional development during the PhD: a set of qualifications that will define your curriculum vitae (CV) or résumé and appeal to future employers. You can then begin planning the specific steps that will allow you to reach that goal.

Finding Job Postings

It is never too early to begin looking at job advertisements. You should begin doing so as soon as you begin your PhD program. This will give you a sense of the market. You can then direct your energies toward becoming qualified and competitive for the positions of greatest interest to you or begin broadening your career options if your preferred jobs seem more difficult to obtain than you had hoped.

Before beginning, review your answers to Exercise 1.1 in the previous chapter. You will want to research the full range of possible jobs with which you could be happy, and maybe even some jobs that you are not so sure about. Most people underestimate the variety of different jobs available. Researching jobs will be a learning experience, and if you cast your net widely, the research process may prompt you to expand your list of the kinds of jobs with which you might be content. For instance, reading about a post at a teaching-focused institution in an attractive part of the country may prompt you to reconsider your commitment to a research-focused university, or finding that some interesting nonprofit or corporate employers allow full-time remote work may prompt you to consider working outside the academy.

When you are ready to look for jobs, the first step is knowing where to look. Recognize that in most fields, whether academic or professional, there is no single source that lists all jobs in the field. Therefore, you must identify and consider multiple sources of job postings. My disciplinary specialty is international relations, a sub-discipline of political science. When I search for international relations jobs, I am consistently surprised to find that the International Studies Association, the American Political Science Association, and *The Chronicle of Higher Education* have almost completely different lists of openings. If I am on the market for a new job, I check each of these regularly.

You will need to develop your own list of websites to check periodically as you learn and track the job market. Job posting websites and publications exist at four levels of specificity:

- General
- Disciplinary
- Sub-discipline / specialty
- Employer

General websites aggregate large numbers of postings by focusing on a type of profession or category of employer. For instance, *The Chronicle of Higher Education* (https://jobs.chronicle.com/) and Jobs.ac.uk (https://www.jobs.ac.uk/) aggregate job postings for all types of academic positions, including both faculty and administrative posts. USAjobs (USAjobs.gov) has openings from across all departments of the US government, while UNjobs (https://unjobs.org/) lists openings at the United Nations and other international organizations. Idealist (https://www.idealist.org/en/) publishes job postings in the nonprofit sector. Minority Postdoc (https://www.minoritypostdoc.org/jobs) is cross-sectoral, listing postdocs and other job opportunities for employers interested in expanding the diversity of their applicant pool. These websites can be good places to start because they are widely used by employers. The challenge is that because they have so many postings, you may have to choose your search terms carefully, run multiple searches, and sift through a larger number of less-relevant options.

Disciplinary websites have a slightly narrower focus, aggregating jobs related to a specific type of academic training or professional domain. Major professional associations based around academic disciplines, like the American Psychological Association (https://www.psyccareers.com/), International Studies Association (https://www.isanet.org/Professional-Resources/Employment/Jobs), or American Sociological Association (https://www.asanet.org/academic-professional-resources/job-bank), often maintain their own jobs listings. This also occurs in some practitioner fields. For instance, Devex (https://www.devex.com/jobs/search/) aggregates job postings from across the international development field. As you develop your professional identity, you will probably spend most of your time using one or more of these sites. They will still offer you a wide range of options, but usually with much more manageable lists of openings.

Sub-discipline or specialty listings are targeted toward people working in a specific domain of research or action. For instance, the Association for Research on Nonprofit Organizations and Voluntary Action (ARNOVA) (https://www.arnova.org/networking/opening_search.asp), of which I am a member, maintains a job listing for positions – both academic and practitioner – related to studying nongovernmental organizations and improving their management. Such sites can be useful because they highlight positions for which you may be particularly competitive since you presumably have the specialty the employer is seeking. They are also helpful if you work in an interdisciplinary specialty, since they may bring to your attention jobs that have been posted on disciplinary websites that you do not normally check.

Lastly, most employers maintain public listings of the current positions they have available. If there is a large nonprofit or particular government organization you are interested in working for, you may find dozens of positions listed on their website. The list of current positions at any given university may be shorter, but if you are trying to find positions in a particular geographic area, you may find it worthwhile to bookmark the employment pages of the local academic institutions and check them regularly.

Some of these options may strike you as more useful than others but starting out you should familiarize yourself with the full range of job listing venues. Where jobs appear is dependent in large part on where the search committee for a position chooses to submit the job advertisement. As noted, this can make the job listings quite patchy.

In general, the larger aggregators may help you find more opportunities, but sometimes there are so many postings that it can be difficult to locate everything that is suitable to you. Disciplinary listings often have a much higher density of suitable postings, but if you have an interdisciplinary specialty, they will not contain everything for which you are qualified. Specialty listings will give you a still higher density of suitable listings, but again may exclude positions that suit you but do not exactly match the specialty. For instance, I often get job postings from ARNOVA, but ARNOVA will not send me advertisements for general positions in political science or international relations for which I might also be qualified.

Many organizations maintain listservs, mailing lists, and other tools that can deliver job postings directly to you. This can be quite useful, especially if there is a specialty organization that suits your interests. The person leading the search or someone on the search team may even post the advertisement themselves, allowing you to email them easily with queries about the position.

The key is to develop an appropriate data pipeline, and to not limit one's options through a scarcity of good data. You should spend some time doing Internet searches for jobs in your field and see what websites you find. You may discover blogs or twitter feeds discussing where to look for jobs. I recommend that you also ask your dissertation supervisor and any committee members you have about how they found their current jobs or where they look at job postings currently. You may be surprised to learn that many faculty members continue to read job postings even after landing a tenure-track job or receiving tenure, but they do. Academia is a highly atomized profession, meaning that workers have a lot of individual responsibility for their own career success. It is not uncommon for faculty to apply for other positions in an effort to move up to more prestigious or better-paying posts, get closer to extended family, or even just live in a more interesting location.

The bottom line is that you should obtain as much data as you can on the best places to look for jobs. Where possible, you should subscribe to organizations' mailing lists or listservs, especially if they send a periodic email just focused on jobs, so that you have a continual flow of information on the job market. Some organizations use RSS feeds that can be pushed through Twitter if you prefer getting information that way.

Lastly, be aware that the number of postings may be time-sensitive and follow specific annual cycles. When you are researching the job market, it is fine to look at old postings. Even if the searches have been closed, you can still get a sense of the job requirements. However, you should use job tracking to learn when the types of jobs in which you are interested are most likely to be advertised. In the US, for instance, most tenure-track academic positions are advertised between August and October for positions beginning the following August. Additional posts are advertised in the spring for an August start, but these are often term-limited positions (e.g., a one-year visiting professorship) that schools use to cover sabbaticals or fill gaps created by faculty who have taken jobs elsewhere. In Europe, permanent faculty positions are more typically advertised between January and June for a fall start, with many positions posted in late spring after public universities have learned what their budgets will be for the next year. Practitioner positions are advertised year-round, but some also follow organization funding cycles.

EXERCISE 2.1: FINDING AND READING JOB POSTINGS

Get started in planning your professional development by taking the following steps:

1. Identify at least two websites that regularly post job openings in which you are interested.
2. Identify at least one listserv or other electronic outlet (e.g., blog, Facebook account, Twitter account, etc.) where jobs are regularly posted in your preferred discipline or field.
3. Subscribe to an email list or feed that will send job postings in which you are interested to your inbox or phone on a weekly or monthly basis.

Assessing a Job Advertisement

Once you have found several good sources for job advertisements, the next step is to assess some of the advertisements you find. Many job postings are surprisingly vague. This can happen when search committees want to cast a wide net or do not want to limit the applicant pool by requiring too many specific qualifications. Institutions may also be bound by law to advertise their openings in some sort of widely read venue, but constrained by the word length limits of the advertising space. The search committees who draft a posting may be bad writers, or the posting language may represent an awkward compromise between competing factions within the institution. Regardless of the reason, it will fall to you to sift through the language for indicators of what the employer really wants.

I advise you to read the advertisements with a blank document open on your device, or even print them and mark them up as you read. You will note several types of information:

- Credentials
- General competencies or skills
- Specific accomplishments or experiences

Credentials are typically your degree. Usually, you will be looking at positions that require a PhD in one of several fields. For example, a position in a political science department may require a degree in political science, international relations, or public administration. Practitioner positions in development may require a PhD in development, sociology, anthropology, or a related field. Some UK institutions will be interested in whether candidates have completed a Post Graduate Certificate in Higher Education (PGCHE). Practitioner employers may be interested in other professional credentials.

General competencies or skills include things not all holders of the required degree might have. Examples include "a knowledge of qualitative research design" or "ability to design and implement large-N surveys" or "ability to teach courses online." Sometimes these will be phrased as a statement of character or interest, for example, "a commitment to innovative teaching," but employers are looking for more than a few enthusiastic statements in your cover letter. They are looking for a candidate whose interests and passions have led them to develop particular skills.

Accomplishments or experiences go a step further. They ask about what you have done. Typical examples include "three years of experience in the field" or "experience managing teams." Sometimes the request is implicit. For example, when an ad asks for a candidate with "a passion for girls' education," the hiring committee is not really interested in the candidate's feelings. They want to know how the candidate's interest has been manifested in their professional work, volunteering, or other activities. Specific accomplishments and experiences allow an employer to know that your competency or interest is not merely theoretical. From an employer's perspective, the best evidence that you can do something in the future is a record of having done something similar in the past.

Academic positions often request experience teaching in a specific discipline, ensuring that candidates actually know how to teach and have completed (or at least begun) the often-challenging process of learning to teach before coming to the hiring institution. For practitioner positions that might attract newly minted PhDs, employers may add an experience requirement because they want to make sure that candidates are really interested in practitioner work rather than just seeking refuge from a tough academic job market (Jensen 2016).

As you read through an ad, identify the specific or implicit credentials, competencies, and experiences the employer is seeking. Then think about how these pieces all fit together. Employers are hiring for a specific purpose. They have an ideal hire in mind. It may be a hard-charging researcher who wins lots of grants, a pleasant colleague who is loved by the students, or a detail-oriented manager whose team completes contracts on time and within budget. The verbiage in the advertisement is the employer's best effort to attract applicants that fit that mold; see if you can discern what the mold is.

EXERCISE 2.2: ASSESSING A JOB ADVERTISEMENT

1. Identify at least two advertisements for positions you would like to hold within one year of completing the PhD. These job advertisements can be up to a year old; they do not have to be current.
2. Inventory the qualifications the employer is seeking. Consider:
   a. Credentials
   b. Competencies or skills (e.g., research ability or language fluency)
   c. Accomplishments or experience (e.g., previous leadership roles or time in the field)
3. What is it that the employer wants the candidate to be able to do?
4. How will the requested qualifications, skills, and/or experiences signal to the employer that the candidate can do the job well?
5. What do you think the CV of the employer's ideal job candidate looks like?

Assessment of Recent Hires

Job advertisements will tell you the minimum credentials, skills, or experience necessary to qualify for a position. But what you really want to know is what it takes to actually get hired. Knowing this will help you decide what you need to do to become competitive for the positions you want by the time you go on the market. Learning this information requires uncovering a bit of tacit knowledge and discerning the level of competition. Assessing the CVs of recent hires can help you do both.

The writers of job advertisements assume a lot of tacit knowledge on the part of the reader. For instance, position descriptions in academia very often include a phrase requesting "evidence of an active research agenda." But what this means at an Ivy League institution where faculty teach just three courses each year is very different from what it means at a teaching-oriented institution where faculty teach seven or eight courses. The search committee at the research-oriented school may be looking for publications in top journals or a book contract with a top-tier university press. The committee at the teaching-oriented school may be content if you have two or three conference papers that you plan to turn into published articles. You can encounter similar vagueness in the practitioner world. A requirement for "experience working in the field" could mean a semester-long internship, a year of doctoral fieldwork, or three years of leading and managing projects. The job posting alone may not clarify the employer's expectations, but employers assume that applicants know what they intend and quickly discard any applications that do not meet their unwritten minimum standards.

Knowing the implicit minimum standards is not the only problem; competition also influences the level of qualifications needed to succeed. Search committees will take the best candidate they can find. If the market in your field is very competitive, candidates may take positions for which they seem overqualified. To extend the academic example above, the search committee at a teaching-focused university may go into a search with low minimum standards for candidates' research outputs. But if their applicant pool includes several applicants who are both stellar teachers and exceptional researchers, they will naturally choose one of them. Thus, you need to know what other candidates are bringing to the table.

The way to learn these realities is to examine the CVs of recent hires. If you are looking for an academic position, review the faculty roster and skim the biographies of junior faculty until you find the two or three people most recently hired by the department. If you are looking for a practitioner position, you may be able to find a biography and possibly a CV by looking in the institution's organizational chart for people holding a position similar to the one you are seeking. You should also search for the organization and relevant position titles through a platform like LinkedIn, where people post their job experience and CVs. If you are looking at a large employer that has several people holding your prospective job title or rank, you may find that one or more of them have a profile posted there.

Once you find two or three people who hold equivalent positions and, ideally, have been hired recently, find their hire date (either by looking at their profile or the dates of employment written on their CV) and subtract any publications, work experience, conferences, or other achievements that occurred post-hire. What is left is the CV they probably had when they were selected for an interview. Use these CVs to set your goalposts: you want to be at least as well qualified as the most recent hires when you yourself go on the job market.

If you have time, I also suggest reviewing the CVs of others within the organization. You will often find patterns among the employees that reveal something about the culture of the organization. In a practitioner organization, you may find that many employees have similar prior professional experience, for example having previously worked for the same branch of government or volunteered with the Peace Corps. In an academic department, you may find that faculty are all members of the same professional organizations, publish in the same journals, or have prior professional experience as practitioners.

Hiring committees are often looking for someone who will "fit in" to the current organizational culture. Human resource professionals even promote this approach on the premise that employees who do not fit in well are more likely to leave, costing organizations money through staff turnover (e.g., Bouton 2015). Unfortunately, a focus on cultural fit can allow hiring committees to act on inherent biases or even hide deliberate discrimination (Nelson 2019). This has created historic injustices for minorities, women, and others who do not fit in so well with the dominant cultures of different organizations (Wolfe and Dilworth 2015; Nelson 2019). This book cannot solve that problem, but it can help make clear the rules of the game. In addition to focusing on the signifiers noted above, figure out what the culture looks like in the organizations in which you are interested. Is the culture marked by previous overseas service? Membership in certain organizations? The use of certain types of research methods, datasets, or theories? As much as possible, figure out how to acquire similar signifiers so that a hiring committee sees you as an insider when you apply for a job.

EXERCISE 2.3: ASSESSING RECENT HIRES

1. Identify two or more employers for whom you would like to work when you complete your PhD. Look at their organizational charts or recent job postings to identify which kinds of positions are usually held by new PhDs.
2. Identify two to three recent hires for these positions and find their CVs or bios.
3. Assess their professional qualifications at the time of their hire. Consider:
   a. Professional experience (including teaching experience for academic posts)
   b. Subject matter or methodological expertise
   c. Publications
   d. Conference presentations
   e. Grants
   f. Language skills
4. Look at the CVs of others within the organization, e.g., managers, associate directors, or associate and full professors. Note any patterns in terms of work experience, professional memberships, publication venues, or research methods or theoretical approach. Is there a "type" that seems to fit in well? What is that type?

Reflecting on Your Desires

Looking at job advertisements can be a daunting experience. Some students will feel inspired and dream about the jobs they could have, but many will wonder if they can ever live up to the expectations of the job market. Whichever camp you fall into, I offer you this advice: reflect on why you are here.

The PhD is gateway to a wide variety of careers to which most people do not have access. Unfortunately, the environment of the university can make it difficult to remember or appreciate the full range of options available because you are surrounded by people – your professors – who have all made the same choice: to pursue a career in academic research. PhD-granting institutions are almost always research-focused institutions, and the faculty involved in training PhDs typically have strong research agendas. A friend studying at an elite institution once had a senior faculty member tell her that "the reason we're all here" was to "become famous" meaning that they would be known for their research. Yet this is a questionable goal. After all, you can be famous in some academic niches when just 30 people know of your work.

Reflect on what you really want to do once you have the PhD, not how you want to be seen or what will please your advisors. Do you dream of teaching at a small liberal arts college where students are invited to faculty members' homes for dinner? Do you want to work in interesting locations abroad? What do you love most: research or teaching or leading teams or managing projects? Do you work best with a flexible schedule or do you like the structure of a regular workday? Focus on the jobs that will allow you to do what you want and provide the most energizing environment. Or, to borrow from Mark Batterson, think about what makes you "mad, glad, or sad" and look for jobs that will allow you to work on the things you are passionate about. Remember too that your decisions affect not only you but also any family that you have or plan to have. Becoming an elite researcher can entail significant personal sacrifice. There is no shame in wanting a good work-life balance and a summer schedule that allows you to spend time with your children.

That being said, I also encourage you to aim to be overqualified for whatever positions you plan to seek, particularly if you plan on seeking an academic job. Academia is rife with stories of would-be faculty who never succeed in winning a permanent position and instead eke out a living cobbling together adjunct contracts or limited-term positions. This offers neither security nor good work-life balance. In the next chapter, we will discuss how to acquire the qualifications necessary to compete for the job you want and help you develop a game plan for acquiring the appropriate signifiers during your doctoral studies.

Recommended Readings

Berkley Career Center (2021). Academic job search: Finding job announcements. Available at: https://career.berkeley.edu/PhDs/PhDJobs.

McDonald, D. (2018). Academic careers you may not have considered. *Inside Higher Ed*, 21 May 2018.

Polk, J., & Wood, M. (2018). Preparing for a nonfaculty job. *Inside Higher Ed*, 8 August 2018.

Additional Resources

Brooks, A. (2021). The secret to happiness at work. *The Atlantic*, 2 September 2021.

Fionova, I. (2021). 3 Mental shortcuts that could undermine your job search. *Inside Higher Ed*, 28 June 2021.

Smith, C. (2020). The importance of informational interviews. *Inside Higher Ed*, 3 June 2020.

Developing a Roadmap to Marketability   **3**

Now that you have reviewed job ads and the CVs of recent hires, you should have a general sense of what employers in your preferred fields seek in a new employee. You may also be confused or frustrated. While employers may sometimes ask for quite specific accomplishments, like "five years in a supervisory role," more often they ask for something vague, like "a commitment to undergraduate teaching" or "a robust research agenda." How then do you signal your suitability for a position?

The answer involves a fair bit of tacit knowledge because there is a hidden hierarchy to many of the accomplishments you could use to signal your qualifications. For instance, writing a chapter in an edited volume published by a trade press (this means an academic press not affiliated with a university – e.g., publishing with Palgrave MacMillan rather than Stanford University Press) and publishing a peer-reviewed article in a respected journal can both signal your ability to produce publishable research, but the article will be valued more highly than the book chapter.

Therefore, the first part of this chapter will discuss four of the most common qualifications sought by employers for PhD positions: research ability, professional experience in the field, teaching ability, and the potential to win funding. For each of these areas we will discuss different accomplishments that can signal to employers that you possess the desired qualification and those accomplishments' hidden hierarchy.

Some of the information in the first four sections may be a bit overwhelming if you are new to academia or professional research. There are a wide variety of research outputs, professional positions, teaching roles, and funding sources in academia and other research professions. You are not expected to

DOI: 10.4324/9781003262831-3

acquire or occupy all of them. However, I have sought to make the lists here fairly comprehensive in order to orient you to the field and make you aware of the possible options and their relative value. The important thing is not to memorize these lists, but instead to know that there is a hierarchy. As you make professional development decisions in the future, you can then refer back to these lists and consult additional sources, like senior colleagues, for guidance that is tailored to your particular career path.

The information in the first four sections will also help you as you review others' CVs in the future. Once you know the relative value of different accomplishments, others' CVs may seem less intimidating. For instance, seeing a new hire with eight publications may set a high bar, until you realize that only two of them are articles in peer-reviewed journals (high-value, difficult accomplishments) while the rest are book reviews (lower value accomplishments unlikely to carry too much weight). I encourage you to reflect on the CVs you have viewed as you read this chapter, interpreting them in light of the information here.

The latter part of this chapter focuses on how to integrate the acquisition of those signifiers into your doctoral studies. Once you know what employers are seeking, you should be able to develop a list of the kinds of signifiers you want to acquire and a plan for how and when to acquire them. The key is to acquire them in such a way that your professional development enhances the quality of your dissertation and keeps you on track for a timely graduation rather than distracting you from your research or delaying your progress. This portion of the chapter will show you how.

Research Ability

An ability to do research is fundamental to most jobs that require a PhD for employment. Not all jobs will require you to use this ability yourself. Instead, you may be employing others' research as you write policy guidance or teach courses, or you may be commissioning others to do research and analyzing their outputs. However, the best way to signal to employers that you understand research is to show that you are a successful researcher yourself. The most common signifiers of research ability are:

- Peer-reviewed publications
- Dissertation/thesis
- Conference papers
- Publications in the popular press

These outputs can be used to showcase various aspects of your subject matter expertise, methodological skill, or capacity for innovation. For certain outputs, publishing or presenting your work in more selective venues can demonstrate the quality of work.

While we focus here on your individual accomplishments, do not lose sight of the fact that research is actually a communal endeavor. It is the collective work of thousands of researchers around the world that moves forward human knowledge. We do so imperfectly, making many mistakes along the way. It is through scholarly debate, the testing of old ideas, the inclusion of new perspectives, and the proposal of new theories that our knowledge is corrected, refined, expanded, and improved. When you have research outputs, it signals that you are entering in the community of researchers and participating in that collective endeavor. Research outputs signify that others in the community recognize you as a peer because publishers, journal reviewers, and conference organizers have accepted your work for publication or presentation. Outputs also signal to hiring committee members, who are themselves probably researchers, that your research is substantial and that when you tell them about your planned research contributions you are describing next steps in a path you have already started on, not spinning tales about your hopes and dreams. With that in mind, as you read the following subsections, think about what each of the outputs below communicates to future employers about your participation in and contribution to the research community.

Some of what you communicate is about more than just your research quality. Some venues will signal your affiliation with a particular academic discipline or field of research. For instance, if you are studying in an interdisciplinary field but plan to apply for academic positions in traditional academic departments, publishing in traditional disciplinary journals can help increase your marketability. If you want to be known as a subject matter expert on public health or Middle Eastern politics, presenting your work at conferences that focus on those subjects will highlight your subject matter expertise. Certain journals and conferences are more oriented toward practitioners than academics and can help you position yourself for a practitioner job. White papers, policy briefs, and popular press writing on contemporary issues can also emphasize your ability to participate in policy debates and your capacity for public engagement. Reviewing the research you did in Chapter 2 can help you find patterns in the research outputs of people in your preferred future professions or at your ideal employers. Following the same pattern yourself can help signal that you are an insider in the field.

Peer-Reviewed Publications

Peer-reviewed publications are typically the most valuable type of research output for enhancing your employment prospects. These are most commonly articles published in academic journals. Journals usually send their submissions in anonymized ('blind') form to two or more scholars with knowledge of the article's subject or methods, who then provide feedback to the editor on the article's suitability for publication. Some journals, most notably law reviews, use review by a board of editors in lieu of this external review.

Books, book chapters, and white papers also count as peer-reviewed publications, although they may not be as rigorously reviewed as journal articles. A book is reviewed by an editor at the publisher, and the publisher usually sends your book proposal and later some or all of the final product out for external review. Chapters published in edited volumes are nominally peer-reviewed; here the peer is the volume editor and any external reviewers to whom the publisher sends the completed volume. Papers published in a working paper series or white papers published by a think tank or similar organization also benefit from the assumption that they were reviewed by a series editor or subject to an internal review process.

Be wary of publication opportunities that are not peer-reviewed in some way. Sometimes you will receive invitations to conferences that have unusually expensive registration fees but promise that your work will be published in a volume of conference proceedings. You may also receive invitations from journals you have never heard of, expressing enthusiasm for your research and asking you to submit a piece. If you read deeply enough or visit their website, they will often boast of being "open access" with "page fees paid by the authors or their institutions." These are essentially pay-to-publish schemes and should be avoided (Economist 2020). There are legitimate open access journals in some fields and they do have publication charges, but usually they proliferate when there is abundant external funding and the publication fees can be paid through grants. If you work in such a field, you probably know it already. You should never pay personally to publish your work.

Peer-reviewed articles and books are highly valued because they are rigorously reviewed. They also provide the best opportunities for the dissemination of your ideas. Only popular press publications reach a wider audience, and these rarely allow for deep discussion. Thus, peer-reviewed publications show your potential to impact your field and other researchers' acknowledgment of the value of your contributions.

Some peer-reviewed publications are valued more highly than others. The distinguishing factor is mainly the rigor of the peer review. Reviewers and editors at a highly selective journals and presses will expect submissions to conform to a higher standard in terms of novelty, methodology, theoretical clarity, and significance of outputs.

For journals, in addition to selectivity, you should also consider the discipline, focus, and audience. Most journals are associated with specific academic disciplines or subdisciplines, or with particular subject areas. Publishing can thus be used to show your disciplinary affiliation or highlight your subject matter expertise. If you are working in a niche subdiscipline where everyone reads certain journals, publishing in those journals can help show that you are an insider in the field. Conversely, publishing in a journal focused on an academic discipline can emphasize your disciplinary affiliation. Some journals specifically target practitioner audiences. We will discuss journal selection more in Chapter 9.

HIERARCHY OF RESEARCH PUBLICATIONS

1. Book contract with a top university press
2. Article in a "Top Journal" (top 5–10% journals in your field)
3. Article in a Tier 1 journal (usually the top 25% or 33% of journals in your field)
4. Article in a Tier 2 journal (ranked in the middle third of journals in your field)
5. Book chapter in a volume edited by a well-known scholar or published by a well-ranked press
6. Article in a Tier 3 journal (lowest third of journals in your field)
7. Book chapter in an edited volume with a low-ranked press
8. White paper, policy brief, or working paper published by a recognized organization in an established working paper series

---

Venue quality can often be discerned via rankings. Most disciplines will have a formal or informal ranking of journals. Journal Citation Reports, available through your library's access to Web of Science, is the most respected standard in many fields. You can ask a librarian about how to access it. The SCImago Journal Rank (SJR) (https://www.scimagojr.com /journalrank.php) covers more journals and can also be useful. It is also open access, whereas Journal Citation Reports requires that your library hold a subscription.

Not every journal is ranked. Sometimes new journals do not have a sufficient publication history to be listed. Other journals may be too niche. High-quality outliers will still typically be published by a well-known academic publisher (i.e., a publisher that also publishes highly ranked journals that you recognize) and include well-known experts in your field on their editorial board. Be wary of any unranked journal that does not meet both criteria.

There are also rankings of book publishers. As a graduate student, book publication is typically less urgent. However, as you near the end of your studies, you may begin looking at book publishers for your dissertation research. Publisher rankings are typically assembled by surveying scholars in your field about the perceived prestige, impact, or importance of different publishers (e.g., Garland and Giles 2011). You may be able to find them in a peer-reviewed research piece examining the state of the profession; you can also find informal rankings on academic blogs. As with academic journals, the more selective or highly ranked a press is, the more most employers will value it.

You can also use these rankings and standards if you are invited to submit a book chapter to an edited volume. The editors may not have a book contract yet, but you can ask them where they intend to submit the work and where they hope to see it placed. You can also look at the scholarly profile of the editors; edited volumes with prominent editors are more likely to be well-regarded by future employers, may be more widely read, and will probably attract a better publisher.

White papers and working papers tend to have lower value than articles, books, and book chapters due to their less rigorous peer review process. However, the value is increased if they are published by a highly respected organization, especially if you are looking to impress a practitioner audience.

The list provided in the box on page 28 gives my (somewhat subjective) view of the relative value of different publication types. Note that a book is not always more prestigious than a journal article, since journal articles are more rigorously peer-reviewed. A lot depends on the relative rankings of the press and the journal.

What about book reviews? Graduate students are often offered the opportunity to review books, especially if one of their advisors or instructors is editing a journal that has a book review section. You may even see book reviews listed alongside peer-reviewed journal articles on the CVs of some junior professors. However, book reviews do not signal research ability

(Musgrave 2021). They do show that you can write at a publishable standard and are participating in the scholarly community (Brienza 2014). If you are uncertain of your writing ability or do not yet have enough data or theoretical knowledge to write a full-length journal article of your own, a book review may be a good way to get started and build confidence. That being said, you should not let writing a book review displace an opportunity to write a research publication, develop a conference paper, or make progress on your dissertation.

Dissertation or Thesis

Your doctoral dissertation or thesis is another opportunity to show your research ability. Its value is notably lower than published work because it is common (everyone on the market will have one) and it is hard for a prospective employer to know how rigorously your work was reviewed. However, your dissertation can be useful for demonstrating subject matter expertise and methodological expertise. As you review job postings, you will note that even within a given discipline there may be strong interest in certain specialties. Within my own discipline of political science, for instance, many departments have recently sought to hire experts on conflict and security. Practitioner employers may seek candidates able to address major issues in public policy or work in regions that are attracting significant international attention.

As you progress in your studies, you will also notice that certain methods are common in your discipline. Cultural anthropologists, for instance, gravitate toward ethnography. US political science values quantitative analyses of large datasets. Using the methods that are most common to your discipline can signal insider-ness and make sure that you are conversant with the methods that the hiring committee members use and which they might expect you to teach. However, as you peruse job advertisements you may also note that there are certain types of methodological expertise for which there is high demand and perhaps low supply. Formal modeling skills, for instance, are highly sought after in some academic and professional fields. The ability to use big data is also a growing area of interest to many employers.

You can use this information to maximize the value of your dissertation. Your dissertation will occupy three or more years of your life, so it should be something that you are interested in, and you should prioritize the methods that are most appropriate to your research question. Yet if you have multiple interests or can choose from among multiple methods, choose the question, methods, or combination of the two that will most interest prospective employers. We will discuss this more in Chapters 4 and 5.

Conference Papers

Presenting at conferences shows that you are an active scholar. In many fields, getting research accepted at major conferences is not particularly difficult. Some large conferences have acceptance rates of up to 80%, although others are more selective. Yet even if acceptance is not difficult, presenting at conferences shows that your work is moving past the idea stage and that you are participating in the communal research process. Over time your CV should show a pattern of conference papers becoming published articles. As with other outputs, your conference presentations will show your affiliation with certain disciplines or professions and your engagement with particular audiences. They can also show your subject matter expertise and methods. I recommend that students present at a conference at least once a year beginning in the second or third year of their program.

Popular Press Publications

You may have the opportunity to write in some sort of popular venue. Researchers sometimes write guest columns in major newspapers like *The New York Times* or online venues like *The Huffington Post*. Some new venues like JSTOR Daily (https://daily.jstor.org/) and The Conversation (https://theconversation.com/) focus specifically on showcasing academic voices. The primary value of publishing in these venues is showing that your work is interesting to a wider audience, which can be valuable for employers engaged in policy work or looking to cultivate a more prominent public image. These publications may also showcase some of your subject matter expertise and your ability to relate your expertise to current events. To emphasize your contributions as a researcher, focus on offering evidence-based insights that enhance the public's thinking and be cautious about chasing page views (Brown 2019). Be aware too that while some employers may view this kind of public engagement very positively, others will see it as a distraction from the core mission of the organization or as generating the risk of negative publicity. The CVs of recent hires and more senior employees at your dream employers may give you some sense of what is appropriate.

EXERCISE 3.1: SETTING OBJECTIVES – RESEARCH

Look again at the job postings and CVs you collected for the Chapter 2 exercises. Based on these data answer the following questions:

1. What qualities are most prominent among the research outputs of the employees at your preferred employers: academic prestige, public engagement, policy relevance, methodological expertise, or something else?
2. Which kinds of research outputs (e.g., journal publications, presentations, policy briefs, etc.) do your preferred employers seem to value? Look at both what outputs junior employees had before hiring (if you can discern this from their CVs) and what they have produced since being hired.
3. Besides a completed dissertation, which of the research signifiers here do you most want to acquire?

Professional Experience

Professional experience is highly sought after in practitioner fields and is increasingly valued for academic positions. For practitioner roles, professional experience shows that you are already familiar with the culture and inside knowledge of the profession, things like government contracting procedures, risk management practices, or unwritten norms of behavior. A record of time spent in remote field locations lets employers know that you will not quit after your first case of homesickness or dysentery. Managing subordinates is a skill unto itself, and not one that you will typically learn in a PhD program. Academic institutions may care less about some of these things than non-academic employers, but many departments recognize that experience as a practitioner gives you insights that can make you a better researcher and a more engaging teacher, as well as knowledge and connections that can help with winning grants or assisting students in finding jobs.

Previous roles that can signal some or all of these attributes include:

- Team leader or manager
- Program officer, researcher, or analyst
- Program assistant or similar support role
- Intern or volunteer

The exact titles for positions will vary across fields, but generally correspond to different levels of responsibility: leader, independent worker, assistant, and very junior assistant.

Your professional experience is typically most useful if it is in the field in which you are seeking employment or one closely related. While some skills, like leadership, are highly sought after regardless of the field in which they were gained, most employers are looking for someone who has worked in their specific field. Your previous employer's size or budget, structure, and location of operations may also be relevant.

The most valuable experience typically involves some sort of leadership role. A leadership role shows that you not only have key professional knowledge, but that your expertise is strong enough that you can supervise others in carrying out their own tasks. Leaders may have responsibilities that other employees do not, such as dealing with funder reporting requirements or hiring rules. Leadership is also its own skill, and employers looking to hire someone for a leadership role will be looking for evidence of that skill.

Experience as program officer, researcher, analyst, or in a similar position is also quite valuable. These roles typically suggest that an employee does substantive work, sometimes with minimal supervision. The employee knows the field and has skills specific to the profession. She or he may also have experience working overseas or away from the home office on different projects.

Somewhat less valuable is working at the assistant level. Whether this is as a research assistant in a lab or a program assistant at a nongovernmental organization, assistants are assumed to have lower levels of skill and to need higher levels of supervision. Often assistants are relegated to support roles where they have less opportunity to learn some of the core skills of the profession. In the international development field, for instance, program officers are typically responsible for designing and implementing aid programs and may do work overseas, while program assistants manage things like logistics or staff travel and stay at the home office. Holding such an assistant position shows your interest in and commitment to the profession. Assistants also learn the culture and some practices of the field through exposure, even if they are not key decision makers or actors themselves. This sort of entry-level job is far better than having no experience in the field, but it may be hard to jump from this level to a leadership role, even if you earn your PhD.

Lastly, you can gain experience by interning with an organization or serving as a volunteer. The value of this experience will be highly variable depending on what you do and how it is related to your planned profession. If the role you are seeking involves managing volunteers, for instance, having been one yourself may be highly valuable. Sometimes volunteering engenders close, personal interactions with an organization's beneficiaries or grassroots membership, giving volunteers a ground-level perspective that professional staff may lack. Some organizations also devolve substantial responsibility to volunteers. At a minimum, volunteering or interning shows employers that you have an interest in and exposure to the field and some knowledge of its culture and practices.

Do not be discouraged if you are seeking a professional job but lack the expected experience. Many employers will accept the PhD or another advanced degree in lieu of several years of professional work. If you have the opportunity to volunteer, consult, or intern during your PhD, you should seize that opportunity to begin building a track record of involvement in the sector and to develop professional contacts. However, you can also reflect on the ways that you can leverage your PhD training to gain at least some of the skills and expertise that an employer would otherwise expect you to gain from professional work (Banoo and Gutmann 2018). By carefully selecting your dissertation topic, methodology, or field site, for instance, you can gain insider knowledge, relevant methodological expertise, or field experience and language skills.

EXERCISE 3.2: SETTING OBJECTIVES – PROFESSIONAL EXPERIENCE

Look again at the job postings and CVs you collected for the Chapter 2 exercises. Based on these data answer the following questions:

1. Is professional experience expected by your future employers, treated as a bonus, or not discussed at all?
2. If professional experience is expected or desired by your ideal employers, why do you think it is valued? What exactly are they looking for? Consider things like leadership ability, professional knowledge, connections, specific skills, subject matter expertise, and cultural or linguistic competency.
3. Are there ways that you can acquire the expected professional experience (if you do not have it already)? If not, are there other ways you can demonstrate the desired competencies or expertise?

Teaching Ability

If you are looking for an academic job, employers will want to know about your teaching ability. Ideally, they hope you will excite students about the subjects you teach and contribute to student satisfaction. At a minimum, they want to be sure that your teaching will not be a source of student complaints. They also usually want to know that you can fill key holes in the department roster. This means teaching core courses (sometimes called "service courses"), like introduction to the discipline or introductory methods, that all students in the major must take. It can also include advanced courses in specific subdisciplines if the department is understaffed in those areas. In addition, some employers will be interested in whether you can teach online.

Employers are primarily interested in how much responsibility you have had for any of the previous teaching you have been involved in. They are looking for indicators that you can take on the responsibilities of a full-time instructor, who must design courses, develop lesson plans, manage a classroom or online learning environment, and grade student papers. With that in mind, the hierarchy of teaching experience looks like this:

* Instructor of record
* Teaching assistant (TA)
* Guest lecturer

The instructor of record is the person with primary responsibility for teaching a course. Their name appears on students' course listings as the course instructor. This role connotes a high level of responsibility. The instructor of record typically writes the course syllabus, designs the key assignments, teaches the classes, does the grading, and calculates students' final grades. They keep office hours and deal with student problems. Your university may use graduate students as instructors of record for some courses, especially if your university has teaching fellowships that provide funding for graduate studies. Sometimes universities will hire their own graduate students to fill adjunct instructor roles. Adjuncts are part-time instructors who are paid for each course or section they teach. If your own institution does not use adjuncts or hire graduate students for these roles, you might be able to work as an adjunct for another university in the area. We will discuss how to find such positions in Chapter 11.

Being an instructor of record will give to you the most experience and offers prospective employers the greatest assurance that you can teach at the university level. The experience will also give you a chance to hone your teaching philosophy; many positions ask job candidates to submit a written teaching statement explaining their teaching philosophy as part of the application packet. Lastly, you will get teaching evaluations from your students, which some employers also request as part of their application packet.

A teaching assistantship gives you experience in some of the responsibilities of being a course instructor but not all of them. TAs rarely write syllabi, but many schools use them to teach break-out seminars for smaller groups of students, allowing them to plan lessons and develop classroom management skills. TAs also often assist in grading. A good instructor will seek to mentor their TA, explaining to them how and why the course is taught and inviting them to teach some classes. Other instructors may assign little more than clerical work, asking their TA to photocopy exams papers, post material online, or run scantron sheets through a grading machine. A prospective employer will not know from your CV how much teaching experience you gained as a TA, but if it was substantial you can convey this in your cover letter and in conversations during an interview.

Guest lecturing or guest teaching (delivering a single lecture or lesson in someone else's course) is a great way to get started in teaching, but it has much lower job market value than either of the two previous options. Guest lecturing shows some interest in teaching and some ability to write a lesson plan and manage a classroom but says nothing about your ability to teach an entire course or handle other instructor responsibilities. If you are near the end of your studies and have no opportunities to TA or become an instructor of record, guest lecturing is better than nothing at all. If you are early in your studies, consider guest lecturing as a steppingstone toward becoming a TA or an instructor of record. You can ask instructors you know if they have a lesson you could teach in one of their undergraduate sections.

An increasing number of employers are interested in your ability to teach online. Being a TA or instructor for an online course can increase your marketability for positions that include an online teaching load. Teaching face-to-face and online are overlapping but distinct skills. Teaching face-to-face requires certain abilities, like classroom management, that are not always needed online, whereas good online teaching requires honing your ability to keep students engaged without the accountability of regular classroom attendance. Because most universities still prioritize face-to-face instruction, I recommend that you start by TAing and teaching face-to-face courses. However, if you have the opportunity to also teach online, doing so can help you stand out on the job market.

EXERCISE 3.3: SETTING OBJECTIVES – PROFESSIONAL EXPERIENCE

Use the job postings you collected for the Chapter 2 exercises to answer the following questions:

1. Is teaching a major responsibility for your planned future profession?
2. If so, what kinds of courses do employers expect you to teach – what are their subjects and are they in-person or online?
3. Do prospective employers indicate how they expect you to signal teaching ability? For introductory positions, many may not request anything specific; however, some may request teaching evaluations or even sample syllabi.
4. What teaching roles are available at your institution that would help you gain the expected teaching experience?

Grant Writing

Numerous academic and non-academic employers will be interested in your ability to win grants. Grants are the lifeblood of many nonprofits and development organizations, and even commercial organizations may seek government or foundation funding to support special projects. Some government units also seek grant funding from internal government pools or private donors.

The ability to write grants is rarely required for new PhDs, unless it is part of a non-academic position that also requires significant professional experience. However, many advertisements seek an employee with the potential to win funding. Some signifiers of this potential include:

- Significant external funding for your own research
- Participation in a team that wins significant external funding
- Studentships and scholarships
- Conference or research travel funding

Some countries offer significant government funding for doctoral student research. The most prominent example in the US is the National Science Foundation Graduate Research Fellowship. If you win such an award, it shows that you can write a grant and that your research is sufficiently innovative and well-designed to win major funding. Besides government funding, you may also be able to apply for grants from foundations, think tanks, or nonprofits to support your work. These will vary in their selectivity, but winning any external funding shows that you have both grant-writing skill and fundable research.

If you have a position as a research assistant or work closely with an instructor leading a major research project, you may have the opportunity to participate in writing grant applications for their work. If these grants are successful, this can enhance your marketability, especially if the grant funds the research you are conducting for your doctorate. Such success shows that your research has funding potential and that you have some experience with the grant-writing process. It does not demonstrate conclusively that you can win funding on your own, but it gives you a good start in convincing a hiring committee that you can.

Studentships and scholarships fund the coursework part of your studies and may cover your tuition or living expenses during dissertation writing. They focus more on your qualities as an applicant and less on your proposed research. Winning one shows that you stand out among future scholars and have the ambition to apply for funding but shows relatively little about the fundability of your research.

Some funders give small grants specifically for research travel, and some conference and workshop organizers offer small grants to pay for students to travel to present their work. Winning these sorts of grants shows that your work has interest to others and is better than the competition, especially if you win funding from someplace besides your own university (i.e., "external funding"). Winning these grants also shows your ambition and proactivity as a junior scholar.

EXERCISE 3.4: SETTING OBJECTIVES – GRANT WRITING

Based on the job postings and CVs you collected for the Chapter 2 exercises, answer the following questions:

1. Is grant-writing experience expected by your future employers, treated as a bonus, or not discussed at all?
2. What kinds of grants are others at your prospective employer winning or managing? Does the focus seem to be on research funding, project funding, or other funding types?
3. Do the job advertisements seek employees who have already won grants or merely someone with the potential to win funding?
4. What kinds of grants would help you develop the necessary grant-writing experience or build a track record of successful funding?

Awards

Awards provide prospective employers with an additional measure of the quality of your work. By themselves, they are no replacement for research outputs or teaching or professional experience, but if you have those signifiers, awards can magnify their value. Common examples include:

- Teaching awards
- Conference paper awards
- Dissertation awards

Teaching awards include "Teacher of the Year" type awards, which some universities have for teaching assistants as well as instructors of record. Some universities have a teaching award just for adjunct instructors. Conferences often have an award for the best graduate student paper presented at a conference. For larger conferences, different sections (i.e., groups of scholars within a certain subdiscipline) may have their own graduate student paper awards. Applying for these awards usually requires submitting your paper a bit early (maybe as much as one month in advance of the normal deadline) and, perhaps as a result, they may be less competitive than you would expect. Dissertation awards are given for the best dissertation at a university or in a given field. In the latter case, these awards are given by professional associations and handed out at the association's annual conference.

There is no particular hierarchy to these awards, since each type enhances a different signifier. The value of any given award increases depending on how competitive employers perceive it to be. Awards from an external organization like a professional association may therefore hold more value than awards from your own university. However, for areas like teaching, internal awards may be the only kind available.

You should be aware of the value of awards so that you know to look for and apply for them. For instance, any time you apply to attend a conference, you should look to see what graduate student awards are available and when their deadlines are. You should also check your university's website (and any separate websites for your college, school, or department) for graduate student awards and note when in your career you may be able to apply for them. Some awards will require nominations. It is perfectly acceptable to ask the chair of your conference panel, your TA supervisor, or your dissertation advisor to nominate you. This can feel like an uncomfortable bit of self-promotion, but all of these people are quite busy and most will not make the time to nominate you unless prompted. A simple request from you will nudge them into action.

EXERCISE 3.5: SETTING OBJECTIVES – AWARDS

Using the websites for your university and any subunits (e.g., schools or departments) with which you are affiliated, answer the following questions:

1. Are there any awards granted for teaching assistants or part-time instructors? If your university has a unit that trains teachers or TAs, you may need to check their website.
2. Does your university or department offer awards for best student, best paper, or best dissertation? Who is eligible and when are the application deadlines?

Developing a Plan

The exercises above should give you a rough idea of the kinds of signifiers you will need to prepare for the job market. In future chapters we will discuss these in greater detail, examining potential dissertation topics, conferences, publication venues, and funding sources. At this stage, however, the challenge is to develop a roadmap for acquiring signifiers in a way that enhances your progress through the PhD. The goal is to complete your PhD in the expected amount of time (which can vary by country and discipline), while arriving at the end of your studies ready to enter the job market. If the plan to acquire signifiers is well-aligned with your progress through the PhD, acquiring signifiers will feel like a natural component of your progress through the PhD rather than an added burden that impedes your completion. The feedback you receive on your professional outputs – conference papers, publications, grant applications, and the like – will enhance the quality of your dissertation and the associated deadlines will keep your dissertation moving at a good speed.

The first step is to determine which signifiers you need to acquire. Review your answers to Exercises 3.1–3.5. Note which achievements you have already and which ones you still need to acquire. If you choose, you can use Exercise 3.6 to further refine your self-assessment.

EXERCISE 3.6: CV ASSESSMENT AND SELF-ASSESSMENT

Gather a group of three to five other students with similar career interests. Have each person bring a job advertisement for a post in which they are interested and one to two CVs from recent hires that they have found online. Make sure the posts are suitable for newly minted PhDs.

1. Select one of the job advertisements and imagine yourselves as the hiring committee for that job. Using the requirements of the job ad and the hierarchies of signifiers given in this chapter, evaluate the CVs that have been collected.
   - Which candidates look the strongest?
   - Who would you want to interview?
   - Who would not qualify for the position?
2. Discuss your answers to the above questions to understand which signifiers are necessary for a competitive CV.
3. Reflect: how would your CV fare if compared to others in the pile? How would your CV need to look to be competitive for a job that interests you?

The next step is to program these into your doctoral studies, creating a rough year-by-year or term-by-term schedule. Every student should have a timeline for completing their dissertation that includes major milestones in their coursework, dissertation research, and write-up. A student taking the minimum necessary time to complete in the social sciences would have a timeline that looks something like Table 3.1.

Depending on your field of study and area of research, each of the steps in Table 3.1 may take much longer than this table shows. You should develop

Table 3.1 Basic Timeline to PhD Completion

Years		Activities
US	UK/EU	
1–2	NA	Coursework
2–2.5	1	Develop and defend proposal
2.5–3.5	2	Fieldwork, data collection, dataset creation, or building/running models
3.5–4.5+	3+	Write-up, revisions, defense, post-defense revisions

a more detailed version of your own, noting which courses you will be taking each term and, once you have begun planning your dissertation, what research tasks you will be undertaking. You can continue to modify this schedule, refining it to the level of monthly or even weekly tasks as time goes on.

This outline for progressing through your coursework and dissertation forms the backbone of your schedule for the next four to six years. Acquisition of signifiers should be timed around the key events of your dissertation. Working around the dissertation ensures that the dissertation stays on track. It also sets the stage for synergies between the dissertation and your professional development. On the one hand, your dissertation progress will fuel your professional development. The dissertation itself will provide most of the ideas, data, and text you need for your research outputs, grant applications, and even some of your teaching. On the other hand, your professional development will enhance the quality of your dissertation and generate deadlines that keep you on pace.

For these synergies to occur, professional development activities must be timed to match key phases of your dissertation. As a general rule, I suggest pursuing each signifier as soon as you have the opportunity, data, or experience necessary to apply for it. However, not all of this timing is intuitive. In the paragraphs below, I offer my suggestions for less obvious steps.

First Years

Professional development can start in your first term. If you are at a university that requires two or more years of coursework, you should look for internship opportunities or short-term consulting assignments between your first and second year. Many organizations have internships specifically targeted to graduate students. You may need to apply for such positions as much as six months in advance – at the end of your first term or early in your second term.

You should also use the coursework phase of your program to research and apply for studentships or scholarships to fund your studies. You can do this too from your very first term in the program or, for some scholarships, even before you arrive.

If you arrive at school with significant subject matter or methodological expertise (e.g., from a master's degree in the discipline) or if you form a good relationship with a faculty member who teaches undergraduate courses, you can consider working as a research or teaching assistant during the second year of your program, provided that this is still during the coursework phase. This may feel a bit hectic, but the rigid deadlines associated with your own coursework will help keep you on track and prevent your assistantship work from taking over your schedule. Ideally, take a teaching assistantship or research position in which you will be using some of the same literature, data, or methods you expect to use in your dissertation. In this way, you will be gaining marketable experience while also being paid to prepare yourself for the dissertation.

If you think you have done a good job as a teaching assistant and your department or university has a teaching award for TAs, be sure to ask your supervisor to nominate you for it. Make sure to check the deadline and make your request three to four weeks in advance of it, so that they have plenty of time to submit your nomination.

Pre-Candidacy

The beginning of your third year in most US-style programs marks the start of your work on your dissertation. In UK-style programs, you may start as soon as you matriculate. The first major task of your dissertation research will be developing a research proposal. This involves reviewing the academic literature relevant to your research, developing a conceptual framework connecting together the theories you intend to use, articulating a specific research question, and developing a practical plan to answer it. Successfully defending your proposal is the dividing line between a doctoral student and a PhD candidate.

I encourage every student to submit a conference paper proposal as soon as they have a solid idea of the research question at the heart of their dissertation. The paper proposal should be for a review piece, which is a type of paper or article that organizes the existing academic literature on a topic, identifies weaknesses or lacunae in current thinking, and explains what new research must be undertaken for the field to move forward. A dissertation proposal does the same thing, while adding a detailed plan for answering the core research question that has been uncovered. Thus, the additional work needed to generate a conference paper in addition to the proposal is minimal; much of the text will overlap.

To maximize the synergies between the proposal and the paper, you must apply to conferences early. Applications for national and international conferences are often due six to nine months before the conference occurs. The application usually only requires a brief abstract of the paper you propose to present. For most conferences, you do not have to submit a completed paper until two to four weeks before the start of the conference. If your conference paper proposal is accepted, you gain a useful commitment device (the conference deadline) to ensure that you complete your dissertation proposal in a timely fashion (Haggerty 2010). When you present your paper, you will gain feedback from outside your dissertation committee on your work, which you can use to enhance the quality of your dissertation.

Do not forget to seek a travel grant for the conference. Many conferences offer them to graduate students. You should also check on any awards that may exist for graduate student papers and consider applying for these as well. Put the due dates for funding and awards on your timeline.

Once you have presented that paper and defended your proposal, you should seek to publish a review piece. Use the feedback you received at the conference to guide your revisions to your paper. Ideally, you will be able to submit your paper to a journal with less than a week of additional work. This may produce a slight delay in your dissertation writing, but it maximizes the value of the effort you have already put into your proposal and your conference paper. It will probably not yield a Tier-1 publication (although some Tier-1 journals do accept review pieces) but a Tier-2 publication is quite possible and this is a very credible signifier for a new job candidate. If your review is published, it also helps you lay claim to a particular domain of research. If it is clear from the academic record that you are the first to pose certain questions, other scholars may avoid doing overlapping work or they may cite your work, helping to establish your influence as a researcher.

Having a published review piece (or one that is accepted and awaiting publication) will also enhance any funding applications you make. Once you have your dissertation proposal completed, you should look for funders who have an interest in your field. Try to apply for several grant opportunities and seek travel funding for any fieldwork.

PhD Candidate

After you have successfully defended your proposal, you will move on to data collection and analysis. This may involve fieldwork, in which you leave the university to do interviews, collect documents, etc., or may involve working with datasets and models from your desk or materials in a lab. Again, you should be aware of some opportunities here. New datasets, especially if you have collected, cleaned, and digitized data that have not been assembled before, may be the basis of publishable pieces in their own right. The journal *European Political Science*, for example, regularly publishes dataset pieces, in which authors describe their new dataset, how it was assembled, and what it can be used for, sometimes accompanied by some basic analyses using the dataset to demonstrate its utility. Other journals publish research fieldnotes in which authors describe collecting data on new issues or in unusual places and discuss what they are learning about doing research on these topics or in these locales. Writing such a piece usually will require relatively little extra effort while adding value to your CV.

Even more importantly, you should consider developing your preliminary findings as academic articles. Some universities offer a three-paper option for the dissertation, in which the dissertation consists of three academic articles (not all of which are necessarily published or accepted for publication), plus some additional material explaining the links between them. This can be an excellent option. However, even if you are writing a traditional big book dissertation, your chapters may explore different cases, test different hypotheses, or present different analyses. If this is the case, consider developing one or more of them as conference papers and article publications.

As with your dissertation proposal, you can submit conference paper proposals as soon as you have an outline of the expected chapter. Assuming your proposal is accepted, the commitment to turn that outline into a paper will speed your dissertation writing. The conference presentation will be a useful tick on your CV in its own right and the feedback can improve your dissertation.

Submit articles for publication as soon as you have the draft of each relevant chapter complete or after you have received feedback on it at the conference. Even if you have not written a related conference paper, turning chapters into articles should take very little additional time. You will probably just need to add an introduction and a brief review of the literature section, both of which you will be able to write quickly by cribbing from your dissertation proposal. For this marginal expenditure of time and energy (up to a week per article), you will gain feedback from the journal reviewers, which you can then use to improve that chapter of your dissertation. Hopefully you will also gain a publication.

If you are seeking an academic job, consider the final year of your doctoral studies as another chance to be a teaching assistant or as your time to step up as an instructor of record. If at all possible, take on just a single course, to leave plenty of time for your writing up. Teaching preparation can consume an inordinate amount of time, but only if you let it. As we'll discuss in Chapter 11, you should be able to set boundaries around your teaching work. If you spend one day a week teaching, you'll still have plenty of time to write up. Teaching also has the added advantage of appearing on your CV before the task is complete, rather than after. You can list yourself on your CV as instructor for "Introduction to the Discipline" as soon as you step foot in the classroom in September – which is useful, because you may be applying for jobs in October. If you plan to leave academia, look for consulting work or paid research that you can do part-time in lieu of teaching.

Putting It All Together

We can now produce an integrated timeline. Tables 3.2 and 3.3 show sample timelines of activities, one for students studying in American-style programs

Table 3.2 Timing of Professional Development Activities, US-Style Program

Term	Year 1			Year 2			Year 3			Year 4		
	Fall	Spr	Su	Fall	Spr	Su	Fall	Spr	Su	Fall	Spr	Su
Set up job ad feeds	X											
Coursework	X	X		X	X							
Apply for internships		X			X							
Apply for studentships		X	X	X	X							
Intern			X			X						
Begin dissertation proposal				X								
First conference proposal				X								
Apply for TA positions					X	X						
Apply for conf. travel grant					X							
Present first conf. paper						X						
Defend dissertation proposal						X						
Submit first publication						X						
Apply for research grants					X	X	X					
Teaching assistant					X	X						
Dissertation research							X	X	X			
Additional conf. proposals							X	X	X			
Additional conf. presentations								X	X	X		
Submit additional publications								X	X	X	X	
Dissertation write-up								X	X			
Teacher of record								X	X			
Apply for jobs							X	X	X			
Defend dissertation									X	X		

Table 3.3 Timing of Professional Development Activities, UK-Style Program

Term	Year 1			Year 2			Year 3			Year 4		
	Fall	Spr	Su	Fall	Spr	Su	Fall	Spr	Su	Fall	Spr	Su
Set up job ad feeds	X											
Write thesis proposal	X	X										
First conference proposal	X	X										
Defend thesis proposal		X	X									
Apply for studentships	X	X	X	X								
Apply for research grants			X	X	X							
Apply for conf. travel grant				X								
Present first conference paper				X								
Submit first publication				X	X							
Thesis research				X	X	X						
Additional conf. proposals					X	X	X	X	X			
Additional conf. presentations						X	X	X	X	X	X	
Additional publication submissions							X	X	X	X	X	
Apply for TA positions					X		X	X				
Thesis write-up							X	X	X			
Teaching assistant							X	X		X		
Defend thesis and revise										X	X	
Apply for jobs										X	X	

with extensive coursework and one for students studying in UK-style programs without mandatory coursework.

These schedules project the bare minimum time necessary to complete a PhD in the social sciences. Many students and disciplines require additional time. The main takeaway is that you must undertake professional development activities throughout your studies because of the long lag times involved between things like conference application and presentation or publication submission and acceptance. When I was a student, I once had a conversation with a well-respected senior scholar, in which I asked for his input on my PhD timeline. As I explained that I intended to pause my PhD research at different points to write articles, I felt self-conscious about this obvious effort to prepare for the job market, noting that it was "a bit mercenary." He interrupted to correct me. "In academia we don't say it's mercenary," he explained. "It's pragmatic." If you wait until your dissertation is nearly complete before focusing on professional development, you may find yourself uncompetitive on the job market or lingering in your PhD program, all but graduated, while you try to build up your CV.

Competition and Opportunity

At this point, you should have an idea of the qualifications needed for your preferred post-PhD jobs and some sense of when they should be integrated into your doctoral studies. Chapter 4 will help you identify areas of comparative advantage that you can leverage in your research. The nuts and bolts of acquiring most of the core signifiers discussed here will be covered in Chapters 7–11.

Your reaction to the material in this chapter may be one of exhilaration: you have a roadmap to the career you desire and you are excited about earning accolades and building your CV. Alternatively, you may feel intimidated. Just finishing the dissertation seemed hard enough and now so much more has been added to it. My caution to the enthusiastic is to be mindful of the connection between your accolades and your research. Focus on synergies between the two and remember to distinguish between high-value opportunities and low ones. Seek only the best ones.

My encouragement to the discouraged is that while these increased expectations create pressure, they also create opportunity. When employers focus on concrete indicators of ability, your eligibility for jobs is less dependent on the reputation of your school, program, or advisor. A candidate with publications in well-regarded journals, highly relevant research, or appropriate professional experience will receive serious consideration on the job market, regardless of their academic pedigree. Remember too that you do not have to compete in the biggest or most competitive job markets. Instead, you may identify a professional specialty or academic subdiscipline for which you have natural enthusiasm and talent. The start of the next chapter, which discusses comparative advantage, can help you find your niche.

Recommended Readings

Banoo, D., & Gutmman, M. (2018). From detour to deliberate. *Inside Higher Ed*, 1 May 2018.

Jobs.ac.uk (n.d.). Career planning for PhDs ebook: Activities & advice to help you explore your options & succeed in a competitive job market. Available at: https://www.jobs.ac.uk/enhanced/careers-media/career-planning-phd-ebook.pdf.

Kelsky, K. (2012). Graduate school is a means to a job. *The Chronicle of Higher Education*, 27 March 2012.

Additional Resources

Haggerty, K. D. (2010). Tough love: Professional lessons for graduate students. *The American Sociologist*, 41(1), 82–96.

Jobs.ac.uk (n.d.b). The essential guide to moving up the academic career ladder. Available at: https://www.jobs.ac.uk/media/pdf/careers/resources/the-essential-guide-to-moving-up-the-academic-career-ladder.pdf.

Finding Your Comparative Advantage   **4**

The real step toward completing your PhD is the selection of your research topic. Your program may require coursework or comprehensive exams, but I encourage you not to wait until you complete those things before reflecting on your dissertation research. The real value of the PhD is in demonstrating the capacity for novel, independent, and robust research; this is what sets it apart from other graduate degrees. It is worth noting that a PhD from a UK institution with no required coursework is worth just as much on the job market as a PhD from a similarly ranked US institution with two or more years of coursework. It is the dissertation or thesis research that really matters, and this is by far the program component that gives students the most trouble.

The dissertation gets easier (although it is never easy) if you can identify an area of comparative advantage in which to do your research. In general terms, this means an area where, because of your personal background, previous studies, or professional experience, you are more likely than other researchers to be able to identify a good research question and to answer it well. Working in an area of comparative advantage makes it more likely that you will produce high-quality outputs that enhance your future marketability, and it enables you to integrate your past experiences with your present research in a way that builds a unique narrative about who you are as a researcher (your "personal brand") that you can communicate to future employers.

This chapter focuses on identifying your possible areas of comparative advantage. To explain what constitutes comparative advantage, however, we must first discuss the research process and how it works. Once you understand the parts of the research process, we will discuss what comparative advantage

DOI: 10.4324/9781003262831-4

is and how it can help you at different points in your research. The chapter concludes with some questions, examples, and exercises to help you reflect on your own areas of comparative advantage and identify one or more research topics that make maximum use of them.

Comparative Advantage and the Research Process

One of the core requirements of a successful dissertation is producing novel research, i.e., producing work that adds to the sum total of human knowledge. This typically requires answering a research question that no one has ever asked before, or developing an answer to an existing question in a way that no one has previously and getting a more provocative, comprehensive, or convincing answer as a result.

This is a difficult undertaking. You are being called upon to have an idea or insight that no one has ever had before. If you are not daunted by this challenge, you should be. It is by no means insurmountable; if your school accepted you into their PhD program, they believe you can rise to the challenge. However, students get into trouble when they do not take this task seriously enough and blithely assume that their initial ideas are original and research-worthy.

In the next chapter, we will discuss specific techniques for taking a general topic of interest and identifying within it a novel avenue of research. This happens through deriving a specific, relatively narrow question that is innovative in both its theory and its data or methods. This process is easier, however, if you are working with a topic or methods with which you already have some familiarity or insight.

In economics, comparative advantage is used to describe a domain in which one producer can create a product more efficiently and cost-effectively than another or create a better product for the same expenditure of resources. For example, an appropriate climate and good soil may give certain countries a comparative advantage in growing oranges or making wine. Expert knowledge and advanced technology may give a company a comparative advantage in producing new medicines or complex chemicals.

In the PhD context, every student has certain personal characteristics that will allow them to do research more efficiently and accurately when working on certain topics or questions, thereby giving them a comparative advantage over other scholars exploring the same issues. Emphasizing comparative advantage moves our thinking away from being "the best" in a given program, year, or market and reorients us toward finding an avenue of research that is uniquely suited to us. Doing so allows us to do better research and also to tell a story about how our experiences and research intersect that will be appealing to future employers.

Steps in the Research Process

Identifying comparative advantage in the PhD requires some understanding of how new knowledge is produced. If you are new to the PhD, you may be unfamiliar with the steps in the research process. Knowing what these steps are will help you reflect on ways that your background might give you an advantage at different stages.

Research Topic

Your research begins by identifying a general topic for your research. This should reflect your interests and be fairly narrow and specific because you are driving toward developing a research question that can be answered well in just two to three years of research and because you will need to review the extant literature related to your topic. Choosing something like "African international relations" is too broad. "The role of human rights in relations between African states" or "the role of human rights in relations between African states and former colonizers" is much more precise. You could refine the topic even further, for instance, if you know that you are most interested in a certain subset of states (e.g., West African states or former French colonies) or a particular time period (e.g., the first decade of the global war on terror).

Review of the Literature

Once you have a reasonably narrow research topic or even a preliminary research question, you must begin to review the academic literature on the topic. You first goal here is to determine the novelty of your proposed research. Some academics refer to this as finding "a gap in the literature," but that is misleading. There are very few topics that have received no research, unless you are working on something quite niche, obscure, or new. Moreover, no topic exists in isolation. Even if you were studying the environmental impacts of a never-studied fishing community on a small island, your research would still be connected to – and hopefully contributing something new to – the broader literatures on environmentalism, livelihoods, community dynamics, fisheries, or the anthropology of island communities.

Therefore, rather than focusing on finding a gap, you should seek to problematize the existing research. This means examining what has been done previously on a topic and determining whether there are weaknesses or limitations in the literature that suggest a need for new research. If there are, then your critique is the novel starting point for your work. In essence, you are arguing that the previous research is wrong or limited, and that you have an idea for correcting or expanding it. We will discuss problematization more in the next chapter.

While problematization is the foundation of novelty, there are multiple additional ways in which your research can be novel. You may be applying or developing a new theoretical perspective, gathering new data, or applying new methods or analysis. Establishing this novelty involves first finding everything that has been written on your particular topic (you can see here why a narrow topic serves you well), then reading or skimming everything to determine whether your ideas or approach are new, and finally reflecting on how your contribution could improve on what has come before.

Developing a Research Question

Once you have reviewed the literature and identified its limitations, you will write a research question that clearly responds to the limitations or weaknesses you have identified. For many disciplines, your research question will focus on a causal dynamic, i.e., the ways in which certain variables lead to a certain effect, often expressed as $A \rightarrow B$. Usually this means a how or why question, like "How did $A \rightarrow B$?" or "Why did $A \rightarrow B$?" For example, "How did 9/11 and the global war on terror affect US efforts to promote human rights in autocratic African states?" Some disciplines may also entertain more descriptive "What" questions, such as "What do current trends suggest about future levels of political party affiliation among young voters in the US?" (White 2017).

Data Collection

Data collection involves gathering the information needed to answer your research question. This can include collecting information directly yourself or accessing information others have already collected. Common qualitative techniques include interviewing participants in or witnesses to important events, running focus groups, or observing a particular phenomenon, like how children play in mixed-race settings or how youth conduct themselves at political rallies. You may write and administer surveys to gather information from a broad group of people, use software to collect information from news outlets or social media, or work with archival texts. Quantitative researchers may convert qualitative data, like survey responses or social media posts, into numeric data or use pre-existing datasets, like from a government household survey. Sometimes quantitative researchers build their own datasets by combining data from multiple sources. Research can involve travel, whether domestically or overseas. Even quantitative researchers working with existing datasets sometimes travel abroad to gain access to government archives and data (e.g., Jerven 2013).

Data Analysis

Once you have collected your data, you will need to analyze them. In essence, you will be identifying trends in the data and determining how different categories of data ("variables") are related to each other, e.g., how earnings relate to voting behavior. There are many different ways analysis can be conducted, and the researcher must choose a method that is appropriate to both the data and the research question. Quantitative researchers have a host of statistical techniques available to them, ranging from very basic frequency counts (e.g., how many people with certain characteristics showed a specific behavior) to linear regressions to more complex means of identifying associations and testing their strength. Qualitative researchers may look for connections between data in interviews, observations, or text or use discourse analysis to examine tone and meaning. Some researchers carry out visual analysis of imagery, such as that used in advertising, protests, or propaganda. Other methods abound. You should get a sense for which methods are most common in your field through the review of the literature and any methods courses in your coursework.

Final Write-up

Once the researcher has analyzed her or his data, the researcher must distill those findings into a concrete answer to the research question. This answer should be linked back to the problem identified in the literature to show how the research challenges, confirms, or advances aspects of previous thinking. In some disciplines, the findings will also need to be applied to current policies or real-world problems to generate policy guidance.

Sources of Comparative Advantage

As noted earlier, comparative advantage is created by those characteristics that enable you to complete your research more quickly or efficiently than others or allow you to produce a higher quality product. This can occur at any stage in the research process. Ideally, you will develop a research agenda that combines multiple characteristics for a stronger comparative advantage. To help you think about these, this section discusses how different sources of comparative advantage can enhance your performance at each stage of the research process.

Research Topic

The first opportunity for comparative advantage is choosing a research topic connected to your identity, previous experiences, or personal interests. While it is dangerous to assume that the experiences or observations of any one person are generalizable to the larger population or capture the whole of a phenomenon, people who have grown up in a particular community or been actively engaged with a particular issue naturally know more about it than those who have not. For instance, someone who has lived and worked in a rural Thai village will know much more about the culture and economics of such a place than someone who has not – and someone who grew up there probably knows more than someone who has only lived there for a few months. Similarly, someone who has participated in protests or served in combat almost certainly knows more about protests or combat, at least in some dimensions, than someone who has only read about these things in books. Their experiences will not capture all of the phenomenon – they may know what it is like to be a protestor but not a police officer, or what it is like to be a helicopter pilot but not an infantryman – but the experience they do have has a depth that can never be replaced by book knowledge. Not only do they know part of the experience well, but they may also have some sense of what the whole of the phenomenon looks like (e.g., that protests can involve multiple groups of protestors as well as law enforcement, observers, and the media) so they can more easily figure out what it is that they do not know and begin researching that. In short, personal identity and life experience can give you a head start because you know more than others and can more easily figure out what you need to learn.

Hobbies and passions can also create familiarity and give you a head start. I know of two professors who have spun a massive research agenda out of their love of beer, examining beermaking and beer drinking using the disciplinary tools of geography (Hoalst-Pullen and Patterson 2017). Another has leveraged her passion for beauty pageants and her work as a beauty pageant judge to write about the sociology of beauty pageants (Levey Friedman 2020). I once even met a rock climber who was doing a PhD on cliff-dwelling birds.

Reviewing the Literature

If you know some of the key authors, seminal texts, and dominant theories on a topic, you will have a head start on reviewing the literature, giving you an advantage when compared to someone who is new to it. Note, however, that to have a real comparative advantage you must have done more than simply take coursework on the topic at the undergraduate or master's level. It is often advantageous to pursue a PhD in a field related to your undergraduate or master's work, but a review of the literature around a research topic is much narrower and more detailed than the readings for a typical taught course. Besides, many people in your field will have taken similar courses. Instead, comparative advantage comes from building on work you have done for a master's thesis (master's dissertation in the UK) or a senior undergraduate thesis, or on research you have done as part of your professional employment. Building on your previous research in your PhD will also help create an intuitive arc to your professional trajectory that may help later in marketing yourself to employers.

Developing a Research Question

The same kinds of personal knowledge and experience that you can leverage in choosing a research topic can also help you identify a problem in the literature or a need for additional research. Recognizing where the previous literature is weak or inadequate usually requires a certain intuitive leap. I often see this result from students' experiences as practitioners. For instance, a close friend was familiar with how the academic literature suggested that foreign donors dominated negotiations with poorer nations receiving foreign aid. Yet in her work as a business consultant, she heard government officials in several such countries describe the leverage they held over foreign donors. These conversations suggested to her ways that the academic literature might be in error and prompted her doctoral research.

Professional experience is not the only place where this occurs. You may be part of a particular racial, religious, or cultural subgroup that you suspect is not adequately understood by most academics. Platt and Hamilton (2017), for instance, write that Black doctoral students often choose race-related dissertation topics because, as they read the academic literature, it is startling and obvious to them the ways it neglects Black experiences.

Perhaps you are not a member of an academically neglected or misunderstood community yourself but tied to it in a way that gives you deeper knowledge than most outsiders. Levey Friedman (2020), for instance, writes of how having a former Miss America as her mother exposed her to beauty pageant culture from a young age even though she was never a competitor. Similarly, former Peace Corps and VSO volunteers and former missionaries often have a deeper understanding of the countries and communities in which they served than academics without similar experiences, even though they are not natives of those communities. This familiarity can again help identify problems in the literature.

Research Design

While not explicitly referenced in our earlier discussion of the research process, research design involves selecting the data collection and data analysis methods appropriate for your research question. I list it here separately because there are certain characteristics that can help you know what data and methods are appropriate for the question you have identified.

Sometimes researchers create inadequate or unrealistic research designs because they are unfamiliar with the existing data or with conditions affecting data collection. You may have a great plan for answering a question using certain data, only to learn that such data are unavailable and that collecting them yourself would require more money and time than you have. Or you may not realize that a certain question you plan to ask is culturally inappropriate or that answering it might place your respondents at risk of persecution.

If you have never done research in a particular region or with a particular culture group, you may be unaware of physical and cultural hurdles that will determine who you can talk to, what you can ask, how many people you can interview, how many events you can observe, or how much time and money it will take to do what you plan. Previous experience working with a particular type of group or in a particular setting will help you create a realistic plan and increase the likelihood that your study generates robust, meaningful results.

Data Collection

As noted, after you have generated a research question, you need to collect or access the data necessary to answer it. You may have experience, identity, or skills that help you collect data more easily or improve the quality of the data you collect, giving you a comparative advantage when working on certain topics or with certain methods.

Professional connections often yield access to data. One summer during my PhD studies I worked as an analyst for a Washington, DC, firm that was leading lobbying around a change in World Bank policy. One of my colleagues had collected extensive data on the policy change, and I recognized from our discussions that the material would make a good case study for my PhD. I asked my employer for permission to use the data, which was granted. The result was a published journal article, coauthored with the colleague who had collected the data, and material for half a chapter in my thesis.

Access can also be linked to identity. My first published academic article was derived from my master's dissertation. (I studied for both my master's and my PhD in the UK, so I did a master's dissertation and a PhD thesis.) I had worked previously as a campus minister for a Christian NGO and decided to do research on the World Bank's policies toward faith-based organizations. While my previous experience did not give me any special insights into the topic, it gave me an identity as part of the community of Christian NGO workers. When I contacted the leaders of Christian faith-based organizations for interviews, they often remarked positively on my previous employer – some of them were even donors to the organization. This established a rapport that made the interviews much easier to get and conduct.

Members of the same faith are not the only ones who share this rapport. I have seen military veterans gain access to military leaders and military or intelligence-related archives. International students often do research in their home countries where they can leverage their status as a local. Members of marginalized communities may be more willing to trust and talk with researchers who come from their community.

You can develop your comparative advantage through your choice of data collection methods. Data collection can have a steep learning curve, and newcomers to a method often struggle before finding their feet. You can leverage any previous experience you have with data collection, provided that the methods you have used previously are appropriate to your research question. It does not matter if your experience was gained in a non-academic setting. For instance, you may have experience conducting interviews as a journalist, administering surveys as pollster, or observing behavior as a law enforcement officer. Other skills and experiences can make it easier for you to learn new techniques. A background in programming, for example, can give you a head start on doing computer-assisted content analysis or scraping web sources for data.

Lastly, language skills are a key basis for comparative advantage. Whether you are communicating with the local population or reading documents, if you are a proficient speaker or reader of a given language, you have a significant edge over researchers who will either need to learn the local language or work via a translator. If the language happens to be one in which academic journals are published and you are doing research of interest to speakers of that language, your language skills can also create additional publication opportunities for your work.

Data Analysis

As with data collection methods, you may have expertise in a particular set of analytical techniques. This may result from your previous studies, especially if you completed master's level research in a field with rigorous methods, or it can be through previous work as a researcher or through other professional experience. Students with a background in programming may have an easier time using software to organize and analyze their data, lawyers are familiar with analyzing legal documents, and so on. If you have previous professional experience, you should reflect on what your profession has taught you and what sorts of data you are familiar with handling.

Naturally, analyzing your data also requires that you understand it. All the characteristics that helped you in picking a research topic and identifying a question, like personal experience with a people, place, or issue, will also help you at the analytical stage because you will more readily understand what the data mean and how to interpret them.

The Power of Comparative Advantage

Focusing on your comparative advantage while planning your dissertation produces a more self-referential approach than most of the advice you will find on selecting a dissertation topic, much of which focuses on steeping yourself in the current academic literature, consulting with faculty, or even finding inspiration in your coursework (Lei 2009). In my experience, students who take these conventional approaches often end up with quite derivative topics. After all, it is hard to find a place to say something new just by reading or studying what has already been said. It also can set you up for a challenging dissertation process in which everything – the theory, the subject matter, the methods, etc. – is new to you, rather than exploiting synergies with your expertise and past experiences. In contrast, planning a dissertation that uses your comparative advantage will allow you to save time, identify a better research question, make fewer mistakes in your data collection and analysis, and develop a more persuasive, robust answer to the question you identify. It will also help you begin establishing a personal brand and develop a research agenda that feels true to yourself.

I recognize that some readers may be passionate about a particular topic, regardless of their lack of experience with it. Passion is important in the PhD, and you should seek to find a topic that you are excited about. After all, you will have to work on this topic for two or more years, and perhaps much longer if you go on to a research-focused academic job. However, I urge you to be realistic about the challenges of working on a topic about which you are largely ignorant and how your topic selection will affect your future marketability.

You should also think of yourself as starting (or continuing) the development of your personal brand as a researcher. This involves finding "those elements that could differentiate or favourab[ly] position" you in your professional life (Ilies 2018). The process is inherently self-referential. When developing a personal brand, "you need to focus mainly on yourself … and try to exude as much authenticity as you can" (Stahl 2018). This can be challenging for some students, especially those from cultures in which personal stories are not shared publicly or where there is a strong divide between the personal and the professional. If that is the case for you, you may want to read ahead to Chapter 13 where this topic is discussed in more detail.

For now, it is enough to know that in many Western contexts it is to your advantage if your CV tells a story that is compelling and easy to understand, including a pattern of regular engagement with certain issues or topics or a progression toward increasing mastery of certain skills (Banoo and Gutman 2018). An undergraduate degree in music and a PhD on the sociology of professional orchestras makes intuitive sense. An employer can imagine the synergies created by the two. An undergraduate degree in music and a PhD on the sociology of working-class taverns in Chicago just raises questions. You can have a good answer to those questions but struggle to find an employer willing to look past the mysteries and give you time to explain.

Comparative advantage also has relevance beyond the dissertation. If you train yourself to identify your areas of comparative advantage in research, it will help you spot new research opportunities as they arise. Over time, you will be able to distinguish between those moments when you are simply learning something yourself for the first time and the moments when you are having a genuine and novel flash of insight, rooted in your perspective and experiences, that will also be new to many other people. The latter represent research and publication opportunities, both in graduate school and in any future research career.

Finding Your Area of Comparative Advantage

To help you identify those characteristics and experiences that set you apart and are relevant to your dissertation, I've devised several exercises (4.1–4.3). Complete as much as you are comfortable with. The intent is not to pigeon-hole you or to assume that your research future is circumscribed by your past. Instead, the goal is to reflect broadly on many possible features and experiences that might give you an advantage in doing research on a particular topic or in a particular way.

EXERCISE 4.1: IDENTITY AND PERSONAL EXPERIENCES

1. Does your family have any notable characteristics? For example, were you raised in a single-parent household, or as the child of refugees, activists, or government officials?
2. What is your socio-economic background?
3. Where have you lived?
   a. Which countries?
   b. Which regions or cities?

    c.   In urban, rural, or suburban settings?

    d.   In settings marked by notable poverty or wealth?

4.   What languages do you speak?

5.   Do you identify with any subcultures or groups, e.g., based on race, ethnicity, shared history, gender, religion, politics, preferences, or lifestyle?

6.   Do you have any hobbies or extracurricular activities that you have performed at a high level? Have you been an instructor or competitor in any sport, craft, or artform?

7.   What are you passionate about? To borrow from Mark Batterson, what makes you "mad, glad, or sad?" How have your passions shaped your activities?

8.   Are there any other characteristics or interests you would like to integrate into your doctoral research?

EXERCISE 4.2: PROFESSIONAL AND VOLUNTEER EXPERIENCE

1.   What jobs have you had, whether paid or unpaid?

2.   Have you worked in any roles that are unusually prestigious, often go unnoticed, or are marginalized or stigmatized?

3.   What sectors of the economy have you worked in?

4.   Have you worked in professions that are not well understood by outsiders, like government or military service?

5.   What subject matter expertise have you gained through professional work? For example, do you know about logistics, public health, child education, or certain foreign cultures?

6.   What sorts of data have you used in your previous work? For example, did you deal with statistics, government records, or legal documents?

7.   Did you collect data or use any research methods in your previous jobs? For example, do you know how to do an interview, run a focus group, observe groups or individuals, assemble a dataset, map terrain, or write a survey?

8.   Did you learn or use any skills that can be applied to data analysis? For instance, did you do project evaluations, write programs to analyze digital data, or run statistical analyses?

9.   What else have you learned from your professional or volunteer work that feels relevant to your doctoral research?

EXERCISE 4.3: EDUCATION AND PREVIOUS RESEARCH

1. What have you studied at the undergraduate and graduate levels?
2. Did you complete a significant research project as an undergraduate or graduate student? On what topic? Using what methods?
3. Have you served as a research assistant or in another research-focused role? What literature did you use? What subject matter or methodological expertise did you gain?
4. Have you presented research at an academic conference or published any of your work, whether as the sole author or with coauthors?

Once you have reflected on these questions, you may want to assemble these characteristics into a chart or grid so that you can see everything at once. You can eliminate the questions that seem less relevant to you. Your goal is to begin connecting the dots and identifying an avenue of research that combines multiple areas of your background and experience.

My initial PhD research topic (which I later refined) was "the impact of faith-based organizations on the representation of developing country stakeholders at the World Bank." This connected my time working in Togo (a low-income country in West Africa), my passion for seeing that low-income country populations have voice or at least accurate representation on the world stage, my experience working in international development, my master's dissertation on faith-based organizations and the World Bank, and a previous publication based on my master's dissertation. I could work on this topic confident that relatively few other researchers would have both my access and experience. I was also familiar with much of the relevant literature and knew about the structure and function of the World Bank because of my master's research. Lastly, because my one academic publication also focused on faith-based organizations and the World Bank, this PhD research topic would help give my CV a clear narrative arc.

Use Exercise 4.4 to brainstorm some research topics of your own. As noted, the goal is to connect several of your characteristics and experiences, whether personal, professional, or research-related. If this is the first time you have really thought hard about your research topic, and especially about making your topic personal, it may take a while to develop something you are happy with. Give yourself some time and continue to reflect on topics for several days. My initial topic reflected weeks of on-and-off brainstorming. Once you have some topics, try telling a friend (or just imagine telling a friend) why you think you can do a better job with this topic than most other researchers. This will help you refine your sense of your comparative advantage and how it relates to each research topic.

EXERCISE 4.4: BRAINSTORMING RESEARCH TOPICS

1. Identify two to three research topics. These should be general areas of research, like "intergenerational dynamics in low-wage work" or "human rights and trade relations in Southeast Asia," rather than full questions. Each topic should meet the following criteria:
    a. Something of genuine interest to you.
    b. Connects at least three aspects of your characteristics and experiences.
    c. Involves some element of mystery, paradox, and public or academic interest – i.e., you see a specific need for more research and have an idea for why others may be interested in your findings.
2. Write or verbalize a short justification explaining why you think you could research this topic better than many other scholars. Reflect on your inside knowledge, access, the methods needed, etc. Explain not just how you can do the work faster or more efficiently, but also why you are more likely to get an accurate answer to any research question you ask.

Your research topic does not have to be too refined or detailed yet. Try to make your possible topics narrow enough to be researchable: "the role of street art in popular protest in the Middle East" is better than "the role of street art in popular protest" (which implies a global scope) or something really broad like "street art." That being said, you will probably identify broad areas of interest first (e.g., "street art") and then narrow them down by reflecting on other dimensions of your comparative advantage (e.g., time as an activist or family connections to the Middle East).

This is just the start. While your research topic may imply that you will use certain data or methods, these choices will become more explicit as you develop your research question. With that in mind, once you have found several topics that seem to suit you, proceed to Chapter 5 where we will discuss how to turn your general topic into a specific research question.

Recommended Readings

Banoo, D., & Gutmann, M. (2018). From detour to deliberate. *Inside Higher Ed*, 1 May 2018.

Holliman, A., & Jones, T. (2018). Identifying a topic for a psychology dissertation: A process map for students. *Psychology Teaching Review*, 24(1), 82–90.

Platt, C. S., & Hilton, A. (2017). Why so much blackness? Race in the dissertation topics and research of black male doctoral students. *Spectrum: A Journal on Black Men*, 5(2), 23–44.

Additional Resources

Ekhlasi, A., Talebi, K., & Alipour, S. (2015). Identifying the process of personal branding for entrepreneurs. *Asian Journal of Research in Marketing*, 4(1), 100–111.

Peters, T. (1997). The brand called you. *Fast Company*, 31 August 1997.

White, P. (2017). *Developing Research Questions: A Guide for Social Scientists*. New York: Palgrave MacMillan.

Developing Your Research Agenda

5

Once you have identified a research topic linked to your comparative advantage, it is time to refine this topic into a research agenda. At this stage of your doctoral studies, your research agenda will revolve around a single research question at the heart of your dissertation. This will typically be some sort of larger, causally-focused question that is complemented by additional sub-questions. For instance, your central question may be "How do government leaders' attitudes towards environmental degradation affect their management of grazing rights for pastoralist peoples in East Africa?" This might be complemented by sub-questions like, "What are government leaders' beliefs about environmental degradation?" or "What political power do pastoralists have relative to other social groups?"

The answer to this central question will be your most important output. Ideally, it will be publishable in a top-tier journal or even as a book. However, the data gathered while answering your sub-questions may also yield conference papers and articles, which can be presented and submitted for publication earlier in the research process. As noted in Chapter 3, the process of presenting and publishing will help you get feedback on your research, making it stronger and preparing you to defend your work. At the same time, presentations and publications will publicize your research agenda, build your CV, help you build your professional network, and give you greater credibility when you go on the job market.

The central question of your dissertation will also set the direction for your future research and publication agenda. Once your dissertation is done, you will likely mine the data you have gathered for additional publications. For instance, you might publish a piece on policy recommendations for

DOI: 10.4324/9781003262831-5

government leaders engaging with pastoralists or for nongovernmental organizations lobbying for pastoralist rights. Perhaps you will meet a colleague at a conference who is studying grazing rights in West Africa or India and you will combine your data to coauthor a comparative piece. Your research can also form a foundation for applying for external funding if that is part of your career strategy. For instance, you might find that international donors managing conflicts between pastoralists and farmers are willing to commission additional research on how to shape local government policies. If you become a practitioner, you may find that you are most marketable for jobs working with pastoralists, environmental issues, indigenous rights, or issues in East Africa because of the expertise you have developed on these topics.

This chapter focuses on how to develop the central question of your dissertation, beginning with a research topic and working toward a specific, researchable question. It also includes guidance on how to leverage your question for additional professional development, especially presentations and publications based on your research.

The Importance of a Good Research Question

The central question at the heart of your dissertation is referred to as your research question and is typically singular, whereas the smaller questions that help you answer it are referred to as sub-questions and are usually plural. Because a good research question is central to writing a dissertation, if your PhD program has coursework on research design or a first-year seminar you may cover developing a research question there. I include it in this book, despite the possible redundancy, because writing a good research question lays the foundation for your research agenda and professional development, and because writing a good research question is itself a core professional skill.

Learning to write a good research question is hard. Once you have done it a few times it gets significantly easier and more instinctual, but when a student is first learning what constitutes a good question, the criteria can seem impossibly opaque. If your advisor uses an instinctual or intuitive process to identify their own research questions, as many do, they may compound your frustration by giving vague feedback like "It's not quite right. Work on this some more." Insofar as this book is designed to both help you as a student and take some pressure off your advisor, it is worth discussing this topic here.

A good research question will set you up for success in your dissertation and future professional endeavors. A poor one will lead to frustration, a low-quality product, and much wasted time. Developing a good research question will require a thorough review of the relevant literature and, in most cases, some preliminary data collection, often from secondary sources. You will revise your research question repeatedly as you progress in these steps. In all, developing a good research question may take 25% or more of your total dissertation-writing time. Indeed, in many programs, the time devoted to developing the research proposal (which articulates and frames the research question and presents a plan for answering it) is often 25%–33% of the total expected research time. If you invest this time well, the actual research will go much more smoothly. Much of the writing you do for your proposal can be transferred into your dissertation with only modest revisions, and the proposal itself may (in abridged form) become a publishable product.

Moreover, your dissertation or thesis is probably not the only research you will ever do. If you go on to a profession with a research component, you will be writing research questions, identifying questions in need of research, or evaluating the questions others propose to examine or claim to have answered. Thus, learning to identify a good research question is an important professional skill.

Subsequent chapters of this book, on things like going to conferences, writing articles, and applying for funding, all assume that you have identified a question that others think is worth answering. If we were to discuss those skills in isolation, without first discussing writing a research question, you might get the erroneous impression that success in those sorts of professional endeavors rests primarily on mastering the right procedures and tricks. Knowing the right procedures and a few tricks is helpful, but those things are secondary to having a good research question and a solid plan for answering it.

Deriving a Research Question from Your Topic

In the previous chapter, we discussed identifying several topics that leverage your comparative advantage. Ideally, these should also be topics about which you are naturally curious and for which you feel that there are unanswered questions, on-going debates, or incorrect or outdated thinking. These features will help you turn your general topic into a specific research question.

To pass your dissertation defense and earn your PhD, your dissertation must make a genuinely new contribution to human knowledge. You cannot know if your findings themselves will be novel until your research is complete. (Assuming that you know what your findings will be is a bad idea, since it may bias your research; your research should ask a question, not demonstrate or prove a claim.) Therefore, the best way of ensuring novelty in your dissertation outputs is to ask a genuinely novel question – a question that is at least a little different from what any scholar has asked before.

You should appreciate that this is a difficult challenge. Thousands of scholars and centuries of recorded research precede you. Recognizing the difficulty of the challenge is the first step toward meeting it. If you think it will be easy, you are more likely to fall short.

Fortunately, there are some standard strategies for surmounting this challenge. One is notably better than the other, but we'll discuss the strengths and weaknesses of each. The first strategy is finding and filling a gap in the literature. The second is to problematize the existing literature by identifying a weakness or limitation in the existing research.

Mind the Gap

A gap refers to a particular topic or issue that no one seems to have examined before or a known topic or issue that has not been investigated yet using a certain method. The idea is that you will fill this gap by taking on this topic or deploying this method. Finding a gap is probably the most commonly recommended strategy for developing a research question (White 2017). Faculty in your own department may ask you what gap your research addresses, and you will read academic articles in which the authors describe identifying a gap in the literature.

The gap strategy ensures novelty through the fact that no one has taken on this particular subject before or used this particular method to examine it. The newness of the data collected or newness of the method is the guarantee of novelty. If you are researching a genuinely new phenomenon, this approach may be appropriate.

However, there are problems with this approach. Most notably, it can make for boring research and unimportant findings (Joy 2013b). If a certain sociological question has been asked in the UK, Canada, and New Zealand, repeating the question again in Australia may fill a gap ("No one has looked at this in Australia!"), but unless you have good reason to think that the Australian results will significantly deviate from the results of the previous studies, the findings probably will not be very interesting.

At other times, gaps exist because they are impossible to fill. Perhaps large sample size ("large-N"), quantitative analysis of behavioral patterns among a population of injection drug users would offer better insights than previous small-scale, qualitative investigations. It may also be unfeasible due to the inaccessibility of the population and incomplete information on who is a member (cf. Bryman 2012). As Patrick Dunleavy (2003) writes, sometimes gaps exist for a good reason.

Because the gap strategy relies on a fairly marginal amount of novelty (i.e., the newness of the data or method is all that makes the research novel), it also entails greater risks. Other students, scholars, and practitioners are doing research at the same time you are. If you are asking a very conventional research question and the only thing that makes your research different is new data or a new method, you may find that someone else publishes that data or deploys that method before you have a chance to complete your dissertation or publish your findings. This is often more likely if you choose to focus on a new or emerging phenomenon. In my own field of NGO research, for instance, the hot emerging phenomenon a few years ago was national government restrictions on the operations of foreign nongovernmental organizations. It was a genuinely new and important phenomenon – but soon after it began attracting scholarly attention, I saw multiple PhD students presenting on it, including three at the same conference.

Problematizing the Existing Research

A much better strategy is to problematize the existing research (Dunleavy 2003). What this means is to find places in the existing literature where you think that the conventional wisdom is incorrect or incomplete. Usually this means that you have identified new data or a new theoretical perspective that suggests a problem with the existing academic thinking. Note that, as I explained above, you cannot predict with certainty the outcome of your own research. Thus, you are not asking "Is the conventional wisdom wrong?" for your research question. If you do that and the answer is "no," you may not have findings worthy of a dissertation. Instead, you must establish the problem with the existing research in the development of your research proposal.

If you look at a widely used theory in your field and you know from your own experience or new data that in some cases that theory is wrong, then that is a starting point for your research. Imagine, for example, that the conventional scholarly thinking on foreign aid suggests that the loss of foreign aid will have negative effects on economic growth, but new data you have identified show that in some countries, certain segments of the economy grow more rapidly after donor exit. Thus, you have a basis for challenging the existing theory and you can expect that your dissertation will generate new theory because you will need to explain why certain sectors in some countries deviate from the standard predictions.

There are multiple other sources of problematization (Marx 1997). Some topics are marked by an active debate, rather than a single, widely agreed view. You can weigh in on one side of that debate using a new theoretical perspective and/or new data. Problematization can also result from a reconsideration of methods. You might recognize, for instance, that previous findings on a topic relied on a certain statistical method that has a recently recognized flaw or weakness. If you think a re-analysis of the data will yield different findings, the methodological problem could be the basis for your problematization. Lastly, problematization can result from using a new theoretical lens to reinterpret existing data. Conventional thinking in your field may rely on a series of assumptions that are not shared by other disciplines. Borrowing theory from another discipline may allow you to challenge those assumptions. For instance, I have often borrowed theory from economics to challenge the conventional wisdom in political science on NGO behavior (Pallas 2019, 2010; Pallas and Guidero 2016).

To compare problematization with gap-finding, imagine yourself walking alongside a brick wall representing the sum total of human knowledge. A gap-filler looks for a place where bricks are missing. Gaps that are both significant and readily fillable are rare; instead, he is most likely to find a few spots missing a brick or two or places where the wall could be built a bit higher. A problematizer looks for places where the bricks are old, crumbling, loose, or defective. The problematizer then chips away at the bricks and mortar until she has created a unique opening of her own to fill.

Problematization gives value to your dissertation. It expands the dimensions of novelty. You are not just bringing to bear data or new methods. You are challenging existing theory and, in all likelihood, will develop new theory (or at least revisions to existing theory) based on your findings. If you also problematize the existing literature by bringing to bear a new theoretical perspective, this added theoretical novelty is part of your research from the very outset. Having multiple dimensions of novelty makes it highly unlikely that another researcher will publish findings that undermine the novelty of your work. Someone else might work with the same data or apply similar theory, but it is unlikely that they will do both.

Because you are challenging the conventional wisdom in an established area of research, an audience for your work is more assured. Others who are already working in this field will be interested in your findings. Yes, there is some risk that established scholars will react poorly to you challenging the conventional wisdom, but most academics embrace the idea that human knowledge is advanced as new ideas revise or supplant older ones. If your research is robustly executed and respectfully presented, the odds of a strong or widespread backlash are low.

Lastly, because your research has both new theory and new data (or possibly new methods), you can attract a broader audience and market your work and yourself more broadly. Your work will be of interest to people who care about the type of data you use (e.g., case studies from East Africa), the kind of questions you ask (e.g., about pastoralists and government), or the theoretical perspective you use (e.g., applying psychology and ecology to issues of public policy). Your work may be more widely cited, and you may have more job opportunities because you have demonstrated broader expertise.

Getting Started

Your goal now is to develop a research question rooted in a problematization of the existing literature. Begin with the list of research topics you developed in the previous chapter. Your first indication of the potential for problematization may be an intuitive sense that there is a latent paradox or contradiction in the conventional wisdom or a personal experience that suggests that the conventional wisdom misses the mark in some way. With that in mind, complete Exercise 5.1

EXERCISE 5.1: CHOOSING WHICH RESEARCH TOPIC

1. Consider the research topics you identified in the last chapter as being within your area of comparative advantage. For each topic, reflect on the following:
   a. What are the variables being examined in the research topic (i.e., the different causes or effects you want to examine)?
   b. Why is the topic interesting to you?
   c. Is there something that seems paradoxical or mysterious?
   d. If you know some of the literature on this topic, are there things that you find problematic in other scholars' findings?
   e. Is there a way that you want to approach this topic that seems different from how others have done so in the past?
2. Using your answers to the above questions, select the research topic that seems to have the greatest potential for novelty and problematization.

Your next step is to develop a preliminary question. Note that this will hardly be your final research question. To the contrary, your research question will be revised multiple times as you reflect on it, get feedback, review the literature, and conduct preliminary research. To take an example from my own research, I was initially interested in examining how faith-based organizations were influencing stakeholder representation in international policymaking. However, as I began preliminary data collection, I discovered that faith-based organizations were having a negligible role in the policy processes in which I was interested. At the same time, a lot of the academic literature I was reading predicted that nongovernmental organizations generally, not just faith-based organizations, would be improving stakeholder representation in international policymaking. Based on these observations, I revised my question to focus on NGOs more broadly.

As with much writing, revising existing text is much easier than staring at a blank page, so take a moment and attempt to write a research question. At this point, your only goal is to write something that is truly a question (not a statement about how you will "prove," "demonstrate," or "show" something). If you are working in a discipline that values causal questions, it is also helpful if your question connects two variables – e.g., "How does A affect B?" – from your research topic.

EXERCISE 5.2: DEVELOPING A PRELIMINARY RESEARCH QUESTION

1. Take ten minutes and brainstorm a research question derived from your initial topic.
2. Examine your question and ask if it meets the following criteria:
    a. Is it phrased as a question?
    b. (Optional) Does it explore or test a connection between two or more variables?

Once you have a preliminary question – even if you feel like it's not a very good one! – you can begin to revise it. You want to work toward something that gets at the mystery, paradox, or problem you identified earlier. Ideally, it will feel interesting and provocative as soon as one reads it, or you will be able to explain why it is compelling and provocative very quickly. Here is an example of how a research question might progress:

- *Topic: how NGOs improve stakeholder representation and promote democracy in global governance.* This topic was more-or-less the starting point for my doctoral dissertation, once I moved past my focus on faith-based organizations. A topic like this makes a good starting point because it has multiple variables that can be connected together. What also made this topic good was an element of mystery or paradox. At the time I was developing my dissertation proposal, the academic literature claimed that NGOs were promoting democracy in international policymaking by speaking for marginalized populations in global policymaking processes. However, my experience in Africa led me to question whether international NGOs – who played the biggest role in policymaking – really understood grassroots needs or made meaningful efforts to gather grassroots input. Therefore, the predictions made in the literature seemed to be in tension with my personal experience.
- *Round 1: how are NGOs changing global governance?* This is the sort of thing I might have come up with as a preliminary question. It gets at one area of the topic, by examining what the actual results of NGO input are, but it does not connect all of the variables.
- *Round 2: how are NGOs making global governance more democratic?* This connects three parts of the topic and emphasizes causality by connecting NGO actions to a specific output – the democratization of global governance. The problem is that it does not capture the tension or paradox in my question. The reader has no reason to expect an answer any different than what the literature predicts.
- *Round 3: the literature says that NGOs are democratizing global govern- ance, but democracy requires giving everyone's voice an equal weight and most NGO influence is actually based on elite power – so are NGO impacts really democratizing global governance?* This version is messy and cum- bersome, but it is finally on the right track. It connects all of the pieces of the research topic. It also problematizes the conventional wisdom by using a new theoretical approach – i.e., by comparing claims of democratization with standards of democracy that require majority rule instead of elite rule. Note that this was not the final research question I used in my thesis either, but something like this – that both captures a causal relationship and identifies a problem with the con- ventional wisdom – is enough to go on.

EXERCISE 5.3: REVISING YOUR RESEARCH QUESTION

1. Examine your preliminary research question and ask if it meets the following criteria:
   a. Is it a question?
   b. Does it integrate all the variables from your research topic?
   c. Is it interesting?
   d. Does it respond to a paradox or problem in the conventional wisdom on your topic?
   e. Is answering this question likely to produce new insights that will advance scholarly thinking, rather than simply adding new data?
2. Revise your question and repeat step 1 until it clearly meets all of the criteria, even if it becomes long or messy.

If this process seems difficult, do not be discouraged. Your goal here is just to develop a workable preliminary version. Even this initial step will take time. Allow your ideas to percolate over several days. Practice summarizing your research by pretending to explain it to a stranger your meet in a pub or coffee shop, giving yourself a time limit of one to two minutes to force yourself to be succinct. Then try it on some friends and see if they feel like they understand what you want to do and why it is interesting to you. These exercises will help you clarify your thinking. At the same time, you can begin reviewing the literature to refine your question.

Refining Your Research Question

Once you have a preliminary research question, it is time to refine it. Your goal here is to develop a research question that meets certain criteria. For most PhDs, your question is required to be (White 2017; Bryman 2012):

- **A question.** You might be surprised at how often students miss this fundamental criterion. A research question that aims to "show," "prove," "argue," or "demonstrate" isn't a question at all. Such a statement sends a strong warning to reviewers that you began your research with a conclusion in mind, rather than letting the data lead you to your findings. You need a sentence that can end with a question mark.

- **Answerable.** Certain types of questions cannot be answered. Questions with a normative component are often unanswerable. If you ask, "What is the best solution to poverty?" the validity of your answer hinges on the definition of "best," which can be endlessly debatable. Questions that ask what is right or good have similar problems. Better to define what you mean by best (or good or right) in your question, e.g., "What interventions yield the most improvement in household income for families living below the poverty line?"

  Be wary, too, of future-oriented questions. I often see this when students propose questions designed to produce new policy guidance, without any plan to test their results. If you ask something like, "How can we maximize the alleviation of poverty for female-headed households in post-conflict agrarian communities?" you are either committing to some sort of experimental design, in which you will test different interventions, or you are going to produce a result that is largely speculative. Your output will be a list of things that other people should do in the future. How can your examining committee know if your answer is correct? A better question is past- or present-oriented, for example a meta-analysis of the impacts of recent interventions. If you are motivated by the desire to change policy or public opinion, reflect on what data or evidence policymakers or the public would need to change their views, and then develop a dissertation question designed to gather that data or evidence. Your findings can then become the basis for data-driven policymaking.

- **Narrow enough to be answered credibly using the time and resources available to you.** Some fantastic questions are so broad or complex that they will take years to answer well. You may not have that kind of time. Similarly, some questions can only be answered robustly using certain methods (e.g., large-N surveys or experimental designs) that can be expensive to implement. Keep in mind that a really robust answer to a narrow question is better than a weak or doubtful answer to a broad question.

  I often see students struggle with narrowing their topic down to something that is specific and researchable because they are interested in many things and want to write a research question that encompasses all of their interests. It may help to think of the research question as a funnel, with a wide top and a narrow mouth. The dissertation is like a bottle, with a narrow mouth and a wide body. The question takes all of your ideas and pulls them together in a way that allows them to fit into your dissertation. Once inside, they can expand again. Thus, home in on the things that link your interests. If your research has a core question that it answers well, you can add to your dissertation other elements, such as a discussion of the implications of your findings for public policy or their relevance to other contexts or cases.

- **Interesting or important.** For some fields this means that your work will be interesting to academics. For others, your work must also have practical implications and be relevant to practitioners. If you are problematizing existing research, it will be easier to meet this criterion since you will be working in a space that others already consider significant. If you are working in a policy-oriented program, you can also find places where policy and practice have gotten ahead of sound academic research, e.g., a place where policy is being made based on a theory that is, in fact, unproven. This can create an important need for research, especially if you think the policy or practice may be in error.

- **Linked to existing theory.** Most disciplines involve some body of theory, which captures explanations or predictions for certain types of phenomena. Your question should reflect how you are planning to use existing theories (e.g., by using them to examine a new phenomenon), or to challenge and possibly revise them (e.g., by showing how a given prediction does not hold in a new case).

- **Linked to previous research.** Academic thinking is essentially a long, ongoing dialogue. For your work to be respected, you need to show that you have considered and understood what other scholars have already done before branching out on your own. You may satisfy this requirement while considering theory. However, theories can often apply to a range of phenomena, while there is a body of literature that specifically examines the topic you want to address. Other scholars may not have considered your exact research question before, but they will probably have considered parts of it, and you will need to engage with their work. For example, while I looked for research that specifically considered NGOs and the democratization of global governance, I also considered research on NGOs and democratization (in national governance, rather than at the global level), on democracy in global governance (without NGO involvement), and on NGO involvement in global governance (in processes other than democratization).

- **Novel.** If you have examined the theory and previous research, you should know if anyone else has grappled with your particular question using the theory and data you intend to use. Your planned research must be original – hopefully in several different ways – in order to qualify for the PhD. Remember that new methods alone do not generate novelty unless they are likely to yield an answer to the question that is original, non-obvious, and credible.

Some of these criteria, like phrasing your question as a question, you will be able to tackle just through repeated revision and reflection on your own. Other criteria, like theory and links to previous research, cannot be addressed in isolation. They require that you review the literature.

Reviewing the Literature

The full details of how to conduct a review of the literature are beyond the scope of this chapter. You can find entire books devoted to the subject. What I wish to highlight here are what your goals are for a successful literature review.

First, you want to ascertain whether any other scholars have addressed your chosen research topic. I often tell students to take all of the key terms from their preliminary research question and plug them into Google Scholar or another academic database and see what has been written. If your novelty strategy revolves around filling a gap, this step is crucial: you may well discover that someone else has already published on your topic. Even if you find nothing on your specific topic, consider widening your search slightly by eliminating one or more search terms. To build on our hypothetical question from the start of the chapter, maybe no one has written about how politician attitudes toward environmental degradation have influenced policies toward pastoralists in East Africa. But you could search for "politician attitudes environment pastoralists" without confining your search to writings on East Africa. Or you might look at whether politicians' attitudes toward the environment influence other policies in East Africa, without restricting your search to policies on pastoralists.

Second, you will want to develop a sense of the conventional wisdom or existing debates on the topic. Read through the abstracts and some articles and get a sense for what sorts of claims people are making about cause and effect. This is especially important if you are taking a problematizing approach to novelty, since you need to understand the conventional wisdom before you challenge it. If no one has written on your exact topic, it does not mean that problematization is impossible. Instead, reflect on the causal relationships implicit in your research question. You might be assuming that public opinion about environmental degradation affects politicians' attitudes or that politicians' attitudes affect pastoralists' rights. Others may have written about these causal chains, even if they have not specifically linked all of the pieces in your question together. Once you know the conventional wisdom, you can reflect further on the problems or limitations you see in it. You may also find that there is a debate, in which case you will want to problematize the arguments of one or both sides.

Third, reflect on what theory is relevant. This includes both theories scholars are currently using on the topic and any theories that have not been used yet but that you want to apply as part of your problematization. You need to understand others' theories well enough to problematize them in a nuanced and respectful fashion. Moreover, if you are using an alternative body of theory, i.e., borrowing a theory from one discipline to problematize the conventional wisdom in another, you will need to understand that theory deeply enough to deploy it well.

Lastly, consider what methods are being used on this topic. Think about both the techniques and the sample sizes. Are other scholars doing small-scale case studies, large-N surveys, experimental designs? You will want to make sure that your planned methods are as good or better than the current methods in the field. For instance, if scholars in your field are currently using experimental designs, you may not get much respect for using observational data. If others are doing multi-country comparative case studies with 100+ respondents, you may not be credible with a single case study with 25 respondents. In general, the more established a topic is, the more sophisticated the methods become and the larger the datasets used are. If you are proposing a method that seems less than cutting-edge, you need to have a good reason for why that method is actually the most appropriate for your particular question, not simply that it is what you have the time or money to handle or the method you feel most comfortable with. If it is not feasible for you to pursue the needed methods with the time and resources available to you during your PhD, you may need to revise your research question.

Framing a Question

Once you have gone through several revisions of your research question and gotten at least a preliminary sense of the literature, you can begin framing your research question: adding sentences that show more explicitly how you are problematizing the existing literature, and that articulate and justify your choices of theory, methods, and data. To start, try completing Exercise 5.4.

EXERCISE 5.4: RESEARCH QUESTION WITH FRAMING

Using what you know of the academic literature, attempt to complete the following steps using the related sentences:

1. *Summarize the main argument of the conventional wisdom.* "The [conventional wisdom/previous research/existing literature/theory] [demonstrates/argues/suggests] X, or such-and-such relationship between X and Y."
2. *Summarize your main critique(s).* "However, [theory and/or empirical example] suggests Z, or a different relationship between X and Y."
3. *Present your research question, now with references to the theory, methods, and/or data you intend to use.* "Using [A: data from – name of data source], [B: insights from theory – name of theory], and/or [C: methods – note planned methods], this dissertation [tests/investigates/asks] [IF/WHY/HOW] [statement of hypotheses or relationship to be tested]."

These three statements will be expanded into three paragraphs as your research progresses. Here is an example (revised for clarity) from my own doctoral research proposal:

> *Dominant political science theories depict transnational civil society as a democratizing force in global governance, remedying North/South power imbalances by improving the representation of developing country stakeholders.*
>
> *However, the majority of empirical research on transnational civil society organizations (CSOs), much of it done by anthropologists in development studies, depicts them as largely unaccountable to low income-country stakeholders. In addition, some new studies indicate that CSOs may act primarily in the interests of their funding populations and most CSOs conducting global policy advocacy are based in the high-income countries of the global North. Taken together, these data suggest that CSOs may act primarily on behalf of Northern interests, thus worsening imbalances in stakeholder influence and undermining the potential for democracy.*
>
> *Because the World Bank is a core global governance institution and has been heavily lobbied by civil society, it has the potential to act as a leading indicator of civil society impacts on global governance. Therefore, this dissertation asks: How has civil society involvement in Washington-based*

World Bank decision making affected stakeholder influence on policymaking at the institution?

If you can complete these three paragraphs, you are well on the way to having a functional research proposal. You will write a complete review of the literature in which your discussion of the conventional wisdom and your descriptions of the problematizing research or data are expanded to several pages each. However, you will still likely summarize your work in three or four concise paragraphs as you present your research question both in writing and orally.

As with your initial question, you will benefit from workshopping your ideas with academic friends (Toor 2010). One of the most useful things I did at the proposal-writing stage of my own dissertation was meet every week with two classmates for lunch. We would each bring three copies of a one-page outline of our dissertation question, using bullet points to highlight the key points in our framing. We would take turns explaining our outlines, answering each other's questions, and receiving critique. Then we would revise, spend more time reviewing the literature, and return the next week for another round.

Leveraging Your Research Question for Professional Development

Once you have a well-developed research question, you can leverage it in multiple ways for professional development. This begins by writing a review and theory piece based on your research proposal and continues as you write conference papers, articles, and field notes based on your research outputs.

I encourage every student to try to develop a paper based on their research proposal. In most academic disciplines, there is a place for conference papers and journal articles that review the existing literature on a topic, analyze that literature to highlight key trends, findings, and assumptions, and draw out common points of agreement or identify limitations that should prompt new research (Paul and Criado 2020). These are typically called review pieces and – as you may have noted – their contents mirror the contents of a research proposal, minus the detailed research plan. Even if you are taking a gap-filling approach to novelty, you can highlight the conventional wisdom on a topic and make a case for exploring and expanding its scope by adding new data (cf. Kelskey 2011). Better yet, if you are taking a problematizing approach, you can begin by summarizing the conventional wisdom and its basis, and then outline a new theoretical perspective that challenges the conventional wisdom and exposes a need for new research. Developing a good review and theory piece takes a lot of thought, but it is all thought that you already need to put into developing your research proposal.

You can submit a conference paper proposal (as we'll discuss in Chapter 7) as soon as you have a strong enough idea for your review piece that you can write a short abstract summarizing it. You will then have several months before the conference to complete your planned work. Presenting your research framing in the review piece will help you gather feedback on it. This will help improve your research proposal, and your conference participation will give you a head start on developing a professional network (Haggerty 2010).

Once you have successfully defended your research proposal and entered into the doctoral candidacy phase of your PhD, the next thing you should do is develop an article version that highlights your analysis of the literature, your critique, and the case for new research. This piece will likely become the first publication of your dissertation. It will probably not be publishable in a top-tier generalist journal (one that covers your entire discipline), but it may well be accepted by a mid-tier publication or a well-regarded specialist journal. (We'll discuss journal selection more in Chapter 9.) This will build your CV and also help stake your claim to your topic and approach, making it less likely that others will poach your ideas. The time needed to create a publishable article from your proposal is quite minimal. Even if you have never published before, it should not take you more than a few weeks of reviewing journal guidelines and revising the text. If you have already developed a paper based on your research proposal to present at a conference, the time required will be even less. Do not neglect this opportunity.

As your dissertation progresses, it is important to continue to pause and publish. When you develop your research proposal, you will likely identify specific sub-questions that feed into the final answer to your research question. As you proceed with your analysis or data collection, the answers to these sub-questions will begin to emerge. Some of the answers will only be important to your final dissertation product, but other findings will be unexpected and intriguing in their own right. You may also develop enough material for a dataset piece, as discussed in Chapter 3. Consider pausing your research periodically to present and publish some of these findings as stand-alone articles. Writing up your preliminary findings may only take a few weeks and can be done during natural breaks in your research (e.g., between conducting focus groups or waiting on access to archives). Doing so will clarify your thinking and the text you generate will often be directly copiable into your dissertation. The goal is to arrive at graduation having already established the relevance of your work in a given field and the expertise you will use to market yourself. We will discuss more about how to do this starting in Chapter 7.

Recommended Readings

McCaslin, M. L., & Scott, K. W. (2003). The five-question method for framing a qualitative research study. *The Qualitative Report, 8*(3), 447–461.

Randolph, J. (2009). A guide to writing the dissertation literature review. *Practical Assessment, Research, and Evaluation, 14*(1), 1–13.

Toor, R. (2010) A writing group of two. *The Chronicle of Higher Education,* 16 December 2010.

Additional Resources

Dunleavy, P. (2003). *Authoring a PhD: How to Plan, Draft, Write and Finish a Doctoral Thesis or Dissertation.* Macmillan International Higher Education.

Marx, G. T. (1997). Of methods and manners for aspiring sociologists: 37 moral imperatives. *The American Sociologist, 28*(1), 102–125.

Webster, J., & Watson, R. T. (2002). Analyzing the past to prepare for the future: Writing a literature review. *MIS Quarterly,* xiii–xxiii.

White, P. (2017). *Developing Research Questions: A Guide for Social Scientists.* New York: Palgrave MacMillan.

Engaging with Your Advisor

6

Other than yourself, the person who will play the biggest role in your professional development during your PhD program is your advisor. Advisors go by different titles depending on your country and institution: advisor, supervisor, or committee chair are common terms. You may have one or two. In some countries, you will also have a committee of academics or PhD-credentialed practitioners who will guide and review your dissertation work.

Your advisor's role is to act as a mentor (Rackham Graduate School 2020). They will help you plan your doctoral research and may be responsible for approving your dissertation proposal. As your research progresses, they will review incremental outputs, like research protocols or draft chapters, and possibly look over your conference applications and draft publications. They will review drafts of the completed dissertation. Finally, they decide when your dissertation is ready for defense and they will either chair your dissertation defense (if you have an American-style public defense) or help select your examiners (if you have a UK-style viva). Assuming that your defense is successful, they will typically be a key reference for future jobs.

With that in mind, it is important that you think carefully about whom you select as your advisor, picking someone with whom you feel you can work and who has the knowledge and standing to advance your dissertation and future career. You will also need to learn to manage carefully the relationship you have with them. While your advisor may be the most important person in your professional life during your three to six years in the PhD program, you will not be the most important person in your advisor's. Therefore, it is important to learn to engage with your advisor effectively, in order to make

DOI: 10.4324/9781003262831-6

maximum use of the time they have available for advising you. This chapter will teach you how to do these things.

Selecting Your Advisor

Not every university allows you to choose your own advisor or advisors. At some universities, advisors are assigned during the application process and students are accepted as much by the advisor as they are by the program. If that is your case, and you feel that you have a good fit, you can skip down to the latter part of the chapter. If you were assigned an advisor and you do not feel like you have a good fit, read on. Some universities will allow you to change your advisor (Wisker 2014), but before taking such a drastic step, you can use the material here to help you make a more objective consideration of the pros and cons of your current advising situation and figure out what you might want instead.

For everyone else, an advisor is usually chosen sometime during the first two years of the PhD program, prior to defending one's dissertation proposal. This naturally begs the question, "Whom should I choose?" It is a difficult question to answer; it is hard to know what will make for a good dissertation advisor when you have never written a dissertation before. As a result, students often make poor decisions. They pick an advisor because they are famous, the most senior person in the department, the least intimidating, or the easiest to get along with. None of these are bad reasons, but they also are not the best ones. Instead, I suggest that you consider two sets of criteria: one set of essential characteristics and one set of "nice to have" secondary considerations.

Essential Characteristics of an Advisor

Remember that your advisor's first and most important job is to help you navigate the PhD process. While it is good to have an advisor who can connect you with jobs or whose name will stand out when listed among your references or someone whose shoulder you can cry on when things get rough, all of that counts for nothing if you cannot finish the PhD. To help you finish the PhD, an advisor needs three characteristics: a commitment to advising, expertise related to your dissertation, and availability. You should also pay close attention to a fourth issue, seniority.

First and foremost, you need someone committed to advising. While your department may require faculty to take on doctoral advising, not all faculty will be equally committed to the task. Stories abound of advisors who never make time to meet with their advisees, do not read the drafts they are sent, or fail to provide feedback for months at a time (Times Higher Education 2017; Kelskey 2014; Roberts, Tinari, and Bandlow 2019). Occasionally, advisors will see all advisee research as an extension of their own agenda. They will make time to advise you, but much of their advice will be designed to re-orient your work toward the topic, questions, or theories they are most interested in. Unless your interests and theirs closely overlap, this is not the sort of mentorship you are looking for.

What you need is someone who, at a minimum, sees advising as a professional obligation that they have a responsibility to carry out well (Brabazon 2013). They will provide timely feedback on your research proposal, intermediate outputs (like research tools or draft chapters), and your final dissertation. They may also review conference abstracts, draft articles, or small grant proposals for you if their time allows. They may or may not be enthusiastic, but they are committed to getting the job done.

Second, your advisor should have expertise related to your dissertation (Archibugi 2021). Note that no advisor will have expertise related to all aspects of your dissertation. This is your own, novel work and by the time you graduate your expertise in your niche area of research should exceed your advisor's. However, it is important that you choose an advisor who knows enough to give the critical feedback necessary to make your dissertation better. This can mean that she or he is a subject matter expert on some aspect of your dissertation: e.g., the country or region in which you are doing research, the theories you intend to use, or the general topic on which your research question is focused. Alternatively, your advisor may be expert in the types of methods you intend to employ (Hyatt and Williams 2011). You will almost certainly need methodological guidance while preparing for your research, regardless of the methods you choose. A faculty member who does not know your subject well can still help you get a robust answer to your research question by reviewing your data collection tools and/or analytical processes. Ideally, your advisor will have both subject matter and methodological expertise. This is not always possible; however, if you are studying at a university with a committee structure, you can often recruit another committee member to guide you in those areas where your advisor is less expert.

Third, your advisor needs to be accessible and available (Hyatt and Williams 2011). Some faculty are managing large grants, book projects, or extensive research portfolios that have first call on their time. Others travel frequently as part of their own professional development (Brabazon 2013; Kelskey

2014). Occasionally faculty will be gone for extended periods for sabbaticals or fieldwork. It is good to have an advisor who is an active researcher and frequent publisher – their knowledge of the field will be more up-to-date and they will have better name recognition when they recommend you for jobs. However, they need to have the time necessary to review your work in a timely fashion and meet with you regularly.

Lastly, think carefully before selecting a very new faculty member as your advisor. Students often gravitate toward younger faculty members, particularly if they seem more empathetic (Carlin and Perlmutter 2006). Yet junior faculty may not have the status necessary to corral a fractious committee or overcome bureaucratic obstacles (Carlin and Perlmutter 2006; Brabazon 2013). The risks depend on the culture of the department and institution. If your department is collegial and junior faculty are well-supported, the risks may be lower. However, if your department is marked by politics or infighting, you may need a more senior advisor who can advocate effectively for your interests.

EXERCISE 6.1: WHAT DO YOU NEED IN AN ADVISOR?

Reflect on the research topic you identified in Chapter 4 and the preliminary question you developed in Chapter 5. Use the following questions to reflect on the expertise you need in your advisor.

1. What sort of subject matter expertise are you seeking in an advisor?
   a. What is your general topic of study?
   b. What literature are you using?
   c. What theories are you using?
2. Do you know what methods you plan to use?
   a. In what setting will you do fieldwork (if any)?
   b. What kind of data will you collect?
   c. How do you plan to analyze them?

Additional Characteristics of a Good Advisor

An advisor who is committed to advising, knows something about your planned research, and is available to advise is the bare minimum. Ideally, your advisor will have additional characteristics that will make your relationship work. These include having a personality and advising style that suit your needs, an interest in your research project, recognition in your field, and a willingness to mentor you in publishing and other professional development activities.

Advising Style

Different advisors have different ways of delivering guidance on your dissertation. Students sometimes refer to faculty members as cheerleaders, mystics, or taskmasters to describe their advising styles. I find this to be a useful typology.

Cheerleaders are enthusiastic about everything. They tend to be generous with their time and they will use it to tell you about how great your work is and how excited they are about your progress. All of their advice is framed as "the next thing to do," giving you a sense of constant forward motion, even when that "next thing" is actually to make revisions that will improve your previous outputs. If you thrive on encouragement, you will love having a cheerleader for an advisor. The challenge of working with a cheerleader is that you may feel unsure about how good your work actually is, since there is rarely any explicitly critical feedback. You may fail to get the incisive correction necessary to improve your work or the pressure needed to maximize your potential (Kelskey 2014; Archibugi 2021).

Mystics are academic sages who love the intellectual journey of the PhD. They are interested in talking with you about what you are learning and what you are thinking. They may frequently recommend more readings or data collection. If you love having deep, thoughtful discussions with your advisor, this type may suit you well. The challenge of working with a mystic is that advisor meetings can become hour-long brainstorming sessions. You may leave excited about all of the possibilities for further exploration but unsure about what your advisor thinks is truly needed as opposed to what is merely an interesting idea. The mystic advisor may also be less focused than other advisors on identifying an endpoint to your research and developing a gameplan to get there. From their point of view there is always more that could be done or more to think about. It may be up to you to declare that it is time to move on – on to the next step in the research, on to the next chapter, or on to your defense.

Taskmasters are very process-focused. When they meet with their advisees, they set specific goals for the work that the advisees should complete before their next meeting and ask them to set specific dates for when that work will be complete. When a student submits work to them, they provide critical feedback, and highlight any major areas for revision. There is a regular cycle of deadlines and reviews. The advantage of working with a taskmaster is that you always know what you need to do to finish the current stage of your work and, in the end, to complete the dissertation. Some students really appreciate this more directive approach (Cassuto 2016). The main downside of working with a taskmaster is the relative lack of affirmation and encouragement. The taskmaster may be more focused on the product than on you as a person. Their critical feedback can also, at times, feel overwhelming.

Not every student needs the same thing. You will find plenty of advice columns and studies purporting to tell you what the best kind of advisor is, but what most of these really reflect are either the author's idiosyncratic views or the responses of a majority of study respondents (e.g., Kelskey 2014; Hyatt and Williams 2011; Roberts, Tinari, and Bandlow 2019). Do not assume one size fits all; what matters most is matching the student's needs and the advisor's style.

These are not the only ways in which advisors differ. Some like to have regular, face-to-face meetings. Others prefer to correspond by email. Some set very strict deadlines; others are more hands-off. If you have done any sort of supervised research or project-based professional work, you should reflect on what you liked best and least about your various supervisors. If you have the option, try to pick an advisor whose approach will work for you.

EXERCISE 6.2: WHAT DO YOU WANT IN AN ADVISOR?

Reflect on your previous experiences receiving supervision, whether in professional work, athletics, previous studies, or other contexts. Answer the following questions:

1. How much supervision do you think you need? Are you a self-starter who does well when minimally supervised, or do you benefit from regular check-ins and deadlines?
2. Is there a supervising style (e.g., cheerleader, mystic, taskmaster) that appeals most to you? Is there one that appeals least?
3. What qualities do you most appreciate in a mentor or coach, like directness, sympathy, enthusiasm, or an ability to "speak my language"?
4. Are there any qualities that would make it very hard for you to work with an advisor?

Enthusiasm, Integrity, Recognition, and Publication Assistance

Several other characteristics can also be beneficial in an advisor. It helps if your advisor has enthusiasm for your project. Usually this will be because they work in a related field, and they are excited about the intellectual merit of your work. Note, however, that you are looking for enthusiasm for your project, not just enthusiasm for you. To be perfectly frank, some students have an easier time with the PhD than others. This does not mean that they are smarter or will become better teachers or professionals, although they may have a more natural knack for doing research. Faculty can often identify these students, and some faculty may prefer to work with them. These students are more likely to keep on pace and do good research, and their draft outputs are clearer and take less time to review. Therefore, faculty members may invite students to become their advisees simply because they are excited about the student. If this happens to you, be cautious. It can be flattering to have a faculty member suggest that they would like to be your advisor – and it can feel intimidating to say no. However, do your best to delay a decision until you have ascertained whether your prospective advisor meets the essential criteria listed above. Take the time, too, to ask them why they are interested in the project. Listen to their answer carefully and look for signs that they are excited because the work intersects with their own research and expertise.

Be wary, too, of "byline bandits" (Brabazon 2013). You do not want an advisor who is excited about your work because they intend to take at least partial credit for it (Kelskey 2014; Rubin 2015). Years ago, it was accepted that a student's advisor would become a coauthor on publications resulting from their dissertation. Many faculty members now view this as unethical, but some still follow to this practice. However, it inflates the advisor's CV at the student's expense. Single-authored publications are usually worth more on the job market than multi-authored ones. Moreover, when a junior academic publishes with a more senior one, it is natural for readers to assume that the more senior scholar played a key role in developing the ideas or planning the research. Read through your prospective advisor's CV for coauthored publications. Then check those publications to see the coauthor's affiliations. Where you find student coauthors, search Google Scholar for the student author or consult your department's listing of recent dissertations to see if it seems like the faculty member was being listed as a coauthor on dissertation-related outputs. (Sometimes faculty invite students to be coauthors on the faculty member's work, which benefits the student.)

If a prospective advisor has a history of getting themselves listed on outputs from advisees' dissertation work, you may still choose to work with them. However, you should discuss authorship of your research outputs before you finalize your advising agreement and try to negotiate keeping some or all of your outputs single-authored. As a general rule, all authors listed on a publication should have done all of the following: (a) contributed to research design; (b) participated in data collection or analysis; and (c) contributed to writing or at least reviewing the final text. With this in mind, you do not want your advisor listed as a coauthor on the major outputs of the dissertation because it implies that the dissertation was not wholly your own. If your advisor does see themselves as a collaborator in your research, ask if you can develop additional publications together that make use of the dissertation data, while leaving any major publications that summarize the dissertation findings as single-authored work.

Another attribute that can be useful is recognition in the field. Having an advisor who is respected in your field can help you with future employment (Brabazon 2013), although this help has limits. If your advisor is a globally known intellectual rock star, their name can conjure job opportunities. However, to be "famous" in academia sometimes means that just a few dozen people in a niche area of specialization know your name. You will most likely be applying for jobs that have a broader focus. An advisor who is famous for studying NGO advocacy or Cold War strategy, for instance, may be unknown to most members of a committee hiring for a general academic job in political science. If you are looking for a practitioner job, a famous academic's name is probably even less likely to be recognized unless their specialization and your prospective employer's work closely overlap.

It is more likely that having an advisor who is recognized in your field will help you build your network or strengthen your CV. They can introduce you to other scholars at conferences. They may be able to recommend your work to colleagues who are assembling a special issue of a journal or an edited volume. If they are proficient grant writers, they may be able to find a way to fund you through one of their current projects. These things will expand your research opportunities or develop your marketability.

Lastly, it is good if your advisor has an interest in mentoring your professional development beyond just the dissertation. Supervising your dissertation is the core requirement of an advisor. They are not required to help you learn to teach, find publication opportunities, or prepare for the job market. Some advisors see these things as part of their responsibilities, and others do not. Some see it as a bonus that can happen if they are not too busy and you do not ask for help too often. If you can find someone who will make the time to review your conference abstracts, recommend journals to which you can submit your work, review your draft articles, or discuss your teaching, that is a significant benefit.

How Do You Know?

Once you know what you are looking for in an advisor, how do you find an advisor with the appropriate characteristics? While there may be many faculty in your department, you probably only have face-to-face contact with a handful of them.

Do not limit your search to just those faculty you know. Begin by reviewing your department's roster. Read each faculty member's CV or look up their publication record by entering his or her full name into Google Scholar. This will give you a good idea of their subject matter expertise. Reading the abstracts of their articles will also give you a sense of their core methods. If you have a course convenor who leads a seminar for new students, you can also request a meeting with that person and ask them whom among their colleagues they might recommend for your topic and methods.

EXERCISE 6.3: IDENTIFYING CANDIDATE ADVISORS

Review the details about subject matter and methods you noted in Exercise 6.1. With these in mind, take the following steps:

1. Review the roster of faculty members in your department. Whose expertise suits your dissertation? Identify at least two to three candidates.
2. Review the CVs or publication records of your top choices.
   a. Have they published in your area or used your methods recently?
   b. Are there any signs of byline banditry?
   c. If you are looking for a non-academic job, do any prospective advisors seem to have contacts outside of academia (e.g., consulting for or receiving grants from government agencies or nonprofits)?

Next, talk with other students. Fellow students will tell you those things other faculty members, if they are being professional, should not: who is overbearing, who is hard to work with, who has a bad temper, who is never around. Take your fellow students' advice with a grain of salt: sometimes students will complain that a professor is too demanding when the student was simply unable to meet deadlines, or a student will deride a professor as having an unpleasant personality when there was simply a personality mismatch. Take whatever data seem reliable and feed them into your calculations.

If you can, take a course taught by a perspective supervisor. This will give you a sense of their demeanor, communication style, and the kind of feedback they give. If you are fairly sure that you would like to have a certain professor advise your dissertation work, you may also seek to work for them as a research assistant, which will give you an even closer view of their supervising style. Make sure that if your RA work overlaps with your PhD work, you and your advisor communicate about which pieces of the research will be considered yours, such that you can use the data or results in your dissertation.

Lastly, take some time to talk with prospective advisors. Good advisors know students need an advisor who suits their research needs and, ideally, their personality and work habits. Far from being bothered that you are interviewing them or shopping around, they will feel like you are taking a wise approach. Be prepared to discuss with them your research plans and ask for their impressions. Ask them about their advising style and their advising experiences. You can do this in a way that is framed as being about your education, rather than a test for them. For instance, you can ask, "What do you expect from your advisees?" "What are the best work habits you have seen your advisees use?" "What dangers or problems should advisees avoid?" Their answers will tell you something about their advising style and their previous experiences.

Note that selecting an advisor is a two-way street. Faculty are not obligated to take you on as an advisee. Faculty may refuse a student because they feel like the topic is too far removed from their own work, because they are planning to travel or take sabbatical, or because the student has developed a reputation for poor work habits. Be aware that faculty talk among themselves. To increase your chances of getting the advisor you want, make sure to work diligently in your classes and during any research assistant or teaching assistant assignments. Be sure to follow faculty instructions completely (not turning in incomplete or superficial work) and produce the requested outputs in a timely fashion (Rubin 2015). Faculty will recognize these as signs of a good future advisee.

Managing Your Advisor

For many students, the idea of managing one's advisor seems, at first, rude or arrogant. We typically manage subordinates, not superiors. However, management applies not only to people but also to resources. Individually, we manage our time, our money, our emotional energy. As a society, we manage clean water and public land. In these contexts, we have something that is available in limited quantity and that takes some effort to develop or maintain. Therefore, we try to use the resource strategically, maximizing its benefit and minimizing wastage. Think of access to your advisor as this kind of resource and you will start to get the picture. She or he is a resource that is available to you, but in limited quantity. You must use the time and attention she or he can give you for maximum benefit.

Why is your advisor's time limited? Viewed from the outside, the academic life can look quite relaxed. Aside from teaching, professors seem to set their own hours. You may see them come into the office mid-morning, casually dressed, and leave early to go get their children from school. Teaching only takes a few hours a week. What else are they doing? First, teaching takes much more time than just the classroom contact hours. Faculty are responding to student emails, maintaining online learning environments, preparing lectures or learning exercises, and grading. When the teaching is done, faculty have service requirements. Students almost never see the service dimensions of the job, but faculty are at least nominally responsible for governing the university (a role which is sometimes challenged or duplicated by the ever-increasing number of university administrators [New England Center for Investigative Reporting 2014]). Faculty handle graduate admissions, review student applications for departmental funding, write the standards for tenure and promotion, and review every proposed course before it is added to the course catalog. Much of this is done by committee, so even faculty who are not leading such activities are obliged to review others' work. Then faculty must make time for research. While expected outputs vary from institution to institution, in my experience faculty in the social sciences at PhD-granting institutions average at least two academic articles or an equivalent output per year. Consider that a typical article-based dissertation consists of three articles. In other words, the amount of research that will consume a student's full-time attention for two to four years a faculty member must produce every year and a half, while also doing their teaching and service. Many faculty work on nine- or ten-month contracts (being tenured ensures that your contract will be renewed), meaning that they are only paid from August or September until May or June. Yet I do not know a single faculty member who does not work during their unpaid summer months. Nearly all of that time is used for research. In short, some faculty may have significant flexibility in how they manage their time (which is why they can come in late or leave early), but the job itself is often more than full-time (Schiebinger and Gilmartin 2010).

Even if your advisor had unlimited time and attention, they would not give you unlimited assistance. Advisors face two competing sets of demands. On the one hand, they have an obligation to you, to help you develop as a scholar and guide you as you navigate the challenges of mastering your chosen subject area and undertaking novel research. On the other hand, they have an obligation to the profession, to test you and to ensure that they do not grant a PhD to someone who is not ready to become an independent researcher. As Liina Lepp et al. (2016: 6) write, many faculty believe that "an adult pursuing a doctoral study must be intrinsically motivated, be able to direct their studies, and take responsibility for the process" and that "working independently for long periods is how a doctoral student becomes an independent researcher." As a result, advisors guide more than they teach. They will tell you that you need more sources for your review of the literature, but they may not tell you which sources. They will tell you that an interview questionnaire needs to be refined, but they will not edit the questions for you. During your write-up of your findings, they will encourage you to deepen or develop your thinking, but they will not always tell you how. Holding a PhD signifies to others that you are able to do research independently, with no one guiding you at all, so forcing you to figure things out on your own is part of the advisor's role.

The bottom line is that most advisors like it if students are pro-active in managing the advisor-student relationship. Active management on the part of the student signals that the student recognizes that the advisor's time is scarce and is using it carefully. This shows value for the advisor's time and respect for their role. Likewise, a student who comes to their advisor with a specific agenda for each meeting, specific questions, and specific requests for feedback is showing that she or he is in charge of the dissertation project and taking responsibility for the outputs. This kind of independence is what advisors are looking to cultivate.

How to Use Your Advisor's Time Well

You should work with your advisor to set clear expectations for the advising relationship. This should include expectations for both your performance and theirs (Rackham Graduate School 2020). While you will have limited power to set the dynamics of the mentoring relationship, you can ask questions that will prompt your advisor to reveal what they expect from you and how they typically operate – a de facto statement of their expectations for themselves. A set of possible questions, adapted from the Rackham Graduate School's guide for faculty members, is given below. (The complete guide is listed under Recommended Readings at the end of this chapter.) You can use these questions or similar ones in your conversation with your advisor.

QUESTIONS FOR YOUR ADVISOR

1. How do prefer to communicate with your advisees – by email, phone, etc.?
2. What are your typical expectations for advisees?
3. How often would you like to meet? Can we establish a regular schedule of meetings?
4. Are there any group/team meetings you would like me to attend?
5. How far in advance of an advising meeting would you like me to send you any materials we will discuss or review at the meeting?
6. Are you willing to review materials like conference proposals or article drafts?
7. If I am sending you materials to review, what is your typical turnaround time? How far in advance should I send them from when I need feedback?
8. Do you expect to be listed as a coauthor on any of my research outputs or for me to contribute to any of your research?
9. Are there any conferences or professional meetings you suggest I attend? Is there funding available to attend them?
10. Are there any times you will be away from campus or otherwise unavailable?

Adapted from: Rackham Graduate School (2020). *How to Mentor Graduate Students: A Guide for Faculty*. Ann Arbor: University of Michigan Rackham Graduate School.

While the expectations you and your advisor set will reflect each of your personalities, needs, and experiences, I suggest that you include the following items or make them a part of your regular habits even if your advisor does not require them.

Meet with your advisor regularly. I would suggest meeting a minimum of once every three to five weeks, at least during term time. Regular meetings will help keep you on track and help keep your work closer to the front of your advisor's mind. The meetings create deadlines for you and your advisor. Often you will be expected to email your advisor some sort of output in advance of the meeting, and your advisor will know that they need to review that output because a meeting is coming up.

Develop a pattern of regular meetings by planning the date of the next meeting every time you meet. Note that your advisor will need time to review any materials you send, so for some meetings you should agree on both the meeting date and an earlier deadline to submit material to your advisor.

Not all meetings need to be the same length. Fifteen minutes can be enough for a short check-in or to answer a single question. Reviewing the outline of your dissertation can take two hours or more. Ask for the time you think you will need so that your advisor can schedule accordingly.

Every meeting should have an agenda. Giving each meeting a clear purpose can make for more effective mentoring (Carmel and Paul 2015). A written agenda details this purpose. It should include a list of topics or issues you would like to discuss and any questions you would like to ask. Often a few bullet points will suffice. You should set this agenda and send it to your advisor about two days before each scheduled meeting. (Many faculty check email sporadically, so they may need two days to see it.) The agenda will jog your advisor's memory, prompt them to review materials you have sent, and nudge them to mentally prepare for your questions. This helps them and ensures that you get maximum value out of your meeting time.

If you need your advisor to answer questions, try to make them as specific as possible, both in the agenda and during the meeting. For example, instead of asking, "What do you think of my methods?" ask things like, "Would you be willing to review my interview questionnaire?" or "Do you think this sampling technique is the best one for maximizing the validity of my findings?" The more specific your questions are, the more precise and useful your advisor's answers are likely to be.

In the meeting, stick to the agenda as much as you can. You can even help your advisor by bringing a printed copy of the agenda for them to each meeting. Most advisors will try to stay on track and if they get the meeting off track they will feel responsible for addressing the items on the agenda even if it takes extra time. You can also gently move the meeting forward by stating, "The next thing I wanted to talk about is…" and mentioning the next item on the agenda. Note, however, that if you get the meeting off track, your advisor may be unsympathetic. Be wary of turning a meeting with your advisor into an extended personal catch-up time. If you spend the first 25 minutes of your planned 30-minute meeting sharing about your family, pets, or recent vacation, do not be surprised if your advisor still ushers you out the door at the 30-minute mark with your questions unanswered.

Set action items. When I first meet with an advisee, I ask them to begin building a month-by-month timeline for their research and writing-up. We discuss how long each part of the project is likely to take, but it is then their job to assemble the pieces into a draft calendar that reflects their available time. You should do the same. Your calendar will shift as your research progresses, but you should update your plans regularly and try to stay on track with the revised deadlines.

Every time you meet or communicate with your advisor, you should tell them:

- What work you have most recently completed
- What you are working on now
- When you expect to complete the current task
- What you will work on next when it is done

Doing this will help your advisor track your progress and help you maintain momentum. Sharing this information in each meeting can prompt a discussion with your advisor about what materials they should expect from you next, when you will send those materials to them for review, what sort of feedback you will need, and when they will give you that feedback. Articulating a plan for what to work on next, once the current output is complete, also assures your advisor that you will be using your time productively while you are waiting for any needed feedback from them.

You and your advisor should also set deadlines for your advisor. If you ask your advisor, "Would you review my research protocol before I send it to the Institutional Review Board?" and they agree, follow up with, "I was hoping to send it within two weeks. Do you think you could have it reviewed by [date]?" Similarly, if you are in the writing-up stage, it is fine to ask your advisor if they can provide you feedback on a draft chapter or section within a certain amount of time. Just be realistic. Many advisors need two to four weeks to fit something into their schedule.

Send follow-up emails. Send a follow-up email after each meeting noting what was discussed, what work you agreed to do next, what work your advisor agreed to do, and the deadlines to which you each agreed. This email serves several purposes. It is a quick-reference guide for your advisor that they can look at when they are preparing for your next meeting. It is a record for you of your commitments. And it is a polite tool for reminding your advisor of their commitments. If your advisor misses a deadline for feedback or other input that you both agreed on, just forward them a copy of your meeting follow-up email, with a note asking, "I was wondering if you had time to do [the planned task] we discussed?" They will read down, see the earlier email, and realize that they are behind. Kelskey (2014) suggests that follow-up emails are particularly important if you have an advisor whose advice seems to change from meeting to meeting. The email record will help remind your advisor of the input they have given you previously.

Do everything you can to complete your work on time. Inevitably you will miss some deadlines. You are doing the PhD for the first time, so you will not always have the experience needed to know how long things will take. However, when you realize that you are going to miss a deadline, tell your advisor and explain the reason. If the deadline was linked to a meeting with your advisor (i.e., you were going to meet and discuss a certain output), decide if the meeting is still necessary. If you are missing a deadline because of some unforeseen problem with the research, you may need to meet with your advisor and talk it out. If you simply need more time for a certain task, ask to put off the meeting and send a set of revised deadlines. Be aware that when you miss a deadline for sending material to your advisor for review, you become responsible for any resulting delay. Reviewing an advisee's work can require an advisor to block out several hours in their schedule. If the advisee does not send their work, it can be two or more weeks before the advisor can again free up the time necessary to give the work a thorough review.

Your Advisor Does Not Understand You

Even if this sounds great to you in principle, you may struggle to implement it in practice. You will probably miss deadlines, turn in incomplete products, and show up at your advisor's office desperately hoping that they will just tell you what to do rather than telling you to "think more deeply." I want to offer you fair warning: when this happens, do not be surprised if your advisor is largely oblivious to your struggles.

The reason is a selection effect. Many people who do not love doing research during their doctoral programs still become professors. They may like teaching and be gifted at it. They may like the academic lifestyle and find jobs at institutions that do not require high levels of research. They may pursue a research agenda until they have tenure, and then refocus their energies on service or teaching. But faculty who become doctoral advisors – people whose job includes training and advising students on how to do research – typically like doing research and are often naturally good at it.

This likely started for them at the doctoral level. It is not that they never struggled during their doctorate, but even when they were struggling, they enjoyed the research process. What might be a crisis for someone else was for them an intellectual challenge, and they knew that with enough thinking and hard work they could devise a solution. Their meetings with their advisors were often a breeze because they were either on track or could explain clearly where they needed help.

This type of capacity is often evident to others. When you go to academic conferences you will recognize these students. They are the people who are hanging out with faculty, and not just when their advisors invite them to a dinner with colleagues. Faculty from other institutions are saying to them things like, "Please send me a copy of that paper when it's published" or "Your work might be a good fit for a special issue I'm editing." Fellow panelists will ask them to keep in touch so that they can be part of a panel submission for the next year's conference.

Yet if this is you, you probably do not recognize it. You are feeling overwhelmed and trying hard to set yourself up for a future job. Every success feels like a lucky break. You probably do not think you are that special. You are comparing your abilities to those of your professors and you know that you have not attained their level.

Thus, there is a paradox. Professors training PhD students have often had an unusually smooth experience earning the PhD, but often do not recognize the unusualness of that experience. They typically enjoyed it at some level and, due to a natural capacity for research, were able to complete their research more-or-less as planned. Yet, because that capacity was natural and intuitive, many – even now – do not think of or recognize themselves as special. They think of their experience of the PhD as normal. When you struggle, they may not be condemning; they are just mystified by some of your problems.

The bottom line is, once again, that you must see yourself as an independent researcher and find the resources you need – including support from peers, advice from other faculty, or articles or books – to help you past the hurdles. If you struggle, remember that even if the research does not come naturally or easily to you, you can still complete your PhD and go on to a rewarding academic career or to success as a practitioner.

Having Agency as a PhD Student

The fact that you bear the primary responsibility for the quality and completion of your PhD also gives you some privileges. Because you are nominally in charge of the process, you have some agency in it. When you set the agenda for your PhD meetings or negotiate deadlines with your advisor for your outputs and theirs, you are exercising this agency. You can also say no to some input or invitations. If necessary, you can nudge your advisor to set your defense date once you think you are ready or, at some schools, petition to have a defense even without your advisor's approval.

David Perlmutter (2013) has written some guidance for junior faculty on how to respond to advice from their colleagues, and I have found his ideas useful in guiding doctoral students in exercising their agency. As you receive input from your advisor, especially if you are uncertain about it, consider the following steps:

1. Listen carefully. Not every piece of advice makes sense at first but avoid dismissing anything from your advisor out of hand. Try to make sure that you understand their reasoning, even if it does not align with your own.

2. "Investigate before you commit." It is okay to respond to input with questions. For instance, if your advisor suggests that you open a new avenue of inquiry or conduct an additional analysis, it is okay to ask them, "Why?" or even "Do you think that is essential to completing my dissertation?" This will help you distinguish between essential revisions and advisor brainstorming. You can also test alternatives. For example, if your advisor suggests fixing a problem in a certain way, you can ask, "What if I did [X] instead?" If you need to, delay. Tell your advisor you will think about it or look into it. If this occurs in a meeting, make the follow-up action item researching the option, not implementing your advisor's suggestion.

3. Get outside advice. You can take advice from your advisor to your committee members or a secondary advisor, if you have one. You can also consult with your course convenor or other mentors. Do not ask them to contradict your advisor; instead, frame your query like this, "My advisor says [X] but I'm not sure how to interpret/implement this. What are your thoughts?" If they think it is bad advice, they will tell you. If they are committee members and they disagree strongly, you can request a meeting of the whole committee to try to find consensus.

4. "Just say no (thanks)." You can decline your advisor's advice on the dissertation. After all, it is your name alone that will be listed as the author of the final product. Turning down your advisor's advice entails some risks and I would advise against doing it early in the dissertation process. However, by the end, you will understand your data better than your advisor. If they suggest a change that seems incorrect

to you, explain to them why you would rather not make it. Often, the conversation will be clarifying for both of you: your advisor will acknowledge your point, but you will realize that you need to explain your work better so that others do not make the same assumptions (and criticisms) your advisor did.

You can also turn down professional development opportunities if they do not fit with your plans. Your advisor may invite you to take on unpaid research assistant work or other tasks, suggesting that such work will give you experience or build your CV. You can decline if the time involved does not match the benefits. For instance, one of my PhD co-chairs invited me to index a volume he was preparing. He suggested that it would be a good professional development experience for me. I was interested, but I explained to him that I was already preparing publications based on my dissertation and indexing the volume would cost me the time I needed for an additional publication. He readily agreed that the publication was the higher value opportunity and was unbothered that I declined to do the indexing.

No matter how well you perform as a PhD student, you may be unable to make things work with some advisors. Unfortunately, faculty members can be belittling, abusive, or exploitative (Cassuto 2016; Miranda 2021). If you find yourself in such a situation, you can work with your department chair or course convener to try to resolve the problem or exercise your ultimate form of agency and seek a new advisor (Cassuto 2016; Wisker 2014).

Beyond Your Advisor

The material in your dissertation should reflect the comparative advantage we discussed in Chapter 4, and the data and analysis in your dissertation form the basis for acquiring most of the other professional signifiers that we will discuss this book, including conference papers, articles, and grants. Your advisor is a crucial resource in developing a high-quality dissertation. Selecting the right advisor and managing the relationship carefully will enhance your dissertation and everything that flows from it. Your advisor may also help your professional development directly by giving input on conference papers or articles or helping you network. However, your advisor is not the only source of input on your research and professional outputs. You can also get input from the wider community of academics when you attend conferences. We'll begin discussing how in the next chapter.

Recommended Readings

Archibugi, D. (2021). Choosing your mentor: A letter to creative minds. *Journal of Innovation Economics & Management*, *36*(3): 103–115. Available at https://doi.org/10.3917/jie.pr1.0099.

Rackham Graduate School (2020). *How to Mentor Graduate Students: A Guide for Faculty*. Ann Arbor: University of Michigan Rackham Graduate School.

Additional Resources

Carlin, D., & Perlmutter, D. (2006). Advising the new advisor. *The Chronicle of Higher Education*, 5 September 2006.

Cassuto, L. (2016). How to fire your advisor. *The Chronicle of Higher Education*, 28 February 2016.

Roberts, L. R., Tinari, C. M., & Bandlow, R. (2019). An effective doctoral student mentor wears many hats and asks many questions. *International Journal of Doctoral Studies*, *14*, 133–159.

Yans, G. (n.d.). 'Rainbow Children': What grad students should know about interracial mentoring. In Brock, R. (ed.), *Higher Ed: Soup to Nuts*. Published online by The Chronicle of Higher Education.

Applying to Your First Conference and Writing an Abstract

7

Once you have a research agenda, the next step in your professional development is to begin attending academic conferences. Ideally, you will begin submitting conference applications toward the end of your proposal-writing process and present your review and problematization of the literature at a conference soon after you have defended your proposal. Other presentations will follow as your research progresses.

Conference presentations exemplify the potential synergies between dissertation completion and professional development. Presenting at conferences will allow you to collect feedback on your work from people besides your dissertation advisor or committee, expose you to new ideas that may be relevant to your research, and give you opportunities to develop your professional network. Conference papers are also important signifiers of professional ability, and once you have written and received feedback on a conference paper you can usually turn it into an article with a modicum of additional effort.

Note that in all of this, we are focusing on presenting at conferences, not merely attending them. There is no section in most CVs for conferences attended. Listening to others present their work can be highly beneficial, but it does not reflect a unique accomplishment. Students who merely attend a conference may find themselves on the periphery of the conference community, without a clear path for breaking into the "scholarly huddle" (Chapman et al. 2009; cf. Kim, Lebovits, and Shugars 2021). In contrast, presenting a paper signals your membership in the scholarly

DOI: 10.4324/9781003262831-7

community and creates bridges for launching conversations and building your network. Given the limitations of time and funding that most PhD students face, I discourage students from attending conferences unless they are also presenting. Applying to present may seem daunting at first, but there are many conferences each year, ranging from huge international affairs to small, specialist workshops. Using the guidance in this chapter, you should be able to find a conference that suits you and will accept your proposal.

In this chapter, we will discuss in more detail why you should attend conferences and what you will get out of attending them. We will then examine what research outputs are suitable for conference submission and when you should expect to present them. Next, we will explore the types of conferences available and how to pick an appropriate one. Finally, we will discuss how to write a successful abstract, which will form the core of your conference proposal.

Why You Should Attend Conferences

On their face, conferences may seem like extra, unnecessary work and expense, especially if you do not intend to pursue an academic career. Conferences can also seem intimidating – places where you risk being publicly critiqued by more senior scholars or where your best ideas may be stolen. For these reasons, you may meet fellow students who do not go to conferences at all. However, this is short-sighted. Conferences are an excellent place to receive feedback on your work, stay abreast of the latest developments in the field, and network with other scholars. Conference attendance can also help build your CV, form a springboard to article publication, provide inspiration, and help you overcome your fears. This section will discuss these benefits. (The next chapter, on participating in and presenting at conferences, will give you guidance on dealing with critical audience members and protecting your intellectual property.)

First and most importantly, conferences are opportunities for you to receive feedback on your work (Gupta and Waismel-Manor 2006). Our research builds on the work of our colleagues and predecessors in the field. The volume of this previous research is often so vast that it is difficult to master it all. Critiques from others help clue us in to what we have missed. Other scholars can also offer suggestions based on their own experience, research, and perspectives, helping us consider our research from new angles. If you study the acknowledgments section of articles in the top journals in your field, you will often find that these pieces thank numerous other scholars for their input. Good feedback makes for better research.

By presenting your work at a conference, you invite this feedback. Most conferences require you to submit a conference paper, usually the length of a typical academic article in your field, a few weeks before you present. Some conferences will feature a dedicated discussant as part of each panel, whose job it is to read and critique the papers and, ideally, identify links among them. Fellow panelists will also read (or at least skim) your work and offer helpful questions or comments. Most audience members are unlikely to read your work in advance, but they will listen to your presentation and respond with questions and comments as well. Often interested audience members will approach you after you present to request a copy of your paper. You can ask these new contacts to send you any feedback they have once they have read it. Not all this input will seem appropriate or accurate, but even where the feedback reflects a misunderstanding of your work, it can help you identify things you need to explain more clearly or discuss in more detail.

In addition to presenting your own work, you will listen to others present theirs (Cooper 2008). Other scholars will also be presenting their new research for feedback prior to submitting it for publication. By attending panels related to your research, you can hear about the latest developments in the field, learn about theories or sources you may have overlooked, and even meet some of the leading lights in your domain of research (Bassey n.d.).

As you present and as you listen, you will have opportunities to build your network (Mata, Latham, and Ransome 2010; Cooper 2008). Often the members of your panel will meet for drinks or a meal to discuss their work. Audience members will approach you after you present and, sometimes, discuss ways your work relates to their own projects. When you are an audience member you can do likewise, approaching the presenters of pieces that interest you. These connections can be invaluable for building your career (Gupta and Waismel-Manor 2006). One of my grad school presentations garnered an invitation to participate in an edited volume and, later, to apply for a postdoc. Conference interactions with a fellow grad student eventually led to us coauthoring two articles together. Now, as a more senior scholar, I have invited graduate students I have met at conferences to submit work for a special issue of a journal or a volume I was editing or sent them advertisements for jobs at my institution.

PAPER OR POSTER?

Many conferences offer the option of presenting a poster instead of a paper. At a poster session, a dozen or more scholars (usually graduate students) stand in a gallery next to posters visualizing their research. Audience members wander through and stop to talk with researchers whose work interests them. Posters can be an effective means of information transfer (Rowe and Ilic 2009). However, a poster presentation lacks the guarantee of feedback you get from being on a panel. The format is also less readily converted into a publication, and a poster presentation often has less cachet than a paper. Given that preparing a poster is just as much work as preparing a paper, I always suggest that students present a paper if they have the option to do so.

Conference presentations are listed on your CV and show that you are an active scholar. As noted in Chapter 3, presenting at conferences recognized by your future employer can help mark you as an insider in the profession. This is true even for non-academic jobs.

Ideally, every conference paper can be developed into a publication. Once you have written a paper and received feedback, revising and submitting the paper for publication can take as little as two or three days of additional effort. Indeed, be careful about attending too many conferences without converting your papers into publications; this can send the wrong signal on your CV, making you look like someone who goes to conferences for vacation rather than a serious scholar (Haggerty 2010).

Conferences provide inspiration (Bassey n.d.). There is something about being surrounded by fellow researchers and hearing lots of new ideas that is exciting. As my time at a conference progresses, I find myself filled with new ideas – research opportunities to explore, grants to investigate, new contacts to follow up with, and ways to improve my own work. If you are feeling stalled or unmotivated, a conference may be just the thing to revive your momentum. The commitment to produce a paper by the conference deadline can also provide the pressure many of us need to get a difficult project done.

Lastly, going to conferences can help you overcome your fears and build your confidence (Gupta and Waismel-Manor 2006). You will gain confidence in your ability to make presentations and speak publicly about your research (Simpson n.d.). You may also begin to recognize the interests and traits you share with other career researchers, helping you to see yourself as one of the group and perhaps helping you overcome the imposter syndrome that plagues many early-career researchers (Bassey n.d.). Your first conference may feel challenging, but once you have some experience, conferences will become more comfortable environments and more professionally fruitful (Chapman et al. 2009).

What to Present and When

If these arguments have persuaded you that you should present at conferences, you will need to know what to present and when to begin applying. You may also be wondering about where you should apply. We will discuss this question later; you need to reflect on what you are presenting before seeking a suitable venue.

You should consider the questions of what to present and when to apply in the context of the timeline you have constructed for your dissertation. Major conferences often have a lead time of nine or more months, meaning that you must submit a proposal nine or more months before you expect to present your work. Smaller conferences and workshops may have shorter lead times, perhaps three to six months, but these times are still significant. No one, especially a PhD student eager to get feedback and proceed with their dissertation, wants to let completed work sit for months while waiting for a chance to present it and receive feedback. As a result, most scholars submit conference proposals long before the work they intend to present is complete. You should do this too. Begin submitting conference proposals as soon as you know what you *intend* to research or write, even if this work has barely begun. If your proposal is accepted, the conference then gains an additional function, alluded to above: a commitment device (Haggerty 2010). As you will no doubt discover, there will be many days during the dissertation process when your motivation will lag and your work will slow. (We'll discuss how to manage your time and motivation in Chapter 12.) Knowing that you will need to present and defend your work in front of a live audience can help you push through the block.

I suggest that students begin submitting conference proposals when they have a second or third draft of their dissertation proposal complete. You do not need to have defended your dissertation proposal, but you need to be deep enough into the literature and preliminary data to know that your question is novel and meaningful, and you need to have had enough meetings with your advisor for you to know that your planned work is unlikely to radically change. Because the key to good professional development during the PhD process is maximizing synergies between the dissertation-writing process and your professional development, you do not want to be committed to writing and presenting a conference paper that is no longer directly connected to your dissertation.

Your first conference paper should be based on your dissertation proposal. A good proposal will review the research, problematize it, and propose a theoretical framework and research plan that will address that problematization. The first three of these elements – a literature review, problematization, and new theoretical framework – are the backbone of what is known as a review article or review piece. Not to be confused with a book review (which examines the pros and cons of a single volume), a review piece aims to capture the current state of research in a field, provides a framework that helps organize the ongoing scholarly discussion, and leverages this framework to pinpoint ways that the field needs to move forward, e.g., by highlighting latent debates, areas of imprecision, or unanswered questions (Paul and Criado 2020; Webster and Watson 2002). Your first conference paper should distill your proposal into a review piece. If you talk to your professors or skim through some journals in your field, you will find plenty of examples of this sort of publication that can serve as a template for your work.

Presenting a revised and abridged version of your proposal as a conference paper will give you feedback on your review of the literature and your theoretical framework. This is useful because most of the material from your proposal will appear again in your dissertation. You may add to it or expand on it, but you will probably copy and paste whole sections of your review of the literature straight into your dissertation. Indeed, if you are writing a big book dissertation (as opposed to one composed of stand-alone articles) you will probably have a chapter dedicated just to reviewing the literature. Thus, even if you have already defended your proposal by the time of your conference presentation, the feedback you receive will still improve your dissertation. Moreover, you can use that feedback to refine your conference paper as you develop it into an article.

The process of submitting conference proposals should continue as you proceed with developing your dissertation. If your dissertation has specific sub-questions to answer, the answer to each question or set of questions will often be interesting enough for its own conference paper. The same is true if you are doing multiple case studies, testing several different sets of hypotheses, or examining two different sets of data as part of a mixed-methods approach. Such natural delineations in your work can help you identify pieces of the larger dissertation suitable for stand-alone conference papers and presentations.

When you begin data collection or begin building your statistical models, you should take the time to submit conference proposals timed so that the conference dates will align with whenever you expect the data collection and analysis to be complete. The conference proposals will push you to convert your data or analyses into written outputs and help you to get feedback on your efforts to make sense of your data. If you think you will have multiple outputs, you can submit proposals to multiple conferences or even submit multiple papers to a single conference – many conferences allow two presentations. Just make sure to include the necessary writing time for the papers in your PhD timeline.

Lastly, as you near the end of your dissertation process and develop a completed first draft of your dissertation, you may want to submit conference proposals that distill your entire dissertation or highlight its key findings. While the review piece based on your proposal and other pieces based on your intermediate outputs may end up published in mid-tier journals, you should attempt to wring at least one really good, top-tier journal article out of your dissertation by publishing a piece that showcases your most robust and important insights. This journal article can start as a conference paper. Although you cannot yet know your findings, it may be useful to reflect on what might be the focus of that culminating paper, to help create a mental category or bucket that you can fill as your dissertation generates data and ideas.

EXERCISE 7.1: MATERIAL FOR CONFERENCE PRESENTATIONS

Drawing on your research question exercises from Chapter 5:

1. Identify the focus or title of a potential review piece based on your dissertation proposal.
2. Brainstorm additional paper topics that may result from your data collection and analysis.
3. Reflect on the focus of your culminating paper. What questions will it answer for academics or practitioners?

Dangers and Solutions

There are some dangers in timing your conference submissions around your projected progress on the dissertation. One is that you will not complete the work you intend to do because of circumstances beyond your control. Maybe your visa does not come through for fieldwork or you cannot get access to the dataset you planned to use. Will you have to withdraw your paper? Will you be publicly shamed? This risk is less serious than it seems at first glance.

Assuming you are still writing your PhD and not giving up, you will find an alternative way forward – e.g., conducting interviews remotely or using a different dataset. Most conferences have a window a few months before the conference when you can revise the title and abstract you have submitted. You should use this window if there have been significant changes in your research plan. However, if your core research questions are unchanged, your paper should still fit with the panel to which you have been assigned and no one is likely to complain. Other scholars understand the challenges of research and they will respect the effort you have made to find a solution.

A second danger is that you will not complete the work because of circumstances you can control. For example, you did not work fast enough, or you did not buckle down and do the writing. My main advice is to not let this be you. Discussants sometimes call out panel members who have not submitted their papers on time, even if just to explain to the audience why the discussant is not prepared to discuss that panelist's work. Remember that the PhD is about the process of becoming credentialled as an independent scholar. Managing your time and finding a way to motivate yourself to get the work done can be a struggle, but it is one you will have to overcome to earn the degree. It can be done; we'll discuss strategies in Chapter 12.

A third danger is that you preview in your conference proposal conclusions that turn out to be unsupported by your data or analysis. After all, one of the problems with submitting a proposal in advance is that you are expected to summarize the results of research you have not actually done! The key thing to remember when this happens is to never try to massage your results to fit your earlier assumptions. This is anathema to good research. Instead, write your paper about the unexpected results of your research, even your null findings. Use the conference window for abstract and title revisions if you know your results early enough. Otherwise take some time at the beginning of your conference presentation to discuss your research process and its unexpected results. If you can explain why you unexpectedly got a null finding or an unforeseen finding, that itself may be interesting to the audience members. In any case, if you are addressing the same research question you discussed in your conference proposal, your findings will fit the panel and be valuable to those who attend.

Picking a Conference

Once you have an idea for your conference paper and presentation, the next step is to pick an appropriate conference. Finding options is fairly straightforward. Conferences and workshops are typically advertised via calls for papers (or just "calls"), that describe the conference focus or theme and lay out the requirements and due dates for proposals. Make sure to read carefully; the phrase "call for papers" is also used to solicit materials for special issues of a journal or an edited volume.

There are a number of websites that aggregate conference calls and let you search among them. The major professional associations in your discipline or field may maintain a list of upcoming conferences. You can also ask your professors about any listservs in your field or subfield; many events – especially smaller workshops – are advertised through these. You should be able to locate some good options through an hour or two of web searches, complemented by conversations with your peers and professors.

EXERCISE 7.2: FINDING SOURCES FOR CALLS FOR PAPERS

1. Identify the major professional association in your discipline or subject area and note its next annual conference or meeting.
2. Identify one or more websites that aggregate calls for conference proposals in your discipline or subject area.
3. In consultation with your advisor or peers, identify and subscribe to one or more listservs or other feeds through which calls for conference papers are regularly advertised in your field.

The real challenge is choosing among the options you find. When you first begin looking at academic conferences, you may be overwhelmed by the number of choices available (Simpson n.d.). Imagine that you are studying at a university in Texas in the field of comparative political science with a dissertation focused on municipal elections in rural towns in Mexico. You find that you can submit a proposal to the Southwestern Political Science Association, the American Political Science Association, the International Studies Association, the Latin American Studies Association, a conference on rural development, or a workshop examining municipal elections across different countries and continents. How do you choose?

In selecting a conference, you should follow several principles. Most importantly, you will want to pick a conference where your paper fits well with the general focus of the conference, such as international studies or rural development. Doing so increases the likelihood that your work will be accepted, but even more importantly, it increases the likelihood that your presentation will be seen by people who are qualified to comment on it and who will give you feedback that improves your work. Those same people will be valuable contacts, and watching their presentations will benefit your growth as a scholar. Second, you will want to pick at least some conferences with strong reputations. Small specialist gatherings can be very exciting because of the high degree of synergy among the participants' work, but you also want to have some events on your CV that future employers will recognize. Review the work you did in Chapter 2 and look for the conferences that are often attended by people holding the sorts of jobs you would like to have. Third, you will need to pick conferences you can afford to attend. If you want to present the same work more than once, these will also need to be conferences where the audiences are unlikely to overlap. Lastly, you will need to avoid scam conferences – high-priced gatherings organized by for-profit entities with little (or even negative) professional value.

REPEAT PRESENTATIONS

There are several legitimate ways to present the same material multiple times. One is to present it at events where the audiences are unlikely to significantly overlap (Dometrius 2008). For instance, you could present the work at a small, topical workshop and again at a big disciplinary event. Another is to present your findings in revised form if there is significant time (6–12 months) between the conferences (Copper 2008). Your work can improve and you can share with the audience how it has evolved. Lastly, you can combine data from an old paper with new data to address different research questions.

Unless your work has changed so much that it warrants a new title, do not change the title of your presentation. This allows prospective audience members scanning the conference program to avoid a repeat, and it creates a more honest CV.

Resist any temptation you may feel to inflate your CV by presenting the exact same paper multiple times under different titles, especially at conferences with overlapping audiences. Doing so is considered bad form and may irritate hiring committees (Dometrius 2008). Moreover, when the members of your audience come to hear you, they forego the chance to hear someone else. If they come and hear the same paper you presented last time, you do them a disservice.

Rather than describing how to assess these factors afresh for every conference, it is useful to discuss how they align in the four types of conferences you will most typically encounter: disciplinary conferences, topical conferences, workshops and symposia, and scam conferences.

Disciplinary Conferences

One way of finding alignment between your work and the conference is to pick a large conference organized in a particular discipline. Whatever your discipline, there is almost certainly a professional group within your country or continent that hosts a regular gathering. The American Anthropological Association, the European Consortium for Political Research, and the American Sociological Association all host annual meetings. So do the South African Sociological Association and the Israeli Political Science Association. These events can be quite large: the European and American meetings often have thousands of participants.

Many of these conferences have a special theme for the gathering, usually related to current events or recent developments in the field. However, your work does not have to fit the conference theme. These conferences are gathering points for everyone in a certain profession or who shares a certain disciplinary perspective, and they are structured accordingly. Often members with a shared interest or sub-discipline will have a section that will organize a track that reviews relevant proposals and organizes the successful ones into panels. You can download conference programs from previous years to see the diversity of papers presented. For some conferences you will need to pick out which sections or tracks you would like to consider your conference proposal during the proposal submission process.

The virtue of these major conferences is that at least some of the attendees are likely to be interested in your research and the conference will be easily recognized on your CV, increasing its reputational value. If you are near the end of your PhD program and getting ready for the job market, you will also find that some employers conduct preliminary interviews at the major conference in your discipline or field. The challenge is that sometimes these conferences have so many panels that some of them are quite poorly attended. And while it is certain that some of the people attending the conference will be interested in your work, it is also certain that the majority attending will not. At a conference of 5000 people, there may only be 50 who are truly interested in your topic. This sharply reduces the odds that a spontaneous encounter in the queue at the coffee bar will yield an important contact.

Lastly, major conferences like these are often held in big cities with good airline connections. This can make travel to the conference cheaper but make accommodation more expensive.

The major disciplinary conferences in your field may be complemented by smaller local versions. For instance, in addition to the massive annual meeting of the American Political Science Association there is also a meeting of the Southern Political Science Association (serving states in the southern US) and of the Georgia Political Science Association (serving political scientists in the southern US state of Georgia). These conferences can represent an inexpensive, low-risk way to gain experience. A paper you present at a local conference can typically be repeated at a national or international one. However, unless you are interested in local or regional issues, the number of scholars whose interests overlap your own may be lower at these local conferences than at major national ones, limiting the quantity and quality of feedback you receive. Your networking will also be concentrated on colleagues in your region, which can be very helpful if you are looking for a local job but less useful for a wider search.

Topical Conferences

Other regular conferences exist among researchers interested in a particular topic. The International Health Economics Association meets biannually. In my own field of NGO research, the Association for Research on Nonprofit Organizations and Voluntary Action meets every year, usually in the US, while the International Society for Third-Sector Research meets biannually, usually in Europe.

In my experience, these more topical meetings involve more practitioners, which can be an important consideration if you plan a practitioner career. They are also sometimes smaller: maybe 600–1000 participants as opposed to 2000 or more at a major disciplinary conference. Often the panels are better attended (although this depends on the willingness of the organizers to not over-schedule) and the audience is more likely to be expert in your topic and interested in engaging in discussion. The number of people truly interested in your research will increase and the odds of meeting them spontaneously improves even more if the total number of participants is smaller. Over time, I have come to prefer these topical conferences as better venues for getting feedback and doing networking. The downside is that they may have less reputational value among people who are not working in your professional subfield. Cost wise, they are similar to big national conferences, but they are sometimes held in smaller cities where hotel rooms and meals are a bit cheaper.

Workshops and Symposia

There are many small gatherings that have a much stronger adherence to a theme or a much narrower focus. These gatherings take the label workshop or symposium to reflect their smaller size. A symposium is like a small conference in that it is organized around a series of panels. However, there is often just one panel at a time and members of the public are usually part of the audience. Workshops are usually closed-door affairs where a group of scholars take turns presenting until everyone in the group has shared their work. Presentation times and discussion periods are typically much longer than in a conference panel and may be complemented by group dialogue on the workshop topic.

Sometimes these are one-off events, convened around a particular topic as part of a grant obtained by the organizers. Sometimes they are recurring. For instance, at the time of this writing, the University of Washington organizes an annual Graduate Workshop on Environmental Politics and the Lemon Project at the College of William and Mary hosts an annual symposium on the legacy of slavery.

The virtue of these events is their tight focus. You can expect high-quality feedback, a highly interested audience, and valuable networking. There are also other benefits. Presenters may speak for longer than at a regular conference and have a longer period for questions and answers. Meals may be arranged and paid for by the workshop organizers so that the scholarly exchange can continue after-hours. The likelihood of having your attendance subsidized or fully paid for is also much higher. Note that the tighter focus can make it more difficult to have your paper accepted; if you are unsure if your work fits, you can email the organizer your topic or title and a short summary and ask if your work seems suitable.

I particularly encourage you to apply to any workshops you find related to your dissertation topic. They can be challenging events because your work will be fully dissected, and you may be expected to read and comment in detail on others' work. However, the richness of the feedback and networking is entirely worth it. Do not assume that such events are reserved for senior scholars either. Often organizers have a commitment to incorporating scholars from across the ranks – including students, early career, and senior scholars – in order to promote cross-pollination and challenge stagnant thinking. The only real downside, besides opening yourself up for intensive critique of your work, is that such workshops may have lower reputation benefits if they are less well-known or are one-time events.

Scam Conferences

Scam conferences are assembled by organizations and businesses that profit from conference organizing. On their face, these conferences may appear interesting and highly topical, with professional websites and attractive locations. Beneath the surface, however, they are high-priced events that are rarely linked to a reputable university or professional association.

These conferences often prey on the pride or ignorance of the unsuspecting. Once you have developed any sort of digital identity as a researcher, even from just a single conference presentation, scam conference organizers will find your email address and send you an invitation to share about your research at their event. It can be flattering, until you realize it is automated spam. Other, more subtle organizations set up websites that look just like legitimate conference events and, without careful digging, they may trick you into believing that they are legitimate.

Scam conferences also cater to the needs or desires of less scrupulous researchers. One of the hallmarks of a scam conference is the promise that your conference paper will be published in the conference proceedings or an association journal. Often there are the paradoxical promises that papers will both be peer-reviewed (suggesting a screening process) and guaranteed publication. They may indicate that paying your conference fee ensures that your proposal will be accepted (at legitimate conferences this process is competitive). For some academics facing a tenure or promotion review, the promise of a guaranteed presentation and publication on their CV may lure them to a disreputable conference. They are not tricked; they are getting what they paid for.

Some researchers also treat conferences as an opportunity to go on a paid vacation. They have no intention of attending the conference beyond the one presentation they have committed to give. In this case, guaranteed acceptance at a conference located in an interesting location can be very appealing. The high cost is irrelevant if their university is paying for it.

Scam conferences have no value for you. You have no guarantee that the other attendees will really know anything about your topic. There may not even be an audience for your panel if everyone else is off sightseeing or swimming at the beach. The cost is high. In the worst-case scenario, an important piece of your work will end up published in a journal or proceedings no one has heard of or respects, and you will lose any chance to publish it in a more legitimate venue.

To avoid such conferences, look for these red flags:

- Unusually high conference fee. Use the major conference in your field as a baseline. Scam conferences may have fees double this amount and a very limited discount for graduate students.
- Lack of any link to programs from previous conferences even though the conference claims to be an annual event.
- Promise or implication that all papers will be published in a proceedings or special issue of a journal, particularly a journal you cannot find or that does not seem to be prominent in your field.
- Doing a web search for the conference organizer reveals that they run many conferences on a broad range of topics.
- Organizers are based outside the country or region where the conference is being held (e.g., an organizer from Bulgaria hosting a conference in Singapore or Montreal).

Just one of these flags is not necessarily disqualifying. Sometimes a conference will have a higher-than-average fee because meals are included in the conference cost or because the organizers are subsidizing the attendance of scholars from low-income countries. Sometimes a small workshop will be convened with the intention of developing an edited volume or a special issue of a journal (although the organizers will not promise publication, since that depends on acceptance by the publisher or journal). Sometimes legitimate organizations will host a conference far from their base to try to make it easier for far-flung members to attend. But if you see more than one of these red flags, you should avoid the conference.

Keeping Track

As with many things in your PhD, it is helpful if you can plan your conference attendance in a strategic and systematic way. I suggest that you keep a spreadsheet of conference opportunities and update it regularly as calls for proposals appear in your inbox and through monthly reviews of the best conference aggregators you find in your field. Your spreadsheet could look something like Table 7.1.

Table 7.1 Sample Headers for Conference-Tracking Spreadsheet

Proposal Due Date	Conference Name	Website URL	Conference Dates	Location/ Registration Cost	Sections/ Tracks to Submit to	Send Proposal? (Y/N)	Date Submitted	Date of Expected Response	Title of Proposal	Notes

A spreadsheet like this will help you capture and compare the opportunities you come across and track the deadlines for submitting your proposals. Knowing when to expect a response (an approximate date is usually on the conference website) will let you know when you should send a follow-up inquiry or assume a rejection. Notes can include your ideas for how to link your proposal to the conference focus or theme (this can be especially important for workshops and symposia) or any special opportunities you want to take advantage of, like professional development events. You may also want to check the conference website for any information on graduate student funding and add a column noting when funding applications are due. Oddly, you may have to apply for funding or a conference fee waiver before you know if your proposal has been accepted.

EXERCISE 7.3: SELECTING WHERE TO SUBMIT

1. Using the resources from Exercise 7.2, build a spreadsheet and fill it in with six or more conferences, workshops, or symposia suitable for your planned work.
2. Reflect on the following:
   a. Which events are most interesting to you? Why?
   b. Which events will give you the best feedback?
   c. Which events are most likely to be recognized by future employers?
   d. How many events do you have time and funds to attend?
3. Use your answers to #2 to highlight those conferences that are your highest priority for submission.

Writing an Abstract

Relatively few conferences require that you submit a complete paper to apply to attend. The vast majority require that you submit a proposal, which consists primarily of a title and abstract for your planned paper (Baker 2017). Thus, the key to successfully applying to conferences is knowing how to write a good abstract.

More than just a summary, an abstract is a microcosm of your work that allows the reader to assess, in just a minute or two, whether you are asking an interesting question, using robust methods, and have interesting findings. Put another way, an abstract makes an implicit argument for why your work is important to the profession and needs to be presented publicly.

The main pieces of a good abstract are as follows:

1) The conventional wisdom. This is a summary of existing research or thinking on your topic.
2) Problematization. Here you identify the problem, limitation, or debate within the existing research that suggests a need for new research.
3) The research question. This is a concise statement of the question you intend to answer in order to address the problem identified in the literature.
4) Research design and methods. Here you tell the audience how your research develops an answer to your research question.
5) Findings. You explain what you found (or expect to find).
6) Significance. You relate your findings back to the literature or to real-world problems. "These findings suggest that literature on [topic] must change/adapt/reconsider..." Or "These findings indicate that the best solutions to [problem] involve..."

Here is an example adapted from a conference proposal I coauthored with Cortney Stewart. The numbers in brackets show how the abstract matches the steps given above:

> [1] Existing scholarship shows that international donors reducing foreign aid to a country frequently seek to devolve responsibility for funding local NGOs to the national government. [2] However, the outcomes of this transition vary widely between contexts; some funding transitions result in a successful government-NGO relationship while others result in an antagonistic relationship. Scholarship on aid reduction has yet to explain this variation. [3] In this paper, we ask, "What factors explain a government's willingness or unwillingness to fund local NGOs during aid reduction?" [4] To answer this question, we generate hypotheses using NGO government relations theory and test them using case study data from the HIV/AIDS sectors in Thailand and Vietnam. [5] We find that NGO-government relations theory provides a convincing explanation for the outcomes of the sector's transition. The theory indicates that for transition to be successful,

the NGO-government relationship must shift from a supplementary one, marked by outside funding for NGOs, guarded attitudes, and restrictive government oversight, to a complementary relationship marked by government funding, collaborative attitudes, and regulations that facilitate NGO activities. [6] These findings suggest that donors need to pay attention to the underlying attitudes of NGOs and government, in addition to laws and bureaucratic procedures, when planning funding transitions.

This structure also works for a review piece, although a discussion of methods, findings, and significance may look slightly different. Instead of drawing on empirical data, the methods develop a theoretical framework that is used to analyze the literature. The findings are the results of that analysis, and the significance section can be used to justify a future research agenda. If the abstract above were adapted for a review piece, it might look something like what is written below. Note that in addition to changing steps 4–6, I have also revised the research question since the goal of the paper is now to set up empirical research, rather than report on it.

[1] Existing scholarship shows that international donors reducing foreign aid to a country frequently seek to devolve responsibility for funding local NGOs to the national government. [2] However, the outcomes of this transition vary widely between contexts; some funding transitions result in a successful government-NGO relationship while others result in an antagonistic relationship. Scholarship on aid reduction has yet to explain this variation. [3] In this paper, we ask, "What factors may predict a government's willingness or unwillingness to fund local NGOs during aid reduction?" [4] We answer this question by drawing together the literature on NGO-donor relationships and NGO-government relations. [5] We find that while scholarship on NGO-donor relations stresses donors' desire to maintain control over NGO activities and manage NGO contracts to achieve donor goals, research on NGO-government relations reveals that some actors within local and national governments may embrace NGOs as partners and allies when NGOs' interests align with their own. These findings suggest that local governments may be willing to fund NGOs during aid reduction when either (a) the government believes it can constrain local NGOs to pursue government objectives or (b) key actors within government view NGOs as sharing their agendas. [6] Further research is needed to test the accuracy of these predictions.

EXERCISE 7.4: A BASIC ABSTRACT

Using one of your ideas from Exercise 7.1, complete the following statements to produce a basic abstract:

1. "Existing research on [topic] argues/claims…"
2. "However, [new data/theory/analysis] indicates/reveals…"
3. "To address this problem/limitation/debate, this paper asks: [research question]"
4. "This paper answers this question using a [research design or data source]" OR "This paper answers this question using an analysis of the literature on…"
5. "These [data/analyses] indicate…[findings]"
6. "These findings suggest that literature on [topic] must [change/adapt/reconsider]…" OR "These findings indicate that the best solutions to [problem] involve…" OR "These findings suggest that future research should…"

Note that the maximum length of the abstract will vary depending on the call for papers. It can be as little as 100 words or as much as 1000; 200–300 words is very common. You may not exceed the stated length, but you also should not be too far under it. A call asking for a 700-word abstract is looking for a high degree of detail; submitting a 200-word version probably will not satisfy the reviewers. Pay attention too to any requests for sources. Abstracts typically do not include citations, but some calls – typically those requesting longer abstracts – require them. If that is the case, read the call carefully to find out if the citations are included in the word count for the abstract.

Once your abstract is written, make multiple passes at revising it. Distilling your work down into such a concise form is tricky, and an abstract that seems perfect when you finally finish it may seem incomprehensible when you review it later. When I was a doctoral student, I would allocate a full day to writing an abstract for a conference. Even now, I typically devote an hour or more to writing an abstract, put it aside, and then devote an hour or two to revising it the next day.

Finally, while the abstract is the core of your conference proposal, recognize that some other information may be required. You will need a title for your paper, which may also be subject to a word length. Some conferences will request that you list three to six "keywords": single words or two- or three-word phrases (e.g., government spending or injection drug use) that will help other scholars index or categorize your work. The application system will also probably ask for some identifying information. The application software may be clunky, and there may be requests for information you did not expect. Complete your abstract and start submitting your application with enough lead time (at least 24 hours before proposals are due) to deal with any problems.

Final Thoughts

Presenting at conferences has many benefits. To improve your research, build your network, and prime the article-writing process, it is good to begin attending conferences early in your studies. Do not worry if you struggle to navigate the application process or if your work feels imperfect. Many conferences have relatively high acceptance rates. Especially for major conferences, one of the main goals is to facilitate dialogue and connections among scholars. Most scholars cannot get funding from their institutions to attend conferences at which they are not presenting, so making the admissions process too selective would undermine this community-building goal. The application materials being evaluated – mostly a short abstract – are also limited, and reviewers may be inclined to give applicants the benefit of the doubt. Lastly, conferences are places to hone work in progress. Therefore, do not worry too much about perfecting your ideas or finalizing your outputs. Find a couple of conferences that seem promising and submit your applications. In the next chapter, we will discuss what to do once a proposal is accepted.

Recommended Readings

Baker, C. (2017). How to write a conference abstract: A five-part plan for pitching your research at almost anything. Available at: https://bakercatherine.wordpress.com/2017/03/15/how-to-write-a-conference-abstract-a-five-part-plan-for-pitching-your-research-at-almost-anything/.

Bassey, A. (n.d.). 7 Reasons why every PhD student should attend academic conferences. Available at: https://authorservices.taylorandfrancis.com/phd-conferences/.

Additional Resources

Cooper, C. A. (2008). Reassessing conference goals and outcomes: A defense of presenting similar papers at multiple conferences. *PS: Political Science & Politics*, 41(2), 293–295.

Dometrius, N. C. (2008). Academic double-dipping: Professional profit or loss? *PS: Political Science & Politics*, 41(2), 289–292.

Gupta, D., & Waismel-Manor, I. (2006). Network in progress: A conference primer for graduate students. *PS: Political Science & Politics*, 39(3), 485–490.

Attending Your First Conference   **8**

Conferences are exciting, dynamic environments. A gathering of hundreds of scholars produces an intellectual ferment that spawns new ideas and connections. Just walking through the halls of a conference or sitting in an engaging presentation, you can feel like you are part of a community of researchers engaged in the massive, collective undertaking of creating new knowledge. You may make friends, develop professional connections, identify potential employers, discover new resources, and return to your university inspired about your work.

Yet participating in a conference can also be intimidating, especially early in your career. Many students are afflicted by imposter syndrome and fear that they are only pretending to be as good as their peers. Even if you do not share this fear, you may worry that your work is not up to the standards of the professors or practitioners alongside whom you will present, that your work will be critiqued harshly, or that your best ideas may be stolen.

This chapter is designed to help you prepare for your first conference experience in such a way as to maximize its benefits while minimizing the stress and risk. If you follow the instructions here, you will feel more relaxed at your first conference because you will know that you have prepared for it thoroughly. We begin by discussing how to manage conference logistics, write your paper, and prepare your presentation. We then discuss things that will happen during the conference: making your presentation, handling audience feedback, and engaging in professional networking.

DOI: 10.4324/9781003262831-8

Managing Logistics

If you are following the guidance of this volume, your conference proposal will reflect a section of your research that you intend to complete anyway. Therefore, when you receive notice of your conference proposal acceptance, you will not need to immediately spring into action to complete your research or paper. Hopefully, the work is already in progress. Instead, turn your attention to taking care of a few logistical tasks. Logistics can be a major source of stress to graduate students planning conference attendance (Chapman et al. 2009), so it is good to get them out of the way. A box on the page 127 gives a complete list of pre-conference tasks in roughly chronological order, and this section will elaborate on the earliest ones.

The first thing you should do is register for the conference. Presenters must register well in advance of the conference or risk being dropped from the program. Most conferences have a steeply discounted graduate student rate, and some have additional discounts for those who register early. You can also investigate whether there are fee waivers for graduate students. Some conferences offer these on a competitive basis, and the application process can be extremely simple.

Many conferences also have travel funding available for graduate students. Some of these require applying before you know if your paper has been accepted. However, if applications are still open, you should apply for funding as soon as you know you have been accepted. Often the process is easy, and winning external funding, even just for conference travel, looks good on your CV. You should also research your institution's funding opportunities as soon as possible; many universities offer some form of conference travel funding for graduate students. Apply for enough funding so that, between the conference and your university, you can cover conference registration, travel, and lodging.

If you win funding, read carefully the requirements for reimbursement. Some funders require receipts for meals and local transport, others pay per diem (a flat daily rate). Some may require you to stay at a hotel instead of renting an apartment or Airbnb room, book your plane ticket at least four weeks in advance, use a preferred airline, or book the cheapest direct flight. Make sure to follow these requirements so that you do not disqualify yourself for reimbursement.

Next, work on housing and travel. Many conferences have so many participants that they fill up the hotels in a city, making rooms hard to find if you are looking for one close to the conference date. When you get your acceptance, check the list of housing options given on the conference website. Look especially for any graduate student options. Some conferences are held on university campuses or similar venues; others are held in large hotels that have extensive meeting spaces. If the conference is hosted in a hotel, avoid booking a room in the same hotel unless you have a generous travel grant or one that specifically covers a room there, because the conference hotel is usually the most expensive option. Instead, find something you can afford that is walking distance or a short trip on public transit away. Make a reservation. Usually this just requires leaving a credit card number on file; you will not be charged until after your stay. There may be penalties for late cancellations, so if you decide for any reason not to attend, cancel your reservation quickly.

CONFERENCE PREPARATION CHECKLIST

- Register for the conference
- Check deadlines for paper sharing/submission
- Request funding
- Make travel/housing arrangements
- Obtain business cards
- Write conference paper
- Apply for paper awards
- Share paper with panelists and discussant
- Upload introduction of paper to conference website
- Send meeting requests
- Check presentation guidelines
- Make PowerPoint
- Practice presentation
- Review program
- Make personal schedule
- Research co-panelists
- Skim co-panelists' papers
- Download conference app
- Subscribe to conference feeds

Booking travel is somewhat less urgent than booking accommodation but should still be done at least six weeks in advance of your travel date. Even if you have travel funding, try to locate a reasonably priced option for travel. You do not have to take the worst option – flying on dodgy airlines, taking redeye flights, or connecting through an endless string of airports – but your funder will look askance if you book a very pricey option when a cheaper equivalent is available.

If you do not have business cards issued by your institution, order them now. Some universities provide them for free, others for a nominal cost. You will want to buy official business cards because they will generally look more professional and because there are legal barriers to reproducing your university's logo without permission. You will need at least 25 for each conference you plan to attend. Make sure to order business cards at least four to six weeks before the conference, to allow for bureaucratic delays, printing, and shipping.

If you know which conference you plan or hope to attend, Exercise 8.1 can help you prepare. Even if you have not submitted any proposals yet, you may want to attempt the exercise using one of the prospective conferences you identified in Chapter 7 to get a feel for conference logistics.

EXERCISE 8.1: MANAGING LOGISTICS

1. When is the conference you plan to attend?
2. What non-conference hotels or room rental options are convenient to the conference venue? *If your paper has already been accepted, reserve a room.*
3. What are your travel options for getting to the conference? *If your paper has been accepted, either book your travel now or note in your calendar when you intend to book it.*
4. What is your university's process for obtaining business cards? How long does it take for cards to be printed and delivered? *Order cards if you do not have them.*

Write Your Paper

As you take care of these logistics, you should also be thinking about your paper. This is especially true if you are using the conference to create deadline pressure that will force you to do your dissertation work. Yet even if your data are already collected, your analysis is done, and the related dissertation text has been written, you will still need time to prepare your paper. Dissertation writing is usually highly detailed, and you will need to revise this to achieve the concision of an academic article. Moreover, regardless of how much text you already have, you will need to prepare an introduction, review of the literature, and methodology suitable for your conference paper.

Most people cannot write effectively for an extended period each day – the mental focus required is simply too much. Therefore, plan on writing for four to six hours a day. Expect to need at least 30–40 hours if you are converting existing dissertation text into a conference paper. If you do not have any text written yet, I suggest budgeting 90–120 hours. If you have not done the underlying analysis or data collection, add still more time. Lastly, remember that your paper will usually be due at least two weeks before the conference. If you wish to have your paper considered for any conference awards, the deadline may be earlier still. Add up the necessary time, factor in a generous margin for unexpected problems, sick days, or special events, and then block out the needed time on your calendar.

Some conferences require that a file be uploaded to their online system by a certain date; others require that it be distributed to your fellow panel members. Check for these deadlines. Even if there are no set due dates, professional courtesy dictates that you send your paper to your panel members about two weeks before the start of the conference. Remember that they will be busy with their own preparation and travel, especially right before the conference. If you do not give them sufficient lead-time, do not be surprised if no one is able to read your work. This will significantly decrease the amount of useful feedback you can get. Some panels also feature a discussant who does not present his or her own work during the session but rather discusses the other panel members' work. Discussants frequently call out panelists who do not submit their work on time. They want the audience to understand that the panelist's late submission, not the discussant's oversight, is the reason why the discussant has not prepared remarks on the panelist's work. Avoid this embarrassment by getting your paper in on time.

EXERCISE 8.2: MAKING TIME FOR PAPER WRITING

1. How much of your conference paper will be existing dissertation material? How much will be new text?
2. How fast do you typically write? How much total writing time do you expect to need to complete the conference paper?
3. Will you be able to write full-time, or will you need to fit writing time around other obligations, like classwork, teaching, or childcare?
4. How much time will you need for revisions after a first draft is complete?
5. What paper awards does your conference offer for graduate students? When is the deadline for consideration?
6. When will you need to start writing to complete the paper by the awards deadline or the conference deadline?

There is no set format for a conference paper. Instead, structure your conference paper like a journal article, since your goal is to revise and publish it. Review the article formats for several top journals in your field, making note of typical length (usually measured in terms of word count) and structure. Typically, articles have an introduction, review of the literature, discussion of the methods, data and analysis, a discussion of the significance of these data, and a conclusion. Some of these sections may be combined, such as the methodology with the data, or subdivided, e.g., a separate section for each country in a multi-country study. Skimming through articles from several journals in your field will give you a feel for what is most common.

If you are using material from your dissertation as the basis for your conference paper, note that you will need to add a clear, concise introduction, review of the literature, methodology, and conclusion. The introduction and review of the literature will identify and frame the specific sub-question or aspect of your main dissertation question that the paper will address. You may be able to copy some of this from your dissertation introduction or dissertation review of the literature, although usually the dissertation text will be too lengthy and detailed to fit within your target word length. Condensing ideas from these parts of your dissertation for use in your conference paper will force you to think about what is most important in those parts of your dissertation, which will help clarify your thinking and perhaps improve those parts of the dissertation text. Similarly, the conclusion you write for your conference paper will help you reflect on the significance of one aspect of your data and analysis; those reflections can later be incorporated into your dissertation conclusion.

Your conference paper need not be perfect. Conferences are a place where you can present work in progress and get feedback on it. However, recognize that you will get the most useful feedback if you have already improved the work as much as you can using your own abilities. You do not want to waste your time collecting feedback that focuses on errors of which you are already aware but have not yet made time to fix. Remember too that your fellow panelists will read (or at least skim) your work and that if audience members are intrigued by your presentation, they may request a copy. To make the best impression possible, complete your paper with enough time for revisions and a thorough proofreading. Reviewing the paper several times over several days is helpful for most people. Remove any typos, insert clear headings, add page numbers, and format your references so that the whole work looks professional.

Apply for Awards

Ideally, you should complete your paper in time to submit it for consideration for any conference awards for graduate student papers. Often there are multiple options: both whole-conference awards and awards offered by various subgroups or sections within the conference. Apply to whichever are relevant to you. It is difficult to predict what an awards committee will find interesting, and the competition may be limited because some students will not have their work ready on time. Therefore, it is strategic to apply to whatever opportunities you can, even if you do not feel confident in your work.

Share Your Paper

You will need to share your paper with your fellow panel members and post a file to the conference website. Send the whole paper to your panel members, including any discussant, with a courteous cover note stating that you are looking forward to an interesting panel. You may wish to include a header or footnote on the first page of your paper stating, "This is a draft document. Please contact [author] at [email address] before citing or circulating." There is a norm against circulating unpublished work that the author has not made public (e.g., via a preprint website), but a gentle reminder never hurts.

If the conference requires that papers be uploaded to the conference website, I suggest that you make a separate copy of your paper where you cut all the text after the introduction. Where the text stops, write, "Please contact the author at [email] to request a complete copy of this paper." This serves several purposes. A good introduction will fully preview your paper, including its motivation, research question, methods, data, and findings, giving prospective readers enough information that they can decide if they want to ask for the whole paper. If people are truly interested in your work, it is good to have them contact you directly so that you can add them to your professional network. This abbreviated document also gives you a file to upload to the conference website. A well-written, well-formatted introduction will signal that a complete work exists; you have not skirted the conference rules by posting a blank file or an outline. Lastly, this strategy keeps your unpublished intellectual capital – especially data and analysis – out of the public domain, significantly reducing the likelihood that your work will be stolen.

Intellectual theft is rare, although it does happen. I have encountered only 2 cases in 14 years as a doctoral student and professor. I think that people are less likely to steal your work and claim it as their own if there is an electronic record of them obtaining the work from you. I would not worry about your work being stolen by people who just hear you present. Others are unlikely to steal your research question or core hypotheses because they know that you have a months- or years-long head start on answering that question or testing those hypotheses.

You would therefore publish your results well ahead of theirs, revealing their work as derivative. Data and results are the most valuable things to steal because these can be repurposed to answer other questions. There will not be enough detail in your presentation to steal them, so if you avoid posting your data on the conference website your intellectual property should be safe.

Prepare Your Presentation

Once your paper is done, work on your presentation. Nearly all conferences have provisions for presenters to use PowerPoint or another form of digital slide show. Your audience will expect to see a digital slide deck, and the visual aid will make your oral presentation easier to follow. Therefore, you should prepare such a deck.

Before you start work on your slides, check the time limit for presentations at your conference. Ten to fifteen minutes is common; however, panelists sometimes agree on a shorter time to maximize discussion. I have also found presentation times to be shorter at virtual conferences. At workshops and symposia times can be much longer (e.g., 30–60 minutes), to allow a very detailed presentation. If the time limit is not stated on the conference website, you will need to contact your panel chair. Even if the time is posted, it can be good to double-check with your panel chair, since chairs will sometimes set times that are shorter or longer than the conference norm.

If you have not created a slide deck before, there are numerous helpful tutorials online. The software itself is also set up to help you, offering templates that will give your work a professional look (24Slides 2018). The content should follow the general outline of your paper. There is typically a title slide, an introduction that explains the impetus for the research, one or more slides discussing the literature and framing the research question, several slides for data and analysis, and a conclusion (Golash-Boza 2018). Outline the key points of your presentation before you start writing slides (Aldritch 2016).

Match the number of slides you have to your available time. A good rule of thumb is a maximum of one slide per minute of presentation time (NCSL 2017). If you have too little time per slide, your ideas will be difficult for the audience to track and you will seem to race through your material. This can give the impression that you have not adequately prepared. Someone who knows their material well understands what is most important in it and can explain it concisely. For this reason, you should also avoid text-dense slides. Use brief text and appropriate images to highlight the key points of your work and then plan to provide more detail verbally (Aldritch 2016). If there are important analyses or visuals that do not fit within your time limit, you may put them after your conclusion as supplemental slides. If an audience member asks a relevant question during the question-and-answer period, you can pull up the necessary slide.

EXERCISE 8.3: PREPARING YOUR PRESENTATION

Determine the typical presentation time for this event or note how much time your chair has allowed each presenter. Then:

1. Make an outline of the key points from your conference paper.
2. Note the maximum number of slides your presentation time will allow.
3. Organize the key points from your outline so that they can fit onto the planned number of slides. If you cannot fit all the content within your slide limit, determine which pieces can be cut or moved to supplemental slides.
4. Working in PowerPoint or other presentation software, write slide text or create visuals that follow your revised outline.

Once your slide deck is complete, practice your presentation. You will probably want some written notes on what you plan to say. Reading from your paper will be too verbose for a short presentation and reading directly from your slides is boring for your audience (Golash-Boza 2018). After all, they can read the slides too. The goal is a verbal presentation that elaborates on the slide material. Time yourself during practice and make cuts accordingly (Golash-Boza 2018). Always think in terms of condensing or cutting material, rather than speaking faster. If you are new to presenting, ask one or more friends to watch you deliver a practice presentation and give you feedback (24Slides 2018).

Finally, save your presentation in multiple formats and places (Aldritch 2016). Save it in PowerPoint format, if possible, since this is the software most commonly found on the conference computers. Also save a copy as a PDF, especially if you are using software other than PowerPoint. Most computers have some sort of PDF reader built in and you can flip electronically through the pages of a PDF just as easily as you can change slides in a PowerPoint deck. Projected on the screen, the appearance is indistinguishable. Save copies of these files to a USB drive, since this is what most conference computers are set up to accept. I recommend getting a cheap USB just for your conference presentations. It is not uncommon for USBs to be lost or left behind in conference computers, and you do not want to lose important files or sensitive information. Also, email a copy of your presentation to yourself or save it in an online space like Google Drive in case your USB is lost or corrupted.

Virtual Conferences

The COVID-19 pandemic prompted many conferences to move to an all-virtual format. At the time of this writing, most conferences seem likely to return to in-person formats. However, all-virtual conferences may become more common, and more conferences may integrate virtual components in the future (Marcos 2020). Virtual conferences and virtual tracks or sections within live conferences can widen conference participation (e.g., by including distant scholars or those with less travel funding), help presentations reach a bigger audience, and reduce the massive carbon footprint created when hundreds or thousands of scholars fly to an academic event (Olena 2020).

If you are attending a conference virtually, your logistics are vastly simplified. However, your presentation may become slightly more complicated. Carefully read your conference's instructions for virtual presenting. You may have to record and upload your presentation in advance of the conference itself (e.g., a week or two before the conference). You may even need to coordinate with your fellow panelists to record a virtual session together.

Make sure to allow adequate time for preparing your video. You will want to select a location with an appropriate background, good lighting, and no distracting noises. Using an external camera or elevating your laptop on some books can help create a video that frames your face well. If you are recording your video solo, you will probably need to make multiple takes before you get one with which you are happy, so be sure to allocate enough time.

Be aware that you may still be expected to be in a virtual room during your conference time slot to engage in a question-and-answer session with audience members after the presentation video(s) have been played. You can use this engagement as a springboard for networking, even in a virtual environment. Networking may be more difficult without face-to-face interactions, but some conferences are experimenting with virtual coffee hours and other, more innovative tools to help virtual conference-goers connect (Kim, Lebovits, and Shugars 2021; Olena 2020).

Prepare to Participate

You now have a way to get to the conference, someplace to stay, and something to present. You have covered the major requirements and can start to relax. What more do you need to do? Most importantly, you should review the conference schedule. Make a note of when you are presenting and where. Once you get to the conference, you will want to figure out exactly where your presentation is. Conference hotels can be confusing, so make a practice trip to the room so that you do not get lost on the way to your presentation. You should also try to figure out which other panels or presentations you want to see. You do not need to fill up your whole schedule – feel free to have a leisurely lunch, catch up on your grading, or do another practice run of your presentation, especially if there are time slots when there is nothing you really want to see (Gupta and Waismel-Manor 2006). However, you should maximize the benefit of being at the conference by attending as many panels as you can that are of genuine interest to you or relevant to your research.

To find appropriate panels, access or download the conference program. I often use simple keyword searches (in my case, for terms like NGO, nonprofit, civil society, or advocacy) to find interesting panels. Increasingly, conferences have online schedule builder functions that help streamline this process. You can also search by presenter name. If there are prominent scholars you would really like to see present or to meet in person, look for them. I often look for former mentors and coauthors with whom I want to keep in touch. Integrate whatever you find into a personal schedule complete with times, locations, and panel information.

Once you know what you intend to see, you may want to download the most interesting papers from these panels. You probably will not have time to read them all, but you can skim the best ones if you have a long plane flight or train ride. Likewise, you should download and at least skim the papers from the other presenters on your panel. This will enable you to comment meaningfully on their papers, which will serve them and make a positive impression. It will also allow you to contribute to the panel discussion if the audience is small or low energy.

You should take a few minutes to do a web search for each of the people on your panel. Read their bios and skim their CVs, if these are available; often they are posted on their university's website. You can plug their names into Google Scholar and, if they have a profile, see what they have published. It makes a good impression if you can signal to others that you are familiar with their work, and you can avoid the embarrassment of over-explaining a topic to someone who is actually quite expert in the field.

Lastly, you may want to download the conference app, if there is one, to your phone and subscribe to the conference social media feeds for instant updates. Many conferences have their own hashtags for Twitter and Instagram. If you are a social media user, you may wish to note these so that you can post from the conference. Remember that future employers may see what you post, so be careful to post and tag only things that are professionally relevant. A picture of you presenting or posing in front of the conference banner is good; a post celebrating the free drinks for graduate students at a conference reception is less so.

Presenting Your Paper

Arrive at your presentation location about 15 minutes early. This will give you time to deal with any technological problems, see the layout of the room, and meet the other presenters and the chair (Gupta and Waismel-Manor 2006).

When you arrive at your room, there may still be people lingering from the previous panel, depending on how tightly the conference is scheduled. If presentations and formal discussion (i.e., a chair calling on audience members) is over, feel free to proceed inside. If the previous panel is running long, leave it to the chair or another senior faculty member from your panel to nudge them along.

Once you enter the room, figure out how to copy your presentation onto the conference computer running the projector. Get your presentation uploaded, take a few minutes to introduce yourself to the chair and fellow panelists, and verify the order of presentations. Typically, it follows whatever is printed in the program – this helps audience members track the progress of the panel – but occasionally there will be changes.

Soon the panel will begin and your turn will come up. Present the way you have practiced. Use your notes and slides and keep to time. Often the chair will have timecards that will show you how much time you have left. Since these are usually only used in the last few minutes of a speaker's time, I suggest keeping open a stopwatch on your phone so that you have a clearer sense of your pace.

If you have worked to keep to time during your presentation practice, you should have no problem keeping to time at the conference. Most people speak faster during the actual presentation than they did in practice. In fact, it can be helpful to take a deep breath after the first couple of slides and consciously slow yourself down if you have been going too fast.

If you have not practiced, or not practiced enough, make sure that you pay careful attention to your pacing. The most important parts of your presentation are normally the last few slides. You do not want to be rushing when you get there or, worse yet, have to skip these parts. Move efficiently through the first few slides and then slow down when you get to the heart of the presentation. If you get a one- or two-minute warning from the chair and have not yet gotten to your key findings, jump ahead to them.

If you run long, the chair will signal you to stop in some way. You can nod or interject "Thanks" to indicate that you have gotten the message. Then wrap up as quickly as possible, even if it means jumping ahead to your final slide. You will see presenters who ignore the chair's timekeeping or put off the chair with interjections like, "I'm almost done," but if the chair must tell you multiple times to stop talking, it looks bad. Going significantly over your allotted time is discourteous. When you go past your allotted time, you are diminishing the audience's opportunity for questions and answers, which is one of the most important parts of the experience for you and your fellow panelists and a highlight for many audience members. Proper planning and practice will prevent this problem.

Comments and Questions

Once everyone is done presenting, the chair will either invite audience questions or turn the floor over to the discussant, if there is one. Ideally, the discussant serves the audience by examining how the papers fit together and can advance current thinking on the panel topic. They may also pose questions to the panelists to help spark discussion. More commonly, unfortunately, the discussant engages in piecemeal critique, offering comments on each paper in turn. Some discussants choose to demonstrate their close reading of the papers or their expertise on the subject by making extensive criticisms. Take notes so that you can use the feedback to improve your paper later and respond to the discussant if the chair gives the panelists time to do so.

If the chair gives you time to respond, try to address only the most salient points in the discussant's critique. There is space to engage in debate with the discussant – you can disagree with him or her – but also keep a respectful tone. You will feel frustrated or chagrined when you hear your paper torn apart publicly, and you may have a strong impulse to defend it. Yet, you do not need to be defensive. Most researchers like to review others' work for themselves; they will not assume your work is bad merely because the discussant criticizes it. They will not think any less of you or your paper even if your work is harshly critiqued.

The fun starts with audience questions and comments. As you will learn, the audience members are supposed to pose questions but sometimes people in the audience just want to share their own ideas. A good chair will manage this, and also control the flow of questions by calling on audience members. You may find that your paper is ignored or that your paper is the subject of nearly every question. There is little you can do to predict this; it depends on the audience.

As much as possible, try to thank each questioner for his or her question (or comment) before responding. If they have been vague or rambling, rephrase their question in your own words, "If I understand you correctly, you're asking if…" Then respond to the question as you understand it. Some questions will be genuine and may even begin with compliments for your work. Others will seem like "gotcha" questions designed to show off the questioner's expertise while exposing weaknesses in your work. Common examples are things like, "Have you looked at the work of Jones? She published on this topic two years ago" or "Why didn't you look at data from this other population? You might have gotten different results."

Regardless of whether the question seems good or bad, if you have a good response, offer it. For instance, "I've seen Jones' work but had concerns about the validity of her findings" or "We did look at that population, but I had to cut our findings from the presentation to keep to time. Here is what we found…" If you do not have a good response, do not bluff or bluster. Instead, give the shortest answer you can, something along the lines of "I appreciate that idea and I'll have to look into it." Another good response is to suggest that you may incorporate the questioner's idea into the next phase of the research. You can even invite a questioner to talk with you more after the panel if you think your response would take too much time and not be of general interest to the audience or if you want to understand their point better. Exercise 8.4 can help you practice.

EXERCISE 8.4: FENDING OFF THE SHARKS

Gather two or more PhD friends who plan to attend conferences soon. Take turns as the presenter and questioners.

1. The presenter should offer a two-minute summary of their work.
2. Questioners should ask sharp, pointed questions, or make critical comments. For example:
   a. *Why didn't you cite [author]? They have written extensively on this topic.*
   b. *Why did you choose [your methods]? Wouldn't [another method] have been better?*
   c. *Will your sample size really give you a valid answer?*
   d. *I don't see how your theory really applies to your data or allows you to reach these conclusions. What is your objective here?*
3. The presenter should offer a concise, professional defense of their work or make a gracious deflection (e.g., "Thank you, I'll have to consider that. Perhaps we can talk more after the panel") in response to each question or comment.
4. Rotate roles until everyone has had a chance to present and defend their work.

Meet and Greet

You may breathe a sigh of relief when the question-and-answer session finally ends, but do not pack up and leave the room yet. Now is the chance to make some personal connections.

If you wait a few moments, you may find that people from the audience approach you to introduce themselves and discuss their interest in your work. Often, they are interested because they are working on similar or related projects. Take the time to talk with them and exchange business cards. Audience members may ask if you will send them a copy of your paper. If you are willing to, it is good to agree. When you email it to them later, you can ask them to send you back any comments they have. Most will end up being too busy to send you anything, but any extra comments you get will be useful.

You can also initiate contact. If there was someone in the audience who had a particularly insightful comment, you may want to introduce yourself to them and thank them. Be sure to also meet your fellow panelists, chair, and discussant if you have not done so already. If any had good questions or comments, you can ask them to send you their feedback on your paper. Often, they have more input than what they had time to share during the panel. Asking explicitly will help ensure that you get as much feedback as possible, which will help you improve your work (Gupta and Waismel-Manor 2006).

Every time you receive a business card, write on the back where you got it and what you intend to send to or to ask the person who gave it to you. This will help make your conference follow-ups more personalized. Keep the business cards you receive in a dedicated space, like a certain pocket of your backpack, jacket, or purse, to help you keep track of them.

Once the panel is over, find a place to decompress. I usually try to avoid attending a panel right after I have presented my own work. Take some time to make notes on the feedback you have received and make a list of action items – things to investigate or changes to consider – that will improve your work. If it helps you process the experience, you may also want to make a list of lessons learned about the presentation experience and things to do or not do next time. When you are ready, jump back into the stream of conference activities.

Networking

While the main purpose of going to a conference is to get feedback on your work, a second important function is building your professional network (Kim, Lebovits, and Shugars 2021; Haggerty 2010). Conferences are a chance to see and be seen, so to speak. Others will become familiar with your work, especially if they see you present across multiple conferences, and you will have a chance to meet scholars whose work is relevant to your own. These encounters can yield important professional development opportunities (Haggerty 2010). Many of my collaborations with coauthors have been inspired by seeing them present at conferences or having them see me present, or by talking over conference meals about our research. Invitations to contribute to an edited volume or a special edition of a journal can result from conference encounters. Conference networking can even lead to invitations to apply for jobs.

How do you maximize your conference networking opportunities? First and foremost, make sure the research you present is as well developed as you know how to make it and that you prepare thoroughly for your presentation. If you have interesting research and present it well, audience members may initiate engagement with you. As discussed above, make sure to linger after your panel to allow those interactions to unfold and make a careful note of who each contact is, where you met them, what they asked for (e.g., a copy of your paper), or what they offered (e.g., a copy of their own recent work). After the conference, follow up with a personal email referencing where you met, thanking them for their interest, and either sharing your work or inviting them to send you theirs.

Not all networking relies on others reaching out to you – although many graduate students may feel that way. Seo-young Silvia Kim, Hannah Lebovits, and Sarah Shugars (2021:2) explain:

> Graduate students often feel they are outside the academic community and must wait for somebody to invite them inside. This isolation is typically felt more acutely by first-generation college students, women and gender minorities, people of color, and others who have been historically excluded from academic spaces. However, graduate students are members of the academic community. Those "waiting to be invited" miss important opportunities to claim space; to invite themselves – and their peers – in.

Kim, Lebovits, and Shugars (2021) suggest that students should move from being consumers of networking opportunities who seek their own advancement to seeing themselves as creators of community who seek the inclusion of others. As community builders, they can develop connections among those who share their experience level, especially other doctoral students, and with those who share their interests, including more senior faculty.

You can initiate contact after the panels you attend with panelists whose work interests you (Gupta and Waismel-Manor 2006). Express your interest in their work, collect their business cards, and make a note on the back of what you intend to request from them (e.g., their conference paper or a recent publication they mentioned during their presentation) and why. After the conference, you will reach out and express again why you were interested in their work and request the materials. Expressing your interest in specific terms – i.e., explaining what you found interesting in their presentation – affirms the value of the recipient's work and helps to make a positive impression. You can also send along copies of any of your own work that has been published or is in press that you think the recipient may find valuable. This can help build others' awareness of your work.

You can also schedule meetups for coffee, lunch, or a just brief chat. Some of this can be done in advance of the conference. If there are scholars at the conference with whom you would really like to talk, send them an email two or three weeks before the conference date requesting a meeting at the conference. People you should consider reaching out to include scholars whose work is related to your own and from whom you would like input; professional mentors, including advisors from your undergraduate or master's education; and fellow presenters from your panel, if their work interests you. Even senior scholars will often make time to talk with a graduate student who shares their interests (Haggerty 2010). Some professional associations also have mentorship programs where they match students and established scholars; if you are part of one, try to meet face-to-face with your mentor at the conference. Be sure to prepare for these meetings, especially with more senior scholars, by reviewing your counterpart's recent work and being ready to discuss it (Gupta and Waismel-Manor 2006).

EXERCISE 8.5: MAINTAINING YOUR NETWORK

a. Make a list of previous advisors, mentors, coauthors, and fellow graduate students with whom you would like to keep in touch.

b. If you have already been accepted to a conference, download the draft program if it is available. (Otherwise, access the most recent program for the conference you plan to attend.) Use the index of presenters to search for people on your list. Note whom you may be able to meet up with at the conference.

c. If your work has already been accepted, send an email to each person on your list, telling them that you will be at the conference and asking to meet there for coffee, lunch, or a short conversation.

You can request a meeting with the chair of the search committee for any position for which you are considering applying. Be mindful that their job is to conduct an unbiased search, so avoid questions and statements that boil down to "How can I impress you?" or "Would you please give me this job?" Instead, ask them questions about the job and their institution or organization: what their students or clients are like, what it is like to work there, or what courses they expect a new hire to teach or what duties they expect them fulfill, etc. These questions will show that you are interested in learning about the job, not just getting hired. The conversation will give you an opportunity to build rapport, and the answers you get should allow you to write a more detailed and well-tailored application.

You can schedule meetups spontaneously. For example, you can suggest that your panel go out to lunch or dinner, even if you all have not planned this in advance. You can also ask a panelist or audience member whose work interests you if they might have a few minutes to get coffee or talk during an upcoming break. You can offer similar invitations to new acquaintances you meet at receptions or use meals to connect with other graduate students (Kim, Lebovits, and Shugars 2021).

Lastly, review the conference program for meetings of specialized sections or caucuses (Kim, Lebovits, and Shugars 2021). These often feature scholars with similar professional interests (e.g., global health) or related experiences (e.g., Latino scholars). Unless otherwise noted in the program, anyone can attend these meetings. There are sometimes also receptions organized by the sections or caucuses. Attending these meetings and receptions can lead to serendipitous connections.

EXERCISE 8.6: MEETING ESTABLISHED SCHOLARS

1. Make a list of scholars whose current work you would like to learn more about or with whom you would like to discuss questions related to your dissertation.
2. Using the draft program or the previous year's program, determine which of the scholars on your list are attending or have attended in the past.
3. If your conference proposal has been accepted, send each scholar a request for a meeting. A sample request might read:

> *"Dear [Scholar], I noted that you will be attending the [Conference] on [Dates]. I will also be attending to present my work on [topic of your paper]. I have found your work on [topic of their research] quite interesting and helpful in developing my research. I was wondering if you would be available to discuss [topic you want to ask about]. Would you have 20 minutes free to meet with me sometime during the conference?"*

In all your conversations, listen carefully to those speaking. Find the points in what they have to say that genuinely interest you and ask meaningful questions about those points. These things help make a positive impression. As Saunders and Joy (2014) write:

> The best tactic when networking is to ditch the pitch – that is, avoid those dreaded, self-absorbed elevator pitches which countless sources insist you must have. Instead, building rapport and establishing a relationship with others involves putting our desired outcome(s) to the back of our minds. That way, we don't distort the conversation by manoeuvring unsubtly to what we really want to discuss.

Avoid speaking negatively about others in the field, even in a casual conversation where you feel you are among friends. Your conference friends are typically people you only see once or twice a year, and you will have little chance to correct misimpressions. Instead, be deliberate about finding and remarking on the positive aspects of others' work.

Post-Conference Follow-up

Once the conference is over, there is a final bit of work to be done. Set aside a day or two for follow-up tasks (Tobin 2021). First and foremost, consolidate any ideas you have had about how to improve your research. This includes feedback you received from your discussant or fellow panelists, new citations your gleaned from hearing others present, funding or publication opportunities you have learned about, and other inspirations. You may not have time to act on all these immediately, but you can note feedback in comment bubbles on your paper or draft chapters and put tasks on a to-do list or calendar so that they do not get lost.

Second, follow up with all the people with whom you made connections at the conference, especially those who requested your research or offered to send you theirs. Go through your stack of collected business cards, read the notes you have written on each, and send personal emails to each.

Finally, make a distribution list of people who are interested in your research. Many articles are published each year, and few people can really keep up with the literature. To make sure your work is used and cited, you want to get it into the hands of scholars who can use it. When your conference paper or related work is finally published, you can send an individual email to each of the people on your distribution list with a copy of the article or a link to the journal website.

Conclusion

Attending conferences can be exhilarating, fun, and professionally rewarding. The benefits far outweigh the risks. You can maximize the benefits (and minimize the risks) by preparing carefully and conducting yourself professionally. If you take care of logistics early, write the best paper you can, and practice your presentation and responding to critics, your conference time will be relatively low stress, allowing you to soak in new ideas, catch up with colleagues, and build new relationships. The feedback you receive on your work will improve your dissertation and help you prepare to publish your conference paper as a journal article. How to do this will be discussed in Chapter 9.

Recommended Readings

Golash-Boza, T. (2018). 6 Tips for giving a fabulous academic presentation. *The Wiley Network*. Available at: https://www.wiley.com/network/researchers/promoting-your-article/6-tips-for-giving-a-fabulous-academic-presentation.

Kim, S., Lebovits, H., & Shugars, S. (2022). Networking 101 for Graduate Students: Building a Bigger Table. *PS: Political Science & Politics, 55*(2), 307–312

Additional Resources

24Slides (2018). The exhaustive guide to preparing conference presentations. Available at: https://24slides.com/presentbetter/preparing-conference-presentation.

Gupta, D., & Waismel-Manor, I. (2006). Network in progress: A conference primer for graduate students. *PS: Political Science & Politics, 39*(3), 485–490.

Olena, A. (2020). COVID-19 ushers in the future of conferences. *The Scientist*, 28 September 2020.

Saunders, S., & Joy, S. (2014). The game of higher education: What's the best way to play it? *The Guardian*, 27 June 2014.

Tobin, T. (2021). How to make the most of an academic conference. *The Chronicle of Higher Education*, 20 September 2021.

Publishing Your First Article   **9**

To maximize your job prospects as a research professional, you will need to become a published author. Publications are the primary research output of most academics, and even those universities and colleges that prioritize teaching over research typically expect faculty to produce occasional publications. In some practitioner positions, the expectations for publication are just as high as they are at a research university. In others, the expectations for publication are lower but publications are treated as important signifiers of subject matter expertise or methodological competence. For these reasons, you should make it your goal to begin publishing your research relatively early in your doctoral career. Successfully publishing your own work will give future employers a clear and convincing signal that you will be able to publish more in the future, are a recognized subject matter expert, or have professional-level methodological ability.

Publications with your dissertation supervisor or other senior scholars on which you are the second, third, or lower author are not an adequate substitute for work that is solely authored or on which you are the first author. If you have sole- or first-authored publications on your CV, additional publications on which you are the second or third author will help increase the overall weight of your publication list and perhaps link your name to more famous scholars. However, if you only have publications on which you are a junior author, employers will question whether you have the skills and ability to produce publishable work independently in the future.

This chapter explains how to publish your first sole-authored journal article. I choose to focus on journal articles because they are the most widely recognized indicator of research competency and are an accessible goal for

DOI: 10.4324/9781003262831-9

doctoral students. A monograph with a good university press may carry more weight, but you will not have enough material for a book until your dissertation is nearly complete. Book chapters, which are published in a volume someone else is editing, typically carry much less weight than journal articles because their review process is not as rigorous. They are also less widely read. Work published in the popular press, like a commentary on a new government policy or business trend, can show subject matter expertise and raise your professional profile, but is not peer-reviewed. Book reviews show knowledge of the literature and engagement with the profession, but they do not demonstrate research expertise. Journal articles provide the right combination of professional benefits in the right timeframe.

You should start the process of publishing articles early. I suggest developing your first article as soon as you have defended your dissertation proposal or completed your first conference presentation, whichever comes first. You should work on subsequent articles during your data collection or data analysis. It can be six months from when you first submit an article to a journal to when you can list it on your CV as having been accepted for publication. It is often much longer. If you aim for highly ranked journals – and you should – you may also endure one or more rejections before your article finds a home.

To publish your first article, you will need to first identify publishable material within your PhD research and select appropriate journals to which to submit your work. You will then need to prepare a manuscript for submission and navigate the journal's online submission process. You will need to interpret whatever feedback you receive and use it to revise your piece before resubmitting it to the same journal or sending it to a different one. When your work is finally published, you will need to publicize it and maximize its visibility. This chapter will cover each of these steps in turn.

Identifying Publishable Material

To publish, you must have publishable material. Most often, this will come from your dissertation research, but you may also have ideas and data from your previous professional work, master's thesis, or teaching experiences. Regardless of the source, what makes material publishable is a combination of two things: novelty and robustness. This section will explain how to judge novelty and robustness, and discuss where you are likely to find material in your dissertation or other experiences that is suitable for publication.

Novelty, as discussed in Chapter 5, means that your material will advance scholarly thinking or debate on a particular topic by bringing something new to the discussion. Most commonly, this means that you have a new hypothesis about the cause or effect of a particular phenomenon, based on a new theoretical perspective, new data, or new analysis. However, new data, new methods, or a new analysis can also yield novelty by themselves. They can be used to challenge a dominant theory, reinforce one side of an ongoing debate, or lend support to an idea that has previously been mostly theoretical. All these contributions can advance scholarly knowledge and understanding of a topic.

Robustness refers to the overall quality of your work. It is not enough to have a good idea. You must be able to convince the reader, via data or logic, that your idea is correct or at least plausible. Often this requires careful argumentation that engages thoughtfully with the existing literature and, for empirical pieces, data and analysis that match the current standards in your field. Sometimes when a field is new or obscure or data are very difficult to access, studies with very small samples and very simple analysis will be publishable because they represent the best data and insights available. However, as research on a topic matures, the standards rise. To be publishable, the quality of your data and the sophistication of your analysis must match or exceed the level of other recent publications in the field.

As you work your way through the dissertation process, there are several things that are likely to meet these requirements. First, your research proposal, particularly your review of the literature, problematization, and resulting research question, can be the basis of a review piece. A review piece is a research article in which the literature itself acts as the data to be collected and analyzed (Paul and Criado 2020). Such a piece includes dozens of sources and offers new insights into the literature by organizing these sources in a way that reveals new links between pieces, and uses these links to generate new theory, make novel critiques, or identify research questions that must be answered for the field to move forward (Webster and Watson 2002). Do not confuse review pieces with book reviews. Review pieces are the same length as other research articles in a journal and are subject to the same type of double-blind peer review. Not all journals accept review pieces – some consider them to be too theoretical – but review pieces play an important role in the profession and they are often found in high-quality journals.

Second, as you begin your data collection, you should be able to identify discrete chunks of data or novel insights that can become their own articles. For instance, if your research involves multiple case studies, each of those case studies may be independently publishable. Similarly, if you are using a mixed-methods approach, the qualitative and quantitative parts of your data may each be suitable for an article. If you are developing multiple models as part of your quantitative analysis, some of them may be publishable independently.

When deriving multiple articles from your dissertation data, you will need to identify a specific research question to be addressed in each article. These research questions can be variations on your main dissertation question or reflect specific sub-questions. Indeed, another approach to deriving multiple articles from your data is to write a separate article for each key sub-question or hypothesis.

Be aware that you may not repeat text between articles. You can use the same data in multiple articles if you are using it to answer different research questions. Senior scholars commonly do this; if they have taken the time to assemble a novel dataset, they maximize its value by using it to answer as many questions as they reasonably can. However, you may not copy and paste text between articles, even if the subject matter overlaps. For instance, each article will require its own short review of the literature. For similar articles you can reuse sources and themes, but you may not recycle the same text.

Third, you should plan an article that summarizes the very best findings of your dissertation. This article should focus on the most polished, refined form of your research question and present a distillation of all your data to make the most robust case possible for the accuracy of your answer. Your articles that break out smaller sections of data or answer sub-questions may only be publishable in mid-tier journals, but this "greatest hits" piece should be targeted toward the best journals in your field. Publishing in a top journal can greatly enhance your marketability if you plan on an academic career. If that is your plan, you may wish to discuss carefully with your advisor your plans for intermediate publications using the dissertation data to make sure that none of these will undermine the novelty and impact of this culminating piece.

In addition, if you are working as a teaching assistant or an instructor of record, you can publish articles based on your teaching innovations. Other instructors in your discipline may be interested in novel ways of teaching tricky subjects or enhancing student engagement with introductory material. Articles that discuss such techniques are part of the Scholarship of Teaching and Learning (SoTL). Your discipline may have several reputable journals that accept such pieces. SoTL articles usually draw on several semesters of instructor observations or student feedback to demonstrate the efficacy of the technique being described. Three or four semesters of data may be sufficient for a publishable article. If you wish to write SoTL articles, be sure to discuss with your university's Institutional Review Board any requirements for using data from your classroom before you start collecting data. Also check with your supervisor if you are a teaching assistant.

You may also consider developing an article based on your master's thesis, especially if it relates to your dissertation work. Reflect carefully on whether your master's research meets the standards of novelty and robustness before devoting time to this task. If it does, you can work on developing an article from it between terms during your first or second year.

This list is not exhaustive. Always be on the lookout for publishable ideas. Sometimes you will chance across data or insights that do not fit well with your dissertation but are still publishable in their own right. For instance, an interview respondent may suggest an additional question for investigation, or you may notice an emerging debate within your field while attending panels at a conference. If you can develop such things into publishable material without significantly delaying your dissertation work, do so. If you cannot, keep track of these ideas as areas for future research. If you are applying for research-focused jobs, prospective employers may ask you about what you intend to research next, once your dissertation is done. These ideas will give you a ready response.

EXERCISE 9.1: IDENTIFYING PUBLISHABLE MATERIAL

1. Reflect on which components of your dissertation are suitable for publication as independent articles:
    a. Identify the focus or title of a potential review piece based on your dissertation proposal. Note your new insights into the literature or new problematization.
    b. Brainstorm additional titles and topics for articles that may result from your data collection and analysis.
    c. List ideas for additional articles not rooted in your dissertation for which you already have data available (e.g., from your master's thesis, teaching, or research assistant work).
2. Evaluate the article ideas on your list in terms of their novelty and robustness. Mark or highlight your three or four best options.

Finding Appropriate Journals

Once you have identified publishable material, you will need to identify several journals to which you can submit the piece you plan to write. Most journals publish articles in a single discipline or area of research, such as political science, public health, or African studies. That area of research can be quite narrow or specific. Some journals also have clear preferences for the types of data used by authors: some publish only empirical studies (i.e., no theory or review pieces) while others embrace theory-oriented work. Some journals have preferences for qualitative or quantitative data or policy analysis.

Journals may favor a particular theoretical perspective, such as critical theory or feminist theory. Because of these variations, it is important that you identify the journals that are most likely to be interested in your work. There are several ways to do this, each of which will be discussed below.

One of the easiest ways to find suitable journals is simply to look at what you yourself are reading and citing. If there are journals in which multiple articles germane to your research are being published, those journals are likely to be suitable venues for your work. Similarly, you can look at journals that are cited by authors you often cite or journals in which those authors are cited. Open some of the main articles you are using in your research and examine the citations lists in those articles: are there any journals that occur repeatedly on those authors' reference lists? Similarly, Google Scholar has a "cited by" function where you can look at an article you have been citing and see who else has been citing it. Look for journals that appear repeatedly or have promising titles.

You can also look for where colleagues or advisors with similar interests have published. If there are certain scholars who have led the way in your specific area of research, locate their CVs or online profiles and see where they have been publishing. Often scholars will publish repeatedly in certain journals that are particularly well-suited to their work.

Lastly, you can look through journal listings in your field. As discussed in Chapter 3, there are several ranked databases of academic journals and multiple systems of rankings (Plume 2018; Belcher n.d.). Your librarian can tell you to which rankings your school has access. Scholars also sometimes publish articles or reports that rank journals in their field or specialty by their reputation or impact. You should see if there are any such articles in your field.

Journal rankings usually focus on a general category, such as political science or sociology. Many of the journals on these lists will be generalist journals accepting research from across the discipline. Such journals are often quite highly ranked, and it is worth considering them, but journals focused on a particular sub-discipline may be more widely read by others working in your area of research. For instance, my overarching professional discipline is international relations and the top journal in the field at the time of this writing is *International Organization* (*IO*). However, my specific area of research is international nongovernmental organizations (NGOs). *IO* publishes work focused on NGOs infrequently, so I do not read the journal regularly. In contrast, I have the table of contents of *Voluntas: International Journal of Voluntary and Nonprofit Organizations* delivered to my inbox so I can review every issue. *Voluntas* is much less well-known than *IO* in the general field of international relations, but *Voluntas* is probably the second-most prestigious journal in the field of NGO studies and the one with the strongest focus on international NGOs. Nearly every article published there has some interest to me, and I know that my fellow NGO researchers – some of whom are not international relations scholars at all – are much more likely to see my work if I publish it in *Voluntas*.

Figuring out the best journals in your sub-discipline will require some work. Small sub-disciplines may not have published listings of journals, but with some diligent searching you may find blog posts or websites where academics have published their personal rankings or used crowdsourcing to assemble an unofficial database.

EXERCISE 9.2: FINDING APPROPRIATE JOURNALS

1. List the journals you have cited repeatedly in your own research.
2. Pick two recently published sources that you have cited frequently or discussed prominently in your own work. Examine the citations lists in those two sources and note any promising venues.
3. Review the official or unofficial rankings of journals in your discipline. Note the titles that stand out to you as possible homes for your work.
4. For each of the journals identified in steps 1–3, visit the journal website and review the journal's aims and scope. Note any journals that seem to be an especially good fit for your work and delete any journals that are unsuitable.

Once you have assembled a list of journals, you can access the website for each journal and find its aims and scope. This brief description of the journal's focus should tell you if your work is suitable. If you are unsure, you can also look at the tables of contents from the last several issues to see if there has been work that has questions, data, methods, or theory similar to your own. Make a note of whatever you find. Particularly in my student and junior professor days, I found it very useful to keep a list of suitable journals. I organized them into rough categories: aspirational journals that were very highly ranked, other journals that seemed to be well-respected and widely read in my sub-discipline, and fallback journals that I thought were acceptable options for pieces I was struggling to publish elsewhere. For each journal, I copied the text of the aims and scope or noted its focus, along with other characteristics like its ranking or selectivity and word limits for authors. With this list, I was able to quickly assemble a list of possible publication venues for each new article I developed, without having to make a new search each time.

Choosing the Right Venue

Once you have a list of potential venues for an article, you must choose among them. Publishing in the right places will maximize the value of having your work published. Most academics mentally rank order the publications in their field in terms of the credibility of the work published there, the difficulty of acceptance, and the overall influence of the venue. As a result, they regard a publication placed in one of the top five or ten journals in their field as a significant professional accomplishment. Such a publication can make you competitive for jobs at elite research institutions, even if you have no additional publications. Therefore, when deciding to which journal on your list you should submit your work first, you should aim as high as you can. A senior colleague once described it to me this way: the hierarchy of publications "is like a ladder," he said, "You have to aim for the very top and bounce down every rung" until you find the best journal that will accept your work. "It's painful, but you have to do it."

Starting out, I did not know this. I looked at journals that published work I often used or had a focus that fit my interests closely and I sent my work there, with no regard to their prestige. Because the subjects on which I was working – international NGOs and the democratization of international policymaking – were relatively niche at the time, these were not always major journals. Twice my work was accepted without revision (an outcome almost unheard of in academia [Belcher 2009]) and often it was accepted with only minor revisions. I thought that this meant that I was doing something right; in reality, it meant that I was underselling my work.

With that in mind, it is important that you select venues for your work with the prestige of the venue in mind. Prestige is not the only factor, as we will discuss below, but it should feature prominently in your decision-making process. You have invested significant time, energy, and stress into your research; you should maximize its career-building benefits. This is more important than publishing in a journal edited by your advisor, responding to a flattering solicitation in your email, or, in most cases, getting something out fast.

Journal Prestige

There are several dimensions to prestige. These include formal rankings and impact factor, wide recognition, and journal audience. Formal rankings can be the easiest to discern. Many journals are ranked by one or more databases using different algorithms and metrics (Belcher n.d.). Journals often list their rankings on their websites. Impact factor is a commonly used metric that reflects how often publications in a journal are cited elsewhere (Plume 2018). What constitutes a good impact factor varies by discipline; find a ranked list that shows the specific impact factors of the major journals in your field to learn what constitutes a high score and what constitutes an average one.

While high ranking is one form of prestige, you also want to be published in journals that are recognized and valued by your future employer. There can be overlap between ranking and recognition: if you aspire to be an academic teaching in a traditional discipline, well-ranked disciplinary journals will also be well-recognized by prospective employers. However, this is not always the case, especially if you are working in a narrow sub-discipline or seeking to demonstrate subject matter expertise in preparation for a practitioner career. People working in narrow specialties, whether as academics or practitioners, may not read the major, highly ranked journals because too many of the journals' articles do not apply to their work or because the methods favored by those journals are not widely used in their field. Instead, they may read other journals that focus on their specific areas of interest. Thus, if you are seeking to market yourself as a specialist or subject matter expert, you should seek to discern which journals are the most widely read and valued by others in your sub-discipline or prospective professional specialty. Look for journals where fellow members of your sub-discipline place their own work, including where staff at your ideal employers are publishing or where top scholars in your field are published. You can ask your advisor or mentors for their opinions. The major professional associations in your subfield may also have one or more journals that they publish; these are likely to be widely recognized.

A third dimension of prestige is the influence of the journal's audience. This can be particularly important if you are planning a practitioner career. Some journals may have only moderate impact factors or be wholly unranked, but be widely read by policymakers and other practitioners. These readers may not go on to cite the work in academic publications, boosting the journal's impact factor, but they will *use* the work in their decision making. Publishing in such a journal may allow you to catch an employer's eye or signal that you are doing applied research. Identifying such journals may be difficult. A good starting point is the journal's aims and scope. Journals with non-academic influence will probably mention a policy focus or a practitioner audience. Other indicators are that high-level practitioners are themselves publishing there or that senior practitioners sit on the journal's editorial board. Conversations at conferences or in online forums can also give you clues. New measures like Plum Metrics and Altmetric attempt to capture things like the social media footprint and non-academic usage of articles published in a journal (Tancock 2017; Altmetric n.d.). You can use these if the journals in which you are interested have them.

EXERCISE 9.3: RESEARCHING JOURNAL PRESTIGE

1. Locate an official or unofficial ranking of journals in your discipline. Which journals are in the top 10% of the list? What is their average impact factor?
2. Which journals seem to be widely read by others working in your discipline or sub-discipline? Is there a professional association in your sub-discipline that publishes its own journal?
3. Are there journals in your field that are widely read by policymakers?

Beyond Prestige

Additional factors to consider besides prestige include rate of acceptance, speed of review, professional identity, and submission requirements. More prestigious journals tend to be more selective, meaning that they have a lower rate of acceptance. While it is important to aim high and be aspirational in your submissions, there is also a balance between aspiration and realism. If you are extracting intermediate outputs from your dissertation or working with small samples, your work may not fit well with the top journals in your field. You may need to start lower on the list with journals that publish more modest research, although you should still aim for the best of these journals. If you are under time pressure because of an approaching graduation date, it may be wise to select a journal with quick review and publication times (cf. Plume 2018). Sometimes these are given on the journal's website or can be gleaned from conversations with peers or advisors.

Establishing professional identity is important for those studying in interdisciplinary programs and those building practitioner careers. The journals in which you publish make "a statement to your community and the world around you" (Chaloux 2016). You want a hiring committee to look at your list of publications and feel like you will fit into their organization. Students who want to be academics and are studying in interdisciplinary programs should recognize that most academic jobs are still in traditional disciplines. You may be studying international conflict management, for example, but the academic jobs available to you will often be in political science, anthropology, or sociology departments. Those departments may be seeking someone who researches conflict and can teach courses on it, but they also need to know that that person is a political scientist, anthropologist, or sociologist who understands the discipline, can advise students, and can teach core courses. Conversely, students with a traditional disciplinary degree who are seeking practitioner jobs will want to avoid being dismissed by prospective employers as ivory tower academics uninterested in practical problems. If either case describes your situation, publishing in journals that are used and read by your target employers will help establish the identity you need for maximum marketability.

Submission requirements vary between journals. The main criterion you need to be aware of is word length. Some journals have very short word limits (e.g., 3000 or 5000 words) and others have very long ones (e.g.,14,000 words). Some journals will desk reject (send back without reviewing) any manuscript over the word limit. Word limit should not always be a major factor in deciding where you submit your work; trimming 1000 words can often improve a piece by making it more tightly focused. However, you will want to avoid a journal that will force you to condense your work so far that you must cut something crucial. I find this to be particularly true for things like articles based on interview data, where sharing findings requires including quotations from respondents.

Scam Journals

You can use the above criteria to refine your list of prospective journals. As you do, be wary of venues that seem too good to be true. Just like there are scam conferences, there are also scam journals (Economist 2020). Typically, these journals entice authors with a prestigious-sounding name and the implied promise of quick, assured publication. They may invite you to submit with a flattering personal email. However, when you explore further, you will discover that many of these journals require a significant payment from the author to publish an article. Open-source publication, in which authors or grant-makers pay for publication so that readers can access their work for free, is common in some disciplines. If it is the case in your discipline, your advisor can tell you. (It is more likely if most of the research in your department is funded by external grants.) You should never pay for journal publication out of your own pocket. Other indicators of a scam journal include a lack of accessible back issues, no editorial board listed on the journal website, or false claims to be ranked in a well-known journal ranking (i.e., you cannot find them in the ranking they claim to be in) (Economist 2020). If you follow the steps given here for finding and selecting journals, you should have few problems with scams. Just be wary of tempting offers in your inbox.

EXERCISE 9.4: MATCHING VENUES TO ARTICLES

1. For each article you intend to write, create a list of at least five possible journals.
2. Rank the journals on each list according to how valuable it would be to your career to publish there. Include one or more aspirational venues (highly regarded but also highly selective), several mid-range journals, and at least one fallback journal (less selective but still recognized and credible).

Complete Exercise 9.4 to generate a list of possible venues for each article you intend to write. When you begin submitting your manuscript, you can start with the most highly selective journal; even if your piece is rejected, the feedback you receive may enable you to hone your work and increase your odds of acceptance at your other choices. Having a clear list of planned journals will help you deal with any rejections, since you will already have a plan for where to submit next.

Preparing and Submitting Your Manuscript

Once the research for your article is complete, you will need to prepare and submit your manuscript. You can only submit a given manuscript to one journal at a time; journals will refuse to review a manuscript that is currently under consideration elsewhere. Preparing the manuscript requires matching the journal's style and format, while submission requires navigating the journal's online submission system and writing a cover letter.

Preparing the Text

If you are extracting text or data from your dissertation, you will need to reconstitute it as a stand-alone article. Most articles have a similar structure: introduction, review of the literature, data, discussion, and conclusion. In some disciplines, there is a standard article structure for the whole field. In others, the specifics vary by journal. Before finalizing your manuscript, skim through several recent articles in the journal to which you are planning to submit. Note the structure of the articles, including the focus of each section and the relative length of each section. Note too the general tone of each piece. You will want to organize and edit your article to match the journal's structure and tone.

Next, consider the formatting of articles in the journal. Look at the heading levels used for sections – are they bold, italic, numbered, capitalized? Look at the format for citations. Check the font and spacing. There will be a link on the journal's website to the journal's submission guidelines. Read these as well in case there have been changes in the journal's preferred format. Match your manuscript to the journal format.

You will need to create an anonymized version your manuscript. Journals reviews are typically double-blind: you should not know the identity of the reviewers and they should not know yours. Therefore, you will need to remove any references that could identify you. For instance, if I have written, "In my previous research, I have noted this phenomenon (Pallas 2019)," I must replace it with "In my previous research, I have noted this phenomenon (Author 2019)." Some journals will require that you replace every self-citation with "Author," but others will allow citations of your previous work to be unchanged if they are not framed in a way that tells the reader you are citing your own work. If you are not sure if you have anonymized things fully enough, do not worry. The editor will simply bounce the manuscript back to you and ask you to make changes before sending it out for review. Keep a non-anonymized version so that you can remember which citation goes where later.

Lastly, you will need an abstract. This should follow the same basic structure given in Chapter 7. However, the word limit for a journal abstract is likely to be shorter than for a conference. Check the word length (it should be in the submission guidelines; otherwise estimate using previous issues) and write accordingly.

STRATEGIES FOR ENHANCING SUCCESS

Several steps during the manuscript preparation stage can improve the odds of your work being accepted at a good journal:

- **Articulate your research question and methods precisely.** Strong research questions and careful methods will increase the likelihood of publication.
- **Circulate your article for multiple rounds of feedback.** Ask advisors, mentors, or fellow students if they would be willing to review and comment on the manuscript. Do not ask the same people to review it twice. Invite input from two to three people, make revisions, and send it to a new audience.
- **Present the work at conferences or workshops.** Ask other panel members to send you their feedback.

Making Your Submission

The online submission process for most journals is tedious and time-consuming. You should budget at least half a day for the process. If it takes less time, you will be pleasantly surprised.

Online submission consists of a long series of forms. You will need to complete basic personal information, including providing your title or position and an institutional mailing address (i.e., whatever address will allow you to receive mail via your department). Journals may ask for a list of keywords that categorize your expertise. You will also need titles and contact information for any coauthors.

Next you will need to provide information about your article. You will need a title which meets the journal criteria (there may be a word limit), an abstract (also meeting the word limit), and a list of keywords that will help others find your article during searches. If you are not sure what to list, look at other articles for examples. You will also be asked for the number of words in your article (this includes the references but usually omits the abstract), number of tables, and number of figures (sometimes with color and black and white listed separately).

You will be asked to write a brief cover letter. This is a chance to tell the editor about your article and why you are submitting it to their journal. Often this should touch on why you think the article will be of interest to the journal's readers. Be brief. A typical cover letter looks like this:

Dear [Editor]:

Attached please find the manuscript, "[title]."

This piece explores [summary of topic and findings]. Because of [reasons], I believe that it may be of interest to [journal's] readers.

The manuscript represents my original work and is not being submitted elsewhere for consideration.

I appreciate the opportunity to submit this manuscript to [journal] and look forward to feedback from the journal's editors and reviewers. Thank you for your time and consideration.

Sincerely,
[Name]

Finally, you will be asked to upload files. Typically, you will be asked to upload an anonymized version of your manuscript plus a non-anonymous version or a non-anonymous title page that includes the article's title and the names and institutional affiliations of the authors. You may also be asked to upload any figures or tables as separate files.

Once you have completed all of this, you will be asked to review your submission and view previews of your uploaded files. Sometimes there are two sets, one PDF version and a second version with embedded hyperlinks. Take special care in reviewing the file previews to make sure everything is still formatted correctly. While doing so, you may notice a few small errors of your own, like formatting the references inconsistently or forgetting to add page numbers. If so, make corrections in the relevant file on your computer, delete the uploaded file, and then upload the corrected version. When everything looks good, take a deep breath and click submit.

Understanding the Decision Letter

You will usually receive a short email from the editor within a week or so of submitting telling you that your article has gone out for review or that it has been rejected by the editor without going to reviewers. If your article is sent out for review, it can be anywhere from six weeks to six months before you get a decision. You can ask colleagues about typical times in your field; the journal's target time to decision may also be listed on its website. It is acceptable to send a polite inquiry to the editor if you have not heard back after the expected time.

When you get a decision letter, the editor will usually tell you in the opening paragraph what the decision was on your manuscript. Additional comments from the editor and reviewers then follow. Decisions come in several types: desk rejection, rejection, revise and resubmit, accept with revisions, and accept. We will discuss each of these in turn and what you should do when you get one.

Before proceeding further, however, let me say a word about reviews. Reviews can be very frustrating to read. Some are so short as to give you little useful feedback. Others complain about everything from your research question to errors in punctuation without distinguishing between major and minor areas for improvement. Sometimes reviewers will disagree with each other in confusing ways. One may praise your research design, for example, while the other tears it to shreds. You will probably also feel like one or more of the reviewers has misread or overlooked parts of your article, dinging you for mistakes or omissions you did not actually make. Adding insult to injury, the language is often blunt to the point of harshness.

You are not alone in the feelings of anger, disappointment, or sadness you have when your reviews come back. It can be worth remembering that the reviews, as harsh and unpleasant as they may be, do serve a purpose. Peer review has been shown to improve the article quality; lengthy reviewer comments may even increase the likelihood that an article will be cited in the future (Belcher 2009).

The most important thing to remember after a painful review is to keep submitting your work. Whether your article is accepted depends in part on who you get as reviewers. One reviewer may love an idea that another one loathes. One may be more knowledgeable about your topic or methods, another less. A senior scholar once shared with me about publishing two articles in one of the very top journals in his field: "I was surprised both times." Continue to submit your work and you should eventually find the combination of editor and reviewers who appreciate it.

Desk rejection. A desk rejection is a rejection directly from the editor. It means that the editor is so certain that your piece cannot be published in their journal that they are saving everyone's time – including yours – by sending it straight back to you. This is disappointing, but it does not necessarily mean your piece is awful. More commonly, it means that your article does not fit closely enough with their scope. I once got an apologetic desk rejection from an editor who explained that the editorial board had recently decided the journal should shift its focus to specialize in just one narrow field of international relations, but had not got around yet to updating the journal's aims and scope on their website.

Sometimes a desk rejection will be related to quality, but read the letter carefully. If you are too disappointed to do so in the moment, come back and read it closely the next day. Is the editor saying "This isn't good research" or just "This isn't good enough for us"? Usually it is the latter, which just means you need to move down a few rungs on the journal ladder before submitting again.

In general, the best response to a desk rejection is to submit your work as quickly as possible somewhere else. The feedback from the editor is unlikely to be very detailed and may focus on things that cannot be quickly fixed. There is no point in trying to make major changes to satisfy someone who does not want to see your work again. Submit it elsewhere until you find an editor who is interested enough to send it out for review.

Rejection. Rejection means that the journal editor, after receiving comments from the journal's reviewers, has decided your piece does not merit publication in their journal and is not interested in seeing a future version of it. Note that this is true even if the editor or reviewers include some positive comments or suggestions on how to improve your work (Belcher 2009).

Rejections sting. You have spent weeks hoping for a positive response, only to hear back that your work was not good enough. Instead of success, you now have two or three sets of comments from the journal's reviewers telling you in detail just how far short your article fell.

As with the desk rejection, your best response is to get it back out fast. Look for the positive comments in decision letters and take those to heart. Sometimes one or more reviewers will like your article even if the others do not. Note if there are any issues that the reviewers and editors all agree on that you think you can fix quickly. Perhaps you can change a few sentences in the introduction to make the claims of the piece more modest or add a short paragraph on limitations. Proofread it again if the reviewers comment on typos and integrate any additional sources they recommend. However, do not spend more than a day making changes. These reviewers are unlikely to see your piece again (there is a very small possibility they may be sent the piece by another journal to which you submit), so there is no need to respond to all their critiques. The next reviewers may want different things.

Revise and resubmit. The name may sound disappointing but a revise and resubmit (R&R) is a positive response. It means that the editor, after seeing the reviews, thinks that your piece has the potential for publication! The reviews may still sting, and the list of requested revisions may be lengthy but, in most cases, if you do what the editor and reviewers have asked you to, your piece will be published. Note that with an R&R, your revised work will go back to the same reviewers for reconsideration when you submit it.

Your first step is to write a note to the editor thanking her or him and the reviewers, and promising to submit a revised manuscript. Usually, the email you have received from the editor gives a deadline for resubmission. If not, ask the editor in your note when the deadline is. Next, you will need to begin identifying what edits to make, revising the manuscript, and writing a response letter. How to do this is described in the next section.

Accept with revisions. This is an excellent response! It means that the journal editor expects to publish your work, but requests that you make some changes first. Some journals use two variations, accept with major revisions or accept with minor revisions, depending on the level of revisions requested. Regardless of which you get, if you make the changes, your piece will be published. Note that if you complete a revise and resubmit, the next decision you get from an editor will often be accept with minor revisions.

Read through the note from the editor carefully to see what she or he is requesting and whether the revised manuscript will be sent back to the reviewers. For accept with minor revisions in particular, final publication is often contingent only on the editor's agreement; the reviewers will not review the manuscript again. The editor will still want you to acknowledge the reviewer comments and resolve any problems they have identified, but you can focus primarily on the changes that the editor has identified as most important.

As with an R&R, you should first write a note thanking the editor and expressing your appreciation for the reviewer comments and your intention to complete the revisions. Note the deadline for submitting your revised manuscript and begin working on the revisions and a response letter.

Accepted. This is the best possible response, and rarely received after an initial submission. More commonly, you will get notice that your piece has been accepted after you have revised a manuscript that received an R&R or an accept with revisions and submitted the revised manuscript. It means that no further changes are needed. You can move it on your CV to your list of published articles, with "Forthcoming" in lieu of a date of publication. Be sure to send a thank you note to the editor and watch your email for notifications about copyright permissions, proofs, or online publication.

Making Revisions and Writing a Response Letter

If your manuscript has received an R&R or an accept with revisions, you will need to make changes to your manuscript before it is reviewed again. In addition, you will need to write a response letter detailing each change you have made and respectfully explaining your reasoning if there are any changes you are unwilling or unable to make.

Your first step should be carefully cataloguing all the changes requested by the editor and the reviewers. Sometimes the reviewer comments can be a bit rambling or have a mix of compliments and critiques. Reviewers are unpaid and the time spent reviewing comes at a cost to their other professional work, so not everyone devotes time to honing and polishing their remarks.

Identify each specific critique and separate them out in a text document, using numbers or bullet points. You should have a separate section for comments from the editor and from each reviewer. Some authors will try to combine points between reviewers where they overlap, but I generally find that it is best to keep each reviewer's points separate, since this document will become your response letter and each reviewer will want to see how you responded to their feedback.

Next, match the requested changes to the relevant sections of your document. In other words, begin thinking about where the changes will go and what they need to be. You can make notes on your list of critiques or in your manuscript. I find that copying reviewer comments into comment bubbles in the manuscript can help me see where the edits need to go and how the critiques overlap.

Not all the requested changes will be quick fixes. For those that require rewriting or rethinking parts of your manuscript, you can complement your comment bubbles with notes in your list of critiques detailing how you will revise or restructure the document to address these more serious issues.

You may need to deal with comments from reviewers about issues that you think you have already addressed in the manuscript. For instance, they may ask you to consider a certain debate or perspective you think you have already incorporated. Rather than arguing the point, take this as an opportunity to clarify or foreground this material so that other readers do not also assume you have overlooked a key issue. Usually adding a few sentences, phrases, or citations to emphasize the material is enough. If you think that they have completely overlooked something you wrote, you can also highlight that to them. Do not say, "The reviewer has overlooked this," since arguing with the reviewers is rarely a good idea; they have more power than you do in this process. My approach is to simply include the overlooked text in the response letter without claiming that I have revised it. For instance, I might write something like this: "*I understand the reader's concern about [issue] and have endeavored to make this point clear. The text on page [number] of the manuscript reads [quote the relevant text].*"

Third, make your revisions. It is good to make the biggest revisions first. These may involve deleting certain arguments the reviewers disliked or significantly restructuring work they thought was unclear. It is best to do that early rather than wasting time on minor fixes that may get deleted or garbled by the big changes. Keep all changes marked using comment bubbles or track changes so that you can find them later when you are completing your response letter.

Fourth, when you are satisfied with the manuscript, prepare your response letter. Take your list of critiques and add a short introduction. It should read something like this:

Dear [Editor]:

I appreciate the time and attention the editors and reviews of [journal] have given to commenting on my manuscript, "[title]." The review helpfully identified ways that the manuscript could be clarified and improved. I am grateful for the opportunity to revise the work and for the invitation to resubmit the revised manuscript to [journal].

In the text below I identify each editor and reviewer critique and present my response, along with excerpts from the revised manuscript showing the changes I have made. Please let me know if you have any questions or further comments.

I look forward to your decision and feedback on this revised manuscript.

Sincerely,
[Name]

After this introduction, you should have sections, marked with headers, for the comments from the editor and each reviewer. Each specific critique should get a bullet point, number, or some bold text to set it apart. You can give each critique a title or summary label if you like, but then copy the reviewer's words noting, "Reviewer 1 states, '[reviewer comment].'" After the reviewer's language, explain briefly but specifically what you have done to address this. For example, "On page 7 I have added a detailed discussion of Rodriguez's (2019) study of this issue. The revised text reads: ..." Then copy in your revised text and any surrounding sentences that are needed to frame it. Put this in italics or offset it as a box quote so that the critiques and the revised text are readily distinguishable from each other.

Your goals here are to convince the reviewers that you have responded to all their concerns and to make the response letter so comprehensive that they do not take the time to reread the whole manuscript again. This reduces the likelihood that they will find new problems or notice your inevitable attempts to placate them while changing as little as possible. However, you will not be able to paste in multi-page sections of the manuscript. For instance, if the reviewers ask for a new introduction or a restructuring of your analysis, you will have to describe what you have done using a few lines of text. For everything smaller than a page, copy and paste the text. Do not worry if this makes your response letter very long. If it is properly structured and formatted, it will be very skim-able, which will make for fast reading.

The response letter is an exercise in respect. The reviewers have power in this process, and you generally should defer to them. Make every change requested unless you think it would worsen the manuscript in a significant way. Minor changes may feel like they disrupt the flow or elegance of your original writing. Maybe adding the requested sources to your review of the literature, for example, makes it less concise. Do it anyway. Your goal at this point is to satisfy the gatekeepers. It is better for your manuscript to be clunky and published than elegant and unseen. Moreover, critiques of our work pique our pride, making it hard for us to be truly rational and objective. The reviewers' comments may be improving your work in ways you cannot appreciate at the moment (Belcher 2009).

If there are any changes you truly cannot make or are not willing to make, note those in the response letter too. It is best if there are only a very few places where you do not take the reviewers' advice. Explain respectfully why you have chosen to take a different approach or why a requested change or addition is beyond the scope of the piece. You may also add language to the manuscript clarifying the scope of your work or its limitations so that future readers, who may share the reviewers' concerns, know that you have considered these issues. Note such changes in the response letter and copy in the relevant text.

Fifth, prepare a clean copy of your revised manuscript, which should still be anonymized. Proceed to the journal's website, where you will need to navigate the submission process again. This time there should be a box to check or a label to pick noting that you are submitting a requested revised text. Upload your manuscript and response letter, along with any tables or figures.

Your manuscript will now reenter the review process, going back out to the original reviewers or, in the case of some accept with revisions decisions, being reviewed by the editor. The timeframe should be shorter, but you can still expect a wait of several weeks before your next decision letter.

After Acceptance

If your research is novel and of even moderate quality, you should eventually find a publication home for it. If you do not get your work into a top or mid-tier journal, do not worry. You may do better on the next one. In the meantime, having a sole-authored publication in any peer-reviewed journal will give you an advantage over job candidates who have none.

Once your manuscript is accepted, you will need to complete several steps. Most importantly, watch for emails from the journal. Usually these will come from a managing editor or an editorial assistant, not the journal's editor-in-chief. These emails will tell you what you need to do next. Usually, you will need to submit a de-anonymized version of your manuscript. You may also need to complete some information related to copyright, giving the journal permission to publish your work.

Eventually the journal will send you a set of proofs. The proofs show what your article will look like when it is published in the journal. Read these carefully. The proofs show how your text has been formatted to fit the journal's look, but they also often contain minor edits or requests for clarification from a copy editor. Ideally, the copy editor is just correcting minor problems. Sometimes, however, the copy editor introduces errors of their own while reformatting your manuscript or making those corrections. If you find things that seem off, compare the proofs with the final, accepted version of your manuscript. Feel free to revert any changes back to your original text if they are problematic, while adding a note explaining why you have done so.

When reviewing the proofs, you may also find language you wrote yourself that you now want to improve. Resist this temptation unless there is a clear error of fact or grammar. The proofs are only a place to correct mistakes, not wordsmith and polish.

EXERCISE 9.5: PROMOTING YOUR WORK

1. Make a list of individuals who have expressed an interest in your work. Include:
   a. Individuals involved in your research (e.g., respondents or data holders).
   b. People whom you have met at conferences who have expressed an interest in your work.
   c. Mentors or colleagues who have provided advance feedback on the work.
2. Research online venues for publicity in your school or department.
   a. Ask if your department publicizes student publications on their website or social media feeds.
   b. Identify the individual responsible for maintaining these feeds and posting new information.

Promoting Your Publication

The journal may publish your work online, ahead of print. Some do this by publishing your un-proofed, final accepted manuscript. Others will post the formatted and proofed version of manuscript even if the print issue in which it will appear has not yet gone to press. This is all for the good, since it makes your work available earlier. If the work is available online, you can add a hyperlink to the article where it is listed on your CV.

Once your work is available publicly, whether online or in hardcopy, you should start publicizing it. While getting published is a key milestone, citations of your publications will become an equally important metric as you advance in your career.

When you are working on an article, you should keep a distribution list that includes everyone you expect to be interested in the research (see Exercise 9.5). This includes respondents who have participated in the research, people who have expressed interest in your conference presentations on the topic, and researcher friends with whom you have discussed the work. Send an electronic copy of your piece or a link to where it is published online to each person, along with a line or two expressing why you thought they would be interested. Note that this means you should write to each person individually, not send out a mass email. There is no shame in this kind of self-promotion if it is done politely. There is a vast volume of literature published each year and few academics have the time to keep track of much of it. The odds of people taking the time to skim your article are vastly improved by you sending it to them.

You can also make finding your work easier by setting up a profile on Google Scholar or one of the several websites that host academic research. The quality and reputation of these sites vary, so ask around about what is most respected in your field. You can also get an ORCID identifier, a digital code which will link your works to you when they are indexed (ORCID 2015). Post a summary of your work on your personal webpage if you have one and post a link on social media if you are a social media user. Even if you are not on social media yourself, you should ask your department to tweet out a link. There is almost certainly someone responsible for your department's social media feeds, and they are usually eager for new content.

Now you can breathe a sigh of relief. Outside of completing the dissertation, publishing your work is the most difficult thing you are likely to do in graduate school and the most important thing for your future marketability for most research positions. Of course, there are still other signifiers you can acquire or skills you may wish to master, including winning funding and teaching students. We will cover these in the next two chapters.

Recommended Readings

Belcher, W. (2009). Parsing the decision letter. *The Chronicle of Higher Education*, Feb 2009.

Economist. (2020). Garbage in: How to spot dodgy academic journals. 30 May 2020 edition.

Paul, J., & Criado, A. R. (2020). The art of writing a literature review: What do we know and what do we need to know? *International Business Review*, 29(4), 101717.

Webster, J., & Watson, R. T. (2002). Analyzing the past to prepare for the future: Writing a literature review. *MIS Quarterly*, xiii–xxiii.

Additional Resources

Belcher, W. L. (2019). *Writing Your Journal Article in Twelve Weeks: A Guide to Academic Publishing Success*. Chicago: University of Chicago Press.

ORCID (2015). Six things to do now you've got an ORCID ID. 23 July 2015. Available at: https://orcid.org/blog/2015/07/23/six-things-do-now-you%E2%80%99ve-got -orcid-id.

Reviews of peer-reviewed journals in the humanities and social sciences. (n.d.). Available at: https://journalreviews.princeton.edu/reviews-of-peer-reviewed-journals-in-the -humanities-and-social-sciences/.

Winning Funding 　　　　**10**

At each stage of your PhD, there will be opportunities to win grants, fellowships, or other forms of funding. You should explore these options. Many applications will take less time than you imagine, and the application processes can help you refine your thinking about your dissertation or the personal narrative you will tell prospective employers.

The most obvious benefit of grant writing is that it brings you money. There is little reason to pay for your own tuition, conference travel, or field research if there is a funder willing to pay for it. Funding can allow you to devote more time to your studies or research and less time to outside work. Having funding may enable you to take advantage of opportunities, like international conferences or research at distant field sites, that you might not otherwise be able to afford.

Grant writing can also bring you recognition. Funders often publish a list of grantees with a note about the specific research funded. The winners of conference funding grants are sometimes listed in the conference program. These modest plaudits can help your professional networking.

Lastly, for some positions, especially at research-oriented universities, the ability to win external funding is a strong preference for job candidates. Leadership positions in many nongovernmental organizations also often include responsibility for writing and winning grants.

Not all jobs have such a high value for grants. Yet even if your preferred employer does not expect grant writing from holders of the position you seek, successful grant writing can be a bonus. Teaching-oriented universities, for instance, may not expect that a faculty member attract external funding,

DOI: 10.4324/9781003262831-10

but they would certainly be happy if she or he could. This is especially true if you can involve students in your research.

In this chapter, we begin by discussing the types of funding that are most accessible to PhD students, and the benefits of each type. Next, we will discuss how to leverage your comparative advantage to find the grants and scholarships for which you will be most competitive. We will then discuss how to maximize your chances of success and when during your PhD you should apply.

Types of Funding

If you go to a seminar on funding hosted by a grants officer from your university, you will almost certainly get a lot of information about project-based research funding from the national government or major foundations. This is the type of funding that is most interesting to professors and has the most value to the university as an institution (Brill 2007). These grants, which typically fund multi-year projects, are often for large amounts of money, have prestige, and, at least in the US, allow the university to extract indirect costs: a percentage of the money that the university takes to fund its own expenses before passing the remainder on to the grant winner. However, this type of funding is hardly the only type of funding available to doctoral students. It may not even be the best fit. Hugo Horta, Mattia Cattaneo, and Michele Meoli (2018), for instance, find that simple tuition funding does more to boost student research performance than winning research project grants. You have to identify the type of research funding that is best for you.

There are four types of funding that most doctoral students should consider: scholarships, fellowships, and studentships; conference funding; research-related travel funding and writing-up fellowships; and research funding that pays for a wider variety of expenses. Each of these types can be leveraged to enhance your progress on the PhD, facilitate professional development, or both. This section will discuss each of these funding types in turn.

Scholarships, Fellowships, and Studentships

Scholarships, fellowships, and studentships are all grants designed to pay for your tuition and possibly your living expenses while you are in graduate school. Some programs automatically award two or more years of funding to all accepted PhD students. Even those that do not, however, typically have at least some funding available on a competitive basis. You should apply for such funding and do so as early as possible; sometimes you can apply before matriculation.

The more money you have available for tuition and living expenses, the less time you will need to spend working as a teaching or research assistant or in an outside job. The result is often increased research productivity, including more publications (Nistico 2015; Horta, Cattaneo, and Meoli 2018). Funded students who pursue publication, as this volume encourages you to do, complete their PhDs faster than unfunded students who also pursue publication (Horta, Cattaneo, and Meoli 2019). Even if teaching, research assistant work, or outside employment is part of your professional development strategy, it will benefit you to have the freedom to take only the best professional development opportunities, rather than feeling forced to take whatever pays.

What sets scholarships, fellowships, and studentships apart from other types of research funding is that they are typically focused on funding you as an individual, based on your distinct characteristics and previous academic performance. The focus and quality of your research are often of secondary importance; for some funders it may not even be a factor at all.

As you look beyond your university, this will become quite evident. There are many organizations that are interested in funding your studies that award funding based on the affinities and interests of the organization. For instance, as the descendent of Italian immigrants, I won a scholarship from the Order Sons of Italy in America (now the Order Sons and Daughters of Italy in America), an organization dedicated to promoting Italian heritage in the US. I had a friend who won a scholarship for Christians pursuing doctoral degrees. Other funding is earmarked for women, racial and ethnic minorities, immigrants, or international students.

Conference Funding

Conference funding subsidizes your conference attendance. As noted in Chapter 8, you should begin attending conferences as soon as you have developed a solid research proposal and use conference feedback throughout your studies to improve your dissertation and jumpstart the publication process. Most conference organizers offer some sort of funding for graduate students. This can be as small as a fee waiver, which covers your registration fees, and as large as free lodging plus travel funding. Conference funding is often awarded competitively, but the application process is usually quite fast and requires only basic details on yourself and your planned presentation. With that in mind, I would suggest that you always apply for travel funding from the conference organizers. It is an easy way to reduce your own costs and add lines to your CV. Sometimes funding winners are even listed in the conference program, giving you an additional bit of recognition and possibly helping you make a positive impression in your conference networking.

Your university probably also has travel funding available to graduate students. Some institutions may earmark a certain amount of funding for each student or award it competitively. The application process is again fairly simple. You will need to provide information on the conference, your expected costs, and the value of attendance for your research or professional advancement. Note that your school may want evidence that you have sought external funding before using school resources, which is another reason to always explore the funding available from the conference organizers. You should also ask about any other limitations your school places on student funding; you may only be able to win funding once per year or only be able to access a certain amount of funds. If your school has such limits, be sure to use the funding strategically to make sure that you can attend the conferences that are most important to you.

Research Travel Funding and Writing-Up Fellowships

If your research involves international fieldwork, the most expensive part of your fieldwork will usually be your travel to and from the field, followed by your lodging while there. Therefore, some universities and external funders provide grants specifically to cover research travel and related living expenses. What sets this apart from regular research funding is that the funders are usually not paying for the research itself. They are just paying for you to get to the field and live there. They are not paying for you to employ translators, rent space to conduct focus groups, or put a survey in the field. As a result, you will have to provide less information about your planned research than in a traditional research grant – although you will need to provide more detail than for tuition or conference funding.

Similarly, some scholarships are focused on funding your writing-up, after you complete your data collection or initial analyses. This can be particularly valuable if you need to take a break from work as a teaching assistant or research assistant to focus on your writing, or if the student funding you initially received from your university has ended. The applications for such funding consider both you and your research, but the focus is likely to be on the findings your research is expected to produce rather than a detailed accounting of the methods that will get you there.

Travel and writing funding can overlap when students are using special archives or document repositories. Universities that hold the collected papers and records of famous people sometimes offer fellowships for students who wish to visit to use those archives. The successful student becomes a research fellow at the institution for one or two semesters, is provided with funding or a stipend to pay for their stay, and is expected to produce research that draws on the materials in the archive.

All these types of funding allow you to improve your dissertation while enhancing your professional development. They may allow you to travel abroad and meet respondents in person, rather than doing interviews remotely or choosing a less ideal (but cheaper to access) field site. They may also allow you to stay in the field longer. These things will hopefully enhance the quality or quantity of your data. At the same time, experience doing fieldwork in a certain region is a job requirement for some practitioner positions and can enhance your job prospects for many others. Lastly, these kinds of grants add more lines to your CV and show that you are able to pursue and win funding.

Research Funding

True research funding can pay for a host of expenses: you can include a stipend for yourself, travel expenses, and research costs like paying for database access, surveys, translation, or local assistants. What makes these applications distinct is that the focus is less on you as a researcher and more on the research itself. The funder will want to know what you intend to produce and how you intend to produce it. Your personal credentials are important only insofar as they signal that you are able to carry out the proposed plan.

Research funding typically involves very detailed applications. You will have to make an argument for why your research is necessary and explain how you intend to conduct it. Much of the material you prepared for your dissertation proposal will feature in a research proposal, albeit in condensed form. Expect to have to produce a detailed methodology and a very detailed budget. Funders want to know exactly what they are paying for. Small-value grants (about 10,000–30,000 US dollars) may have somewhat less detailed proposal requirements, but larger value grants may require very specific, detailed formats. If you are applying for such a grant, you should schedule an appointment with a grants officer from your university for guidance on how to complete the application properly and to learn about any university regulations, including requirements to include indirect costs for the university, that govern how such grants are administered or disbursed.

Winning research funding, especially for large amounts, is prestigious and can provide a significant career boost for both prospective academics and practitioners. Also, some research can only be carried out with external funding. For instance, if you are planning an experimental approach where you will introduce social interventions (e.g., providing vocational training for youth or food vouchers for households in a poor village), you are unlikely to be able to fund the research yourself.

Applying for large research grants requires a much greater commitment of time and effort than other types of funding. Preparing a detailed grant application can take as much time as preparing a journal article. With that in mind, it is important that you make a clear-eyed cost-benefit analysis. Depending on your research and your career ambitions, it may be more advantageous to apply for a small grant with a shorter application process and a higher likelihood of funding, than a large, highly competitive grant with a time-consuming application process (Chasan-Taber 2018). Be aware that this is probably not the advice that you will get from your institution's grants officer. Large-value grants are more beneficial to the institution and grants officers have spent significant time learning how to win them. They may not be tracking the small-value grants that are often more suitable for student researchers. If that is the case, you will have to seek these grants out on your own.

Internal vs External Funding

As I have noted in some of the descriptions above, funding can come from inside or outside your university. These are usually referred to as internal or external funding sources. You should consider both sources for any given funding need. Internal funding is typically much less competitive, making for an easier win, whereas external funding typically has a higher value when listed on your CV. Your institution may also look askance if you apply only for internal funding; it can give the impression that you are exploiting the institution's largess. For these reasons, I encourage you to explore the external options and seek external funding whenever it is readily available (as for conference travel) and save your internal applications to top up the external funding or for significant expenses (e.g., research travel) for which you have been unable to locate a funding source or for which you are uncertain your external funding applications will be successful.

In short, there are many more types of funding available than are discussed in a typical funding workshop and there are a wide variety of sources. You do not need to win a prestigious, government-funded grant to complete your PhD. You may be able to do just as well – or even better – connecting a series of smaller grants for tuition, travel, and research. Over your time in graduate school, you should consider all types and sources of funding.

EXERCISE 10.1: ASSESSING YOUR EXPENSES

What are your projected minimum expenses in each of the following areas for your remaining time in the doctoral program?

1. Tuition
2. Living expenses
3. Conference attendance (plan on at least one conference a year starting in your second or third year)
4. Research travel, if any
5. Research expenses (e.g., access to databases, funding for social experiments, surveys, specialized software, etc.), if any

---

Finding Appropriate Opportunities

Ideally, I would now direct you to a comprehensive database of suitable grants. Unfortunately, no such comprehensive database exists. Many universities maintain their own databases of external funding opportunities, but they are incomplete and may not be regularly updated. I have yet to find a good source of grant information that does not become outdated within a few years. Therefore, you should begin building your own database – a simple spreadsheet will do – capturing funding opportunities that are relevant to you whenever you find them and listing them by funding type and application deadlines, similar to what you are doing with conferences. Table 10.1 provides an example set of spreadsheet headers.

Begin developing your database by examining your university's internal funding options. Internal funding can be particularly good for tuition and living expenses and conference travel funding. Some universities also offer grants to fund student research, including research travel. Your university should maintain an accurate database of university-wide funding opportunities.

Table 10.1 Headers for Funding Application Tracking Spreadsheet

Application Deadline	Funding Type	Max Amount	Name	Funder	URL	Notes

Your school or department within the university may also keep a list that will include funding options only available to its students. Other doctoral students who are a year or two ahead of you should be familiar with the internal opportunities for conference funding or research travel money and can help you learn more about what is available. Begin by accessing these resources and capturing the information in your database.

Once you have done this, you will want to search for external opportunities. The best ways of doing this are different for tuition and living expenses, conferences, and research-related expenses, so we will discuss each of these separately.

Funding for Tuition

The most important thing to realize about external tuition funding is that most funding for tuition and student living expenses is given for some reason besides supporting excellence in scholarship. Many social systems are already based on principles of meritocracy. In theory, the brightest students get into the best universities, earn the best grades, and receive university funding for their studies. There is little reason for most funders to duplicate this system by awarding funding based on the same principles and criteria.

Instead, many external funders focus on areas where they see the meritocratic system breaking down. For instance, they may feel that potential scholars from poor families are underrepresented in graduate programs because they cannot afford to attend, or that intellectually gifted students from disadvantaged backgrounds may not earn the best grades because their education is impeded by difficult social environments or failing schools. Therefore, the funder offers a scholarship not for the "best student," as indicated by overall grades or test scores, but for the best student from a working-class background, for example, or from a poor community.

Other funders may want to help members of particular social groups. I won a grant for American students of Italian descent sponsored by an organization promoting Italian American heritage. One of my PhD students discovered that there was a unique set of scholarships available to children, like herself, who had been born a twin or triplet. Other scholarships are targeted toward persons of particular faiths or scholars from particular parts of the globe.

Regardless of the funder's motivation, the criteria the funder sets limit the population of potential applications. Within the group of students or researchers that possess the distinctive characteristics the funder is seeking, the funder will usually choose the best as conventionally defined (e.g., best grades, strongest recommendations, or most interesting research topic), but first the funder is narrowing down the pool of applicants. This limits competition and increases the probability of success for those who can apply.

With that in mind, your funding search should begin with an inventory of your distinctive characteristics, which may overlap with your previous reflections on comparative advantage (cf., Brill 2007). Do you come from a low- or middle-income country? Are you an immigrant or the child of immigrants? Have you served in the armed forces? What challenges or disadvantages have you overcome? What is your race, ethnicity, or religion? What is your political philosophy? Use the list in Exercise 10.2 to make a detailed list.

EXERCISE 10.2: INVENTORYING YOUR DISTINCTIVE CHARACTERISTICS

Make a list of personal distinctive characteristics. What features may make you different from other students or interesting to potential funders? Characteristics you may want to consider include:

1.   Race or ethnicity
2.   Nationality or country of origin, or ancestors' countries of origin
3.   Religion
4.   Gender
5.   Sexuality
6.   Family history (e.g., recent immigration, first in family to attend college, raised in a single-parent household, child of a military veteran, child of a union member)
7.   Military service
8.   Discipline of study

Once you have completed this exercise, the next step is finding relevant funders. Make a variety of searches for terms like tuition, scholarship, funding, grant, award, or fellowship plus each of the terms on your list from the exercise. Where multiple terms can be applied to the same characteristic, make sure to use each possible term. Likewise, make sure to use both general terms and specific ones. For instance, you may find that there are some scholarships available for all students from Latin America, and some specifically for students from El Salvador or Columbia. Capture all the relevant opportunities in your database.

EXERCISE 10.3: SEARCHING FOR TUITION FUNDING

Using the list of distinctive characteristics you developed in Exercise 10.2, take the following steps:

1. Search for funding opportunities targeted at students having one of your distinctive characteristics.
2. Search for funding opportunities targeted at students that combine two or more of your distinctive characteristics.

3. Enter your findings into a spreadsheet, noting the application due dates of each funding opportunity. Highlight those for which you think you would be especially competitive.

Conference Funding

Conference funding is probably the easiest funding type to locate, because there are relatively few places you need to look. Begin with the conference convener. If the conference is being organized by a large association, there will almost certainly be funding available for students. This can include funding for travel, lodging, and registration fees, but often the funding will cover only some of these. Fee waivers are the most common funding offered, with lodging being second most common. Funding for travel, if available, will probably be in a fixed dollar amount rather than blanket reimbursement for your travel expenses. Other costs, such as food or local transport, are less likely to be covered.

In searching the conference website, be sure to look thoroughly. Some funding will just be for conference attendance. There may also be special programs for students who want to participate in a doctoral student workshop. Such programs may provide more generous funding and can provide you with important additional benefits, like feedback on your dissertation and opportunities to network with other students. In addition, there may be special funding opportunities designed to improve diversity or representation within the organization or the profession. For example, ARNOVA, an organization to which I belong, hosts a special workshop right before its annual conference designed to help "underrepresented groups prepare to enter the field of non-profit, philanthropic, and voluntary action studies" (ARNOVA 2021). Scholars who attend the workshop receive free lodging for the workshop and conference, free conference registration, and a $1000 scholarship.

Once you have exhausted all your opportunities to seek funding through the conference organizer, turn to your university. The deadline for seeking university funding is almost certainly later than the deadline for seeking funding from the conference organizer. This is useful because your university may require or recommend that you seek external funding before using internal resources. You will also be able to calculate exactly how much funding you still need after receiving any funding from the conference organizer.

You may wonder how much money you should seek. If given the opportunity, you should request funding to cover all major expenses, including your registration, lodging, travel, and meals eaten during the conference. While you may end up having to pay some of these costs out of pocket to seize an opportunity to further your professional development, the ideal is to attend conferences for free. That being said, recognize that your university has limited funds and wants to serve the maximum number of students possible. Do not expect them to pay for a more expensive airline ticket just because you prefer a certain carrier or to pay for a room in an expensive conference hotel when you could stay a few blocks away for half the price. Make your funding request complete but also modest. Consult with fellow students a year or two ahead of you; they can give you a clearer picture of the funding practices at your institution.

EXERCISE 10.4: EXPLORING CONFERENCE FUNDING

Pick two conferences from the list you generated in Chapter 7, focusing on national or international conferences hosted by large organizations, since these may have more funding opportunities. Answer the following questions:

1. If you budget modestly, what is your likely total cost of attending before any grants? Include costs like registration, lodging, travel, and meals.
2. What funding is available from the conference organizer?
3. What expenses does it cover (e.g. registration or lodging)? If the funding is given in cash, how much is the funding?
4. What internal funding sources does your university have?
5. How much funding is available internally? Are there limitations on what is covered, how often you can apply, or the total amount you can receive?
6. When do you have to apply for each funding opportunity?

Research Funding

Funding for your research – whether for travel, writing up, or direct research expenses like purchasing database access or fielding a survey – is focused much more on the subject and quality of the research than on your personal attributes. Nonetheless, your best strategy for winning funding is still to find opportunities (a) that align with your comparative advantage as a researcher and (b) where the narrow conditions of the funding limit the number of potential competitors.

I recommend that you think carefully (and consult with your advisor) before using your time to apply for broad, general grants like those offered by the United States government's National Science Foundation (NSF). You are likely to do better applying for small grants from funders who are strongly interested in a narrow field of research (Brill 2007). A narrowly tailored call for proposals means fewer applicants and less competition. Nongovernmental organizations and foundations, for instance, offer funding related to the issues on which they work, such as democracy promotion, climate change, or improving public education. Many government units offer grants that reflect their specific missions and information needs. Travel funding, which typically comes from foundations, may promote research in a particular geographic area. Writing-up fellowships, which are typically sponsored by universities, are often tied to the scholar's ability to use special archives or resources and to contribute to the intellectual life of the institution.

To find these opportunities, you will again need to look in several places. Your institution may have access to a grant opportunity tracking database such as Pivot-RP that tracks research grants and can periodically deliver a tailored set of opportunities to your inbox. If so, you should seek to access it. Your institution's grants officer can tell you how. Pivot, however, is not comprehensive and can recommend unsuitable options. You should add the details of the best opportunities to your personal spreadsheet, but you will still need to make additional searches on your own.

Government funding opportunities should be collected in one or more searchable databases. The grants officer for your university can point you to these quickly. Send him or her a short email requesting the information. You may even ask if she or he would have a few minutes free to meet with you and orient you to the database, in case searching it is not intuitive.

Check the professional associations in your discipline. Look for any funding they offer and any funding aggregators they may host. Also sign up for the organizations' listservs. Some funding opportunities will be disseminated via listserv. Look also for associations and listservs that are narrowly targeted toward your specific area of research. Search for each element of your topic, and also by region and country if your work has a geographic focus.

To find NGO and foundation opportunities, you will have to do still more web searches. Look carefully at your research and reflect on what is distinct about it. Consider, for example:

- Specific subject (e.g., the role of female parliamentarians in Haiti in creating laws against sexual violence)
- General topics (e.g., female parliamentarians or, simply, parliamentarians; laws against sexual violence)
- Policy issue areas (e.g., sexual violence; female leadership)
- Geographic focus (e.g., Haiti; the Caribbean; Latin America; Francophone states; former French colonies)

Using each of these terms or phrases, do a search for funding (e.g., "research grant female parliamentarians"). Make sure to use multiple different terms for funding (e.g., grant, fellowship, or funding), to maximize the scope of your search. Doing a comprehensive search may take you a day once you include time to review each option you find and identify the most appropriate opportunities. This is time well spent. Once you have built a database of opportunities, the application process becomes much more efficient.

EXERCISE 10.5: RESEARCH CHARACTERISTICS

Review the research agenda you developed in Chapter 5. Then:

1. List the distinctive characteristics of your research in each of the following areas:
   a. Specific subject and general topics
   b. Populations of interest (e.g., women, children, nongovernmental organizations)
   c. Geographic focus
   d. Discipline
   e. Policy issue areas
2. Search for research funding specifically related to these distinctive characteristics. Add these items to your spreadsheet, listing the opportunities, their application requirements, and due dates.
3. Highlight those opportunities for which you think your work is most competitive.

Maximizing Success

If you talk with scholars who have been successful in winning major funding, you will find that even highly successful scholars have had more unsuccessful applications than they have had successful ones. Thus, the key to funding success is to make a thorough search and identify as many opportunities as possible. Then, focus on the ones that are most advantageous to you. Look especially for grants that have specialized criteria that suit you but may exclude potential competitors (Brill 2007). If you intend to apply for a research grant, working with a faculty mentor and seeking external review from other faculty members can also be advantageous (Chasan-Tabor 2018; Hopgood 2010).

Unlike journal submissions, you should submit applications for multiple scholarships and grants at the same time. As noted, funding success is a bit of a numbers game, with many failed applications for each successful one. If you are fortunate enough to win funding from multiple sources, there is unlikely to be a problem. Most scholarships are paid directly to you and can be used for a variety of expenses. With research funding, if you win more than one grant for the same set of expenses, you can talk with your institution's grants officer about how to amend your budget to avoid any problems. You can probably expand your scope of work to make sure that all funds are well-used, or perhaps increase your budgeted amounts for living expenses. Only with conference travel should you apply for funding sequentially (first externally and then internally) and seek only what you are certain you need, since your conference expenses are limited and it would be unethical to submit your expenses for reimbursement twice.

Spend some time researching each funder before you apply for funding from them and leverage the experience of applying for one application to apply for others. You should tailor each tuition or research funding application to the specific funder, e.g., using language that reflects their values. However, the core information – your CV, the description of your research, and much of your personal narrative – will remain the same. Creating tailored applications using the same basic material is good practice for future job applications and interviews, in which you will need to tell a story about yourself or your research that resonates with a particular audience. After you have honed your materials through several rounds of funding applications, you will find it much faster to apply for new opportunities, making it easier to seize new ones that come your way.

Funding and the PhD Roadmap

It is important for students to look for funding regularly and become familiar with the major funding sources (Hopgood 2010). I suggest that you review the options for funding and update your personal database at least once a quarter. Put a reminder in your calendar. Also, include application deadlines in your calendar and budget the time needed for applications in your PhD timeline.

Funding applications should fit into your PhD roadmap at several stages. At the beginning of your PhD, you should be applying for as much scholarship or fellowship funding as practical. The time you spend seeking funding for tuition and living expenses will be more than offset by the time you save not having to take on additional paid work, especially work that is unrelated to your professional development or dissertation research (cf., Nistico 2015). You may still take on research assistant or teaching assistant positions if they are part of your strategy for maximizing your future marketability, but it is valuable to have the agency to choose only those positions with clear benefits for your preferred career path (Borrego et al. 2021).

Once you have a working draft of your proposal – something your advisors think you are close to being able to defend – look at conference funding. Look especially for funded PhD seminars connected to major conferences in your discipline or subdiscipline; these will give you money and intensive feedback on your dissertation. Other conference funding, whether internal or external, can also help you attend conferences and get feedback. The conference or workshop presentations and the funding awards will add lines to your CV. You should continue to seek conference funding during the remainder of your dissertation; do so every time you apply to a conference.

Once you have defended your proposal, you should seek any research funding you need. Research funding can improve the quality of your dissertation by allowing you to spend more time in the field or access additional resources. If you need research funding, it is important to apply for it early because the grant application process will be time consuming, and it can take several months for a funder to review your application (Hopgood 2010).

As you draw close to the end of your research, apply for any funding you need for dedicated writing-up time. This will help you maintain your momentum and also bolster your CV.

More than Fame and Fortune

Winning funding can be an important professional signifier and a useful way to subsidize your studies. However, the process of applying for funding is about more than adding lines to your CV or even gaining financial resources. It is also practice for the job market. When you enter the job market, you will need to tell employers a story about yourself and your experiences and how you will meet their needs. The process of applying for studentships, fellowships, research funding, and the like will help prepare you for that. Honing your CV for studentships will give you a polished document that will only need minimal updating for future job applications. Summarizing your research in a concise and compelling written form will prepare you to explain your work during interviews. All of this will give you confidence as you advance in your PhD and your preoccupation with finishing and graduating develops into a preoccupation with a post-graduation employment.

Recommended Readings

Chasan-Taber, L. (2018). 10 Tips for successful grant-writing. *The Chronicle of Higher Education*, 14 February 2018.

Additional Resources

Kelsky, K. (2011). Dr. Karen's foolproof grant template. *The Professor Is In*. Available at: https://theprofessorisin.com/2011/07/05/dr-karens-foolproof-grant-template/.
Mikal, J. P., & Rumore, G. (2018). 10 Common grant-writing mistakes. *The Chronicle of Higher Education*, 4 January 2018.

Getting Started in Teaching

11

Teaching is a skill, and students contemplating an academic career will want to demonstrate to future employers that they have begun to master it. If you are not planning an academic career or doing any part-time teaching, you can skip this chapter. However, if teaching features in your career plan or is a condition of your studentship or fellowship, you will need some advice on how to proceed.

In many countries, there is little or no required pedagogical training for university instructors, so many faculty members muddle through by imitating their favorite professors, borrowing ideas from colleagues, and leaning heavily on a few practices they have stumbled upon that seem to work for them. The wide variation in instructor performance that results from this can give the impression that some people are just naturally good or bad instructors, making teaching a daunting proposition to those who do not think they are naturally good at it.

Because of this lack of clear guidance on how to teach well and a natural fear of doing poorly, teaching commitments can capture an inordinate amount of time for doctoral students, slowing progress on the PhD. Students who want to teach well seem to assume that more time spent on preparation will lead to a better teaching experience and higher student satisfaction. Thus, the time you spend preparing lessons or grading assignments can easily displace much of your time for research, especially if you are teaching multiple courses each semester.

Fortunately, you can be efficient in your teaching while still teaching well. Scholars of teaching and learning have identified effective, engaging teaching

DOI: 10.4324/9781003262831-11

practices that increase student satisfaction and improve learning outcomes. Some of these teaching practices require much less time than traditional lecture-style teaching. Thus, teaching quality and research productivity can both benefit rather than trading off in a zero-sum game.

This chapter will prepare you to integrate teaching into your time as a doctoral student. It begins by discussing the types of teaching opportunities available to you and how to select teaching options that have maximum synergy with your research and your future career plans. It will then discuss how to excel as a teaching assistant and, next, guide you through the basics of teaching as an instructor of record, including syllabus preparation, lesson planning, and grading. Finally, it will conclude with a discussion of how and why you should set boundaries around your teaching time as a PhD student.

Choosing a Teaching Role

If you start teaching as a doctoral student, you will have two main decisions to make: what role to take and what subject to teach. Depending on your institution, scholarship requirements, and your proximity to other universities, you may have many options or just a few. You will have to make the best choice you can among the options available. This section will discuss teaching roles; the next section will discuss choosing a subject.

Doctoral students are most likely to work as a teaching assistant (TA) or as an instructor of record. Teaching assistants work under an instructor of record and have a limited role assigned to them by the instructor. While the TA is responsible to the instructor for completing the work the instructor assigns them, the instructor is responsible for the course outcomes and for supervising the TA in a way that ensures the quality of the class. That means that if a student has a complaint about how the course was conducted or the grade they were given, that is handled by the instructor and is not the responsibility of the TA.

An instructor of record is responsible for the entirety of a course. Unless a standard syllabus is supplied by the department (as it may be for some introductory courses), the instructor of record creates the syllabus, designs the assignments, teaches each class, and does the grading. She or he is responsible for the course outcomes. An instructor of record will receive student evaluations for the course and deal with any student concerns or complaints.

Each role has advantages and disadvantages for a PhD student. Some of the disadvantages can be mitigated and some of the advantages accentuated by careful negotiation, especially for TA roles.

Teaching Assistant

I generally suggest that students start teaching as a TA and then look for opportunities to become an instructor of record. The main benefit of being a TA is that you can have an opportunity to learn how to engage with students and manage a classroom without the added stress of designing a syllabus or planning every lesson. Engaging with students is often the most stressful part of teaching. I began my university career as someone who had done a fair bit of teaching in other settings and thought that I liked teaching. Yet it took me several semesters before I felt truly comfortable in the university classroom and relaxed enough to enjoy myself. Writing syllabi was easy: it was just organizing ideas in a logical sequence to communicate them well, something all PhD students should be learning how to do. Grading was a grind, but one that could be accomplished by putting enough time against the task. But teaching was stressful. At the start of each semester, I would walk into the classroom a bit tense and uncertain, feeling a bit like I was faking it and that students would eventually see through me and question my authority. As the semester progressed, I would note a tipping point – a day when I finally felt comfortable and confident enough in front of the students to relax, make a joke, or spontaneously deviate from my planned lesson. From that point on, the semester would be more fun. Every semester that day would come earlier until, after several years, I felt relaxed and confident my first day walking into the classroom. If you face similar fears or stress, TAing is a good way to gain experience and begin to overcome them.

The challenge of being a TA is that the experience is circumscribed by the role assigned to you by your supervisor and dependent on their commitment to giving you space to learn. A good supervisor will give you opportunities to design lessons, teach, and do grading. They will coach you through each of those activities and give you feedback on your work. Some universities also use a seminar model where TAs run discussion groups that complement the main lectures delivered by the instructor of record, allowing you to practice your classroom management regularly and even to receive feedback on it if the instructor of record comes to observe you.

Poor supervisors give their TAs either too little or too much to do. One type will put you in menial role, only doing repetitive and uninteresting tasks like grading quizzes, taking attendance, or handing out assignments. This is legitimate work for a TA to do but, if it is all you do, you will learn very little. The other type will ask you to take on most of their teaching responsibilities, including teaching many classes and grading all assignments. They may not even show up for class when you are teaching. You will do nearly all the work, without the benefit of their support and without the credit or pay given to an instructor of record.

Before agreeing to work as a TA for an instructor, talk with other students who have worked for them about their experiences. Also talk with the instructor directly about their expectations for their TAs. If there is experience you would like to gain that is not part of their plan for your work, ask if it is possible to add it. For instance, if they do not mention any teaching time, ask them if there are one or two classes in the semester for which you could design and teach the lesson or if you could lead some optional review seminars to help students prepare for key exams or assignments. If no grading work is mentioned, ask if you can help grade one or more major assignments. The worst that can happen is that the supervisor will say no – and many will say yes. Good instructors are interested in the development of their TAs, and your involvement may even reduce their workload or improve student satisfaction.

Finally, if you are offered a TA position, review the terms of the TA contract carefully. Ideally, it should include expectations for hours worked and salary paid or tuition credit received. If it does not, ask for clarification. It is best to do this by email so that you have a written record of anything that is agreed. If you take a TA role and discover that the instructor attempts to put too much work on you, you can use the hour limits to politely push back, pointing out, for instance, that you cannot grade the final essays for everyone in an 80-person class while keeping to your contractual 15 hours per week. If necessary, you can ask your doctoral advisor for help in navigating such situations; they have an interest in helping you make time to complete your dissertation.

EXERCISE 11.1: TEACHING ASSISTANT OPPORTUNITIES

If you are interested in working as a teaching assistant, undertake the following research:

1. Ask fellow PhD students for whom they have worked as TAs, what responsibilities they were assigned, and how they viewed the experience.
2. Ask instructors whom you admire for their teaching style or subject matter expertise whether they teach any course for which they employ teaching assistants and, if so, how those assistants are hired.

Instructor of Record

Because TAing experiences are so variable, they will not carry as much weight with future employers as having been an instructor of record.

Seeing a TA role on your CV, a prospective employer will not know if you are capable of teaching a whole class by yourself or have done little more than clerical work. Moreover, TAs do not typically receive teaching evaluations. This can make it more difficult to provide the "evidence of teaching effectiveness" that some employers request from applicants. Instructors of record receive evaluations. Thus, working as an instructor of record will allow you to clearly demonstrate an ability to teach and, if your reviews are good, provide evidence of teaching quality. The extra time you put into teaching will also help you develop your teaching philosophy, which some employers may ask you to discuss in your job application.

Working as an instructor of record typically pays much better than working as a TA. Many universities employ part-time instructors who are paid a set fee per course taught. These are often called "adjuncts," "adjunct lecturers," or "contract instructors."

You can seek a position as an adjunct at any university within reasonable traveling distance; you do not need to work at your home institution. The process of obtaining an adjunct position is often somewhat informal. It is perfectly acceptable to email the chair or associate chair of the appropriate department and ask them about any adjunct openings they expect to have in the next term. If you have met faculty from other local institutions, you can also reach out to them as well to ask about adjuncting opportunities. They can direct you to the appropriate person in their department and perhaps put in a good word for you.

If the benefits of being the instructor of record are credit, experience, and money, the downsides are responsibility and time. As an instructor of record, you will need to write a syllabus, prepare a lesson plan for each class, teach each class, grade assignments, and keep office hours. Realistically, this may mean six to eight hours of work per week for every course taught. Many students spend more than that when they are starting out, although I hope you will avoid that by following the advice given later in the chapter. Nonetheless, I would suggest teaching only one or, at most, two classes per semester in order to avoid derailing progress on your dissertation. Once you are teaching three or more courses, you have become a full-time instructor (regardless of whether you have the title or salary) and only a part-time student. This can significantly slow your progress toward the PhD.

Perhaps unfairly, there is a certain stigma attached to individuals who hold adjunct roles for a long period of time without winning a full-time position. This stigma is magnified if a heavy adjuncting load causes you to take an unusually long time to finish your PhD. With that in mind, it is best if you can be judicious about your adjuncting work. Teaching one class per term as an instructor of record for the last one, two, or three years of your PhD can give you an advantage in applying for academic jobs, but too much teaching may be detrimental. Unfortunately, not every student has the option of taking on a lighter teaching load. If your financial situation forces you into a heavy teaching load and a slow completion of your PhD, you may be able to leverage your experience by applying for jobs at more teaching-focused institutions.

EXERCISE 11.2: INSTRUCTOR OF RECORD OPPORTUNITIES

If you are interested in working as an instructor of record, undertake the following research:

1. Ask your department chair if doctoral students are ever hired by your department to work as an instructor of record and, if so, ask how and when they are hired.
2. Do a web search to identify other universities within reasonable travel of your university. Identify those you might like to teach at. Contact the relevant department chairs, introducing yourself and asking when and how they hire adjunct instructors.

Choosing a Topic

You may not have the option of choosing what course you teach, especially if you are assigned teaching responsibilities by your department as a condition of a studentship or fellowship you receive. However, if you do have the choice, you can synergize your teaching with your dissertation work or future job search. There are two ways to do this. The first is by teaching a course that has a high degree of overlap with your dissertation research. The second is by choosing a very commonly taught course that is in demand in most departments.

If you choose a course with a high degree of overlap with your dissertation, you will save yourself time in course preparation because you will be familiar with the readings and core concepts. You may even add to the syllabus certain readings you want to examine for your dissertation but that you have not yet had time to read. It is a bit of an open secret that faculty have not always read every reading they put on their syllabi, and it is fine to use your syllabus as a commitment device to help move you through the literature. Just skim enough of each reading in advance to make sure that it is appropriate for your students (in terms of both content and difficulty level) before adding it to the syllabus. The resulting classes may result in stimulating discussions that advance your own thinking on your topic.

The drawback to teaching on your dissertation research is that dissertations tend to be narrow. Thus, a course that closely overlaps with your dissertation will be fairly specialized. Courses I taught based on my dissertation research included a senior undergraduate seminar on the World Bank and International Monetary Fund, and a graduate class on global civil society. Prospective employers may be interested in offering such courses to their students, but they will also want to know that you can teach the introductory and lower-level courses that are in high demand in most departments. These are courses that students take during their first year in the major or that are taken by non-majors as part of their general education requirements. New hires are often expected to teach these courses.

You can generate synergies between your teaching and your future job search by teaching some of the most common courses possible. Is always useful to have taught "Introduction to [the discipline]" and to be able to talk cogently with a hiring committee about how you can teach the course in a way that gets new students excited about the field. Other lower-level courses, especially those on research design or research methods, also tick important boxes. Experience teaching such courses signals to members of the search committee – your prospective colleagues – that you will be able to pitch in and share the department's teaching burden with them.

An additional advantage to teaching core courses is that your department may offer you a standard syllabus from which to teach, saving you time. Even if there is not one, there is no problem with asking other faculty if they will share theirs so that you can use them as templates or identify useful readings. At many universities, it is acceptable to use a textbook when teaching lower-level courses, supplemented by additional readings. A textbook can give a premade structure to the course, and textbook publishers often provide additional resources, like exam questions, for instructors to use. These things can make your course preparation faster and more efficient.

EXERCISE 11.3: CHOOSING A TOPIC

To help you decide what courses to seek to teach, consider the following questions:

1. Based on your research in Exercise 11.2, what courses are likely to be available?
2. Look back at the job advertisements you analyzed in Chapter 2 and the career roadmap you developed in Chapter 3. What type of teaching experience is expected by your preferred employers? Note that smaller schools tend to need generalists who can teach several core courses, while larger universities may seek specialists teaching in niche areas.
3. How can your dissertation research be leveraged to teach or develop a course?
   a. Are there standard courses in the discipline – even upper-level ones – that are closely related to your research?
   b. If you were to design one or more courses based on your dissertation work, what would they be?
4. What core courses are most frequently taught in your discipline? Which are you qualified to teach?

Succeeding as a Teaching Assistant

A letter of recommendation from your TA supervisor may be very important in convincing prospective employers that you can teach well. This is especially true if you do not expect to have the chance to be an instructor of record before going on the job market. Therefore, it behooves you to seek to do well in the role.

Doing well as a TA is partially about performing well as a de facto teacher-in-training, and partially about being a good employee. Your teaching supervisor is under an obligation to the university to complete a narrow and specific job: teaching a certain course to a certain group of students. They have enlisted you (or you have been assigned to them) to help them with their goal, and your work will be judged by how well you do this.

The most fundamental part of doing well as a TA is making sure that you understand exactly what your supervisor wants and delivering whatever they expect from you in a timely fashion. Therefore, you should meet with your supervisor regularly to discuss the tasks they have for you and mark them on your calendar. Ask questions about anything you do not understand. You should also use these meetings to invite feedback on your performance and ask if there is anything else they would like you to do or anything they would like you to do differently.

Make sure that you show up to class early and having read the day's course readings, prepare thoroughly for any lessons you teach, and complete any grading or other tasks assigned to you on time. If anything comes up that prevents you from coming to class or completing a task, make sure that you inform your advisor as early as possible. Ultimately, you would like your TA supervisor to commend you to future employers not only as a good teacher but also as a conscientious and professional colleague.

In the classroom, you should learn the students' names. This will help you feel more confident, and it will encourage student participation (Mustapha, Rahman, and Yunus 2010). It may also help your supervisor if they have difficulty remembering a student's name, or if they need you to take attendance or track student participation. Learning student names takes dedicated effort. I often print a class roster that includes the students' photos and bring it with me to class. When students are engaged in group exercises and problem-solving activities, I sometimes take a minute and use the roster to quiz myself on students' names and refresh my memory for those I have forgotten. I try to call on students by name, even though this means that I have to ask students for their names frequently over the first few weeks of term. I try to be unashamed of forgetting a name or getting one wrong; otherwise, I might stop using student names just to avoid embarrassment. If you use similar practices, after several weeks you should have the names memorized. You will feel more at home when you can call on students by name, and students may feel better known and recognized. You can use Exercise 11.4 to further reflect on the behaviors you want to embrace in the classroom.

EXERCISE 11.4: INSTRUCTOR BEHAVIORS

Reflect on the instructors you have had during your university degrees. Try to identify which instructors made you most excited about attending class and which damped your enthusiasm. For your best and worst instructors, reflect on the following:

1. How did they teach (e.g., lecture, seminar discussion, problem-solving exercises)?
2. How did they address students in class?
3. What kind of feedback did they give, either in class or on assignments?
4. What else made them good or bad as an instructor?

Conduct yourself professionally outside of the classroom. It is not uncommon for teachers to grouse about students, and TAs are no exception. However, you should be careful about this. Your supervisor is entrusting you with the responsibility of helping their students learn. Your business is building them up, not tearing them down. It is normal to vent after a frustrating day, but be careful not to complain excessively, to stereotype students, or to assume that student performance cannot improve. Often there is a reason why a student is underperforming that has little to do with laziness or lack of motivation. Even if you do not know what this reason is, try to assume the best of them rather than the worst.

Lastly, respect student confidentiality. Your institution probably has rules related to student confidentiality, often linked to state or federal law. Be careful not to discuss students' grades or other sensitive information with anyone other than your TA supervisor or other authorized individuals.

More generally, you should avoid using students' names when discussing negative behavior with anyone besides your supervisor; you do not want to poison future instructors against a student before he or she has even stepped foot in their classroom.

Mentorship and Feedback

Embrace TAing as a chance to receive mentorship. If you are running seminar sessions or study groups, ask your supervisor if they will come to observe a session and give you feedback. If you have arranged to teach one or more lessons, ask your supervisor if they will review your lesson plan before you teach and provide you with feedback on your teaching afterwards. If you are grading papers or other material in which quality can be subjective, ask if you can review some work they have already graded (e.g., anonymized papers from a previous semester of the course), so that you can get a sense for their standards and expectations. Then ask your supervisor to review a sampling of your grades. Make a point of asking your supervisor regularly if there are ways that you can improve your teaching performance. Taking such steps signals that you are committed to learning the craft of teaching, but it is more than just signaling; this feedback will make you a better teacher. Junior academics often feel frustrated by a lack of mentorship and guidance as they advance in their careers. It is good to embrace mentorship while you have it.

You should also arrange your own student evaluation if your university does not have these for TAs. You can create an evaluation form that mimics your university's course evaluation or teaching evaluation. Discuss with your supervisor whether and when you can administer it to the students. The feedback you receive will help you improve as an instructor, and it will give you a record that you may be able to use in your job applications.

Teaching as an Instructor of Record

Teaching as an instructor of record involves much more work and responsibility than serving as a TA. You will need to create a syllabus for the course, including assignments and readings; develop lesson plans; teach each class; and grade assignments. Mastering these skills can take years, and there are numerous articles, books, and videos to help you on your journey. I have listed some resources at the end of this chapter. This section will give an overview of each of these topics to help you get started. My goal is to provide you with key principles that can form a foundation for your teaching and allow you to build a personal style over time.

Writing a Syllabus

Depending on where you have studied and who has taught you, you may have been exposed to a wide variety of syllabi. Some instructors view syllabi simply as schedules for the semester: a list of readings and assignments organized by due date, nothing more. Yet it is helpful to see your syllabus as your first communication with your students, a chance to convey to them your intentions and expectations for the course, including learning outcomes, workload, and assignment performance (Wheeler, Palmer, and Anecee 2019). The syllabus also constitutes something of a contract between yourself and the students (Palmer, Wheeler, and Anecee 2016). If a student complains about your teaching or challenges a grade you have given them, the university will examine your syllabus in deciding the case. If the syllabus includes clear statements about learning expectations and grading standards, it will be easy to defend your actions. If these things are absent, your grading may appear arbitrary and become much more difficult to defend.

How do you construct a syllabus? Think of writing a syllabus as creating a pathway or gameplan that will lead students to achieve the learning outcomes you want. When I review the syllabus with students on the first day of a class, I often tell them, "Some of you probably feel like school is a game: you have to jump through the hoops that your professor wants you to jump through in order to get the grade you want. Well, I am here to tell you that you're right; that is exactly how it is. But if the instructor sets the rules and the hoops appropriately, in the course of playing the game you will also learn what the instructor wants you to learn." If you can embrace this logic, you will see the syllabus not just as an outline for the course but as a way to provide students with challenges (in the form of assignments), feedback (in the form of assessments), and resources (in the form of readings and lessons) to move them along a pathway to the learning outcomes you desire.

Many students recognize this game-like aspect to education, and most of them accept it. What they resent is when the scoring seems arbitrary or unfair. One of your goals as an instructor should be to make your learning objectives and grading standards clear, in order to remove any sense of arbitrariness and ensure that students understand how and why they have earned the grades they receive.

The first step is to develop learning outcomes for the course. Read the course description. Unless you are developing a wholly new course (in which case you will write the description) this is language that comes to you from the university catalog. It tells students what the course is about. As you read and reread the course description, reflect on what competency in the course subject would look like, scaling your expectations to the level of students you expect to teach (e.g., new undergraduates vs. senior-level undergrads vs. master's degree students). Distill your reflections into five to ten short statements about what students should be able to do by the end of the course.

Crucially, these should be abilities or actions that are outwardly observable. Thus, rather than writing that you want students to "Know key events in the Cold War," you should write that you expect them to "Be able to recall and describe key events in the Cold War." Rather than expecting them to "Understand the history of race relations in the US," for example, you could ask them to be able to "Discuss in clear and specific terms the history of race relations in the US." If you want them to "Master constructivist theory," you can write that students should be able to "use constructivism to analyze current events." Using action-oriented language creates measurable learning objectives that set clearer goals for students (Ludwig, Bentz, and Fynewever 2011). Some examples of vocabulary that reflects measurable learning outcomes are given in Table 11.1.[1] If you have time available, you can learn more about specifying learning objectives by reading about Bloom's Taxonomy, a

---

[1] Readers familiar with Bloom's Taxonomy will note that I have elided several categories here. The mixing of Bloom's "understand" and "analyze" categories is intentional. Although these are distinct categories within the taxonomy, professors typically expect students who understand key concepts to be able to deconstruct them or draw connections among them.

Table 11.1 Vocabulary for Learning Objectives

Words that indicate *knowing*:
Recall Articulate Specify Describe Define
Words that indicate *understanding*:
Discuss Explain Recognize Differentiate Compare Contrast
Words that indicate higher levels of *mastery*:
Interpret Apply Analyze Assess Create Develop Write Justify Argue Defend

widely used categorization of learning outcomes (Persaud 2021). I have provided a link to one helpful resource at the end of this chapter.

Second, set assessments that will measure students' progress toward achieving those learning outcomes. Assessments should match the kind of learning you want students to achieve: a multiple-choice exam is good for measuring student recall of facts but less well suited to measuring an ability to apply a concept. More advanced learning outcomes may require writing short or long essays, completing research, authoring policy briefs, creating art, or similar tasks. Appropriate assessments will allow you to judge student success. Ideally, you will conduct assessments periodically during the course. This will help students monitor their own progress and help you judge the effectiveness of your teaching so you can make changes as necessary. Smaller assignments spaced out through the semester may also help students retain their learning longer (Lang 2016). Even if you wait until the end of the course to assess students' learning, aligning the assessments with the learning outcomes is essential to justifying the grades you give students.

Because assessments will motivate students to achieve the learning outcomes, it is important to give students at least some details about what the assessments are at the beginning of the course. Thus, rather than writing that there will be "a test" or "an essay," note that there will be a "multiple choice test covering [specific concepts] from Weeks 1–3" or "an essay in which you will use one of the theories learned in this course to analyze the behavior of key actors in a recent event." Giving some details helps students further understand the learning objectives and know what to focus on in the readings and during class.

Third, select weekly readings or other materials, such as videos or podcasts, that will provide students with the information they need to succeed on your assessments. (Hereafter, for convenience, I will refer to the weekly materials as "readings," with the understanding that non-text materials may also be used.) This approach is sometimes derided as "teaching to the test" because of the impression that it limits teachers' flexibility in meeting diverse student needs. However, in this case you yourself have set the terms of the assessments to align with your learning objectives for the course. Using the assessments to guide your selection of course material will keep your course focused on facilitating students' achievement of those learning objectives.

Your goal in selecting the readings is to serve and equip your students by giving them clear, accessible information that will advance their learning. This may include classic essays in the field, scholarly articles, policy briefs, media coverage, or textbook chapters. Some instructors use videos or podcasts. A variety of types of readings or media will help keep students interested and accommodate students with diverse learning styles and aptitudes. Your main constraint is time: have a realistic assessment of how much time your students have available for studying for your course and do not let required readings exceed this amount. If you assign too much material, students will not be able to read (or watch or listen to) all of it, which will only frustrate you and them. Keep highly motivated students engaged by including additional readings as "optional" or provide multiple possible readings with instructions that students should complete, for example, at least two out of three or three out of four.

Finally, organize all of these in a syllabus format appropriate for your institution. As much as possible, use a "positive, respectful, inviting" tone and a format that highlights the learning-focused nature of your course design; this will help improve student perceptions of the course and make you seem more approachable as an instructor (Palmer, Wheeler, and Anecee 2016, 39; Harnish and Bridger 2011). Michael Palmer, Lindsay Wheeler, and Itiya Anecee (2016), whose article is included in the Recommended Readings, provide some examples of how to do this. The University of Virginia has also created a rubric to "assess the degree to which a syllabus achieves a learning orientation" (Palmer, Bach, and Striefer 2014, 14) that you can use to evaluate your syllabi. Lastly, your university may have standard information that you are required to provide, such as the dates and times of class, your office hours, a copy of the catalog course description, links to university resources for students in need, or a warning against plagiarism. Your department chair or administrator can tell you what is necessary or point you to a university website to consult. Include whatever is required.

Developing Lesson Plans

Once you have a topic and assigned materials for each class session, you will need to come up with a plan to teach the material. You do not have to do all this planning at the beginning of the semester. I often prepare my lessons the week of class, which allows me to review the readings myself and have them fresh in my mind.

Many instructors – both new and experienced – confuse teaching the material with preparing a lecture that communicates it. Teaching is much more than communication: it is facilitating your students' comprehension, assimilation, and retention of the core information. Lectures tend to do so poorly compared to more interactive engagement methods that include "activities that yield immediate feedback through discussion with peers and/or instructors" (Hake 1998, 65). To reserve class time for discussing and applying the material to be learned, the material can be communicated to students – at least in preliminary form – before class through readings or other media (Brame 2013). Making class a place to use the material you have assigned will incentivize students to do the readings. Some instructors also use short, weekly quizzes to help make sure students review the assigned material. If you make the lectures the core source of information in a course, many students will not complete the readings. But if they must do the readings or risk failing a quiz or being caught out in front of their peers during class exercises, more of them will. This also allows students to benefit from repetition: covering the material once outside of class and then again as they discuss or apply it in class.

I encourage you to think of class as a time to make the students do intellectual work, rather than merely consume information. See yourself as a taskmaster and coach, not as an orator, lecturer, or entertainer. Just as a coach will assign drills and exercises to teach their athletes new skills or hone existing ones, think about how you can use in-class exercises to prompt students to deepen their understanding of the assigned material and learn to deconstruct or apply it.

Typically, I do this by using a combination of small group exercises and large group discussion. I assign students a series of questions to answer in groups of three to six students. I then circulate through the classroom, visiting groups to make sure that they are on track. I can help along groups that are struggling by providing hints or pointers and challenge groups that are excelling by offering them additional questions. This works well even in classes as large as 40 students. Students appreciate the additional face time with the professor and pose questions when I visit their small group that they might not ask in front of the whole class. After the allotted time for the small group discussion is done, I reorient the class toward a large group discussion in which I collect and integrate the answers from the different groups so that the students know what the correct answers are. Then we move on to the next round of small group discussion.

In a 75-minute class, I typically have 3 rounds of questions. The first focuses on basic comprehension. For example, I may ask students to define certain terms or concepts or explain their history, knowing that the information needed is in the week's readings. The second round is more analytical, like asking students to explain why a certain organization operates in a particular way or how two different theories compare. What I am looking for here is to push students to make intuitive connections that go beyond just what is written in the readings. The final round typically focuses on application, asking, for example, that students use the week's theory to analyze a current event that I have asked them to read about.

Thinking about your class as a time to force students to answer questions or complete exercises requires a shift away from thinking of class as a time to impart information. However, as you do it more often, it gets easier. To facilitate my preparation, I often ask myself several questions: "Why did I assign today's readings?" "What is the most important thing for students to learn about today's topic?" and "What in the material are they least likely to understand on their own?" I then develop questions and exercises to make sure that the most important and difficult issues are addressed.

The result is that my lesson plans are often one or two type-written pages containing my questions and the expected answers. Sometimes I will also write the time that I expect to start and end each exercise or question set to help me keep class on track. Compared to developing PowerPoint slides and lecture notes, it is much faster and simpler, yet most students enjoy this style of class far more than a traditional lecture. Thus, you can save time, improve student satisfaction, and enhance learning outcomes.

This is not the only way to push students into active learning. There are many non-lecture styles (Nilson 2016). The way I teach involves a combination of what is called a flipped classroom (where students review the content before class and then do exercises in class) and problem-based learning (where students apply material to address real-world issues) (Brame 2013). Some instructors use project-based learning, where students collaborate on a large project throughout the term, including during class time. Research the options, experiment in class, and find something that works for you.

Classroom Management

The challenge of using a more engaged teaching style is that you must interact with your students more. If you are afraid of your students or afraid of teaching, you will not have copious lecture notes to hide behind. You will have to listen and respond to student answers on the fly. The important thing to remember is that you are an expert. Even if you have only read the same material as your students on a given topic, your education and training mean that you will understand that material better. If you have done the readings yourself in the day or two before class, you are unlikely to be caught out by a student question related to the readings. Being an expert does not mean that you are an encyclopedia. If you do get a question you cannot answer, do not be afraid to say, "I'm not sure. Let me get back to you." Then follow up with your answer at the start of the next class. I also sometimes look up the answer during the next small group round if the students do not need so much coaching.

Similarly, being an expert means you can be flexible. If a student volunteers an answer to one of your questions that is valid but not what you expected, include it and even affirm them for their insight. Do not turn class into a game of "guess what the instructor is thinking." In most contexts, students will respect you because of your position; you do not have to prove yourself to them by rejecting their ideas or otherwise dominating the discourse. If you believe in your own authority and expertise, it can help you relax, project confidence, and engage students in a more natural dialogue.

Be careful to be positive and encouraging, especially if you are using an active learning approach that relies on student participation. Students are more inclined to participate when instructors use behaviors that are "confirming, encouraging, and supportive," including calling on students by name, smiling or nodding when students respond to a question, and asking follow-on questions to prompt students to elaborate on their answers (Mustapha, Rahman, and Yunus 2010, 1083). Conversely, negative instructor behaviors, like biting sarcasm or public criticism of students, can discourage student participation and undermine the success of active learning approaches (Demirtas 2016).

As described in the TA section, becoming comfortable will take time. It will help to focus on the basics: have a clear lesson plan, start and end each class on time, learn and use student names. Even if all goes well, it can still take weeks to feel like you are really in control of what is happening in your classroom. In the meantime, be flexible and gracious with yourself. Some weeks will not go according to plan. Students will be unable to come up with good answers to your small group questions and you will be forced to do a mini-lecture to cover part of the material. You may plan to do too much and either have to continue the topic in the next class or give your final set of questions to students as an out-of-class reflection exercise (e.g., "Here are a few more questions for you to think about as you go"). Do not sweat these things. An ability to adapt shows that you are moving toward mastery.

AN OUTSIDE PERSPECTIVE

One of the most useful ways of improving your classroom management is to have an experienced teacher observe you and provide feedback on your teaching. Ideally this will occur during your assistantship. Ask your supervisor for an opportunity to teach and ask them if they would provide you with feedback on your performance.

Observation and feedback are also appropriate when you are starting as an instructor of record. I recommend asking for feedback from a senior faculty member in the department where you are teaching, as they may have more time available and a greater commitment to mentoring than more junior faculty.

Some universities have a Center for Teaching and Learning or similar institution that supports faculty teaching; this center may also be able to provide you with an observer to give you feedback.

Lastly, peer feedback can be helpful. If you know other doctoral students who are teaching, you can observe each other and share ideas.

Grading

Learning to grade is another skill that takes time to master. The main things to keep in mind are that your grades should reflect how well students demonstrate their progress toward meeting the course learning outcomes and that your grades should be consistent.

Good grading starts with the assignment instructions. To help align your grading with learning outcomes, it is good to explain in the instructions or prompt what specific skills or knowledge you are expecting students to demonstrate through the assignment. Note how these are linked to the course objectives (Palmer, Gravett, and LaFleur 2018). I usually copy and paste into the assignment instructions the specific course objectives from the syllabus that the assignment is assessing.

Provide detailed instructions and make time to discuss the instructions and your grading policy with students in class (Davis 1993). The students' efforts to achieve the goals you set (the "jumping through hoops" mentioned earlier) are what will drive them to master the course material. Therefore, do not make the mistake of thinking that students should "figure out" what you want in an assignment as part of the learning process. Student learning is enhanced by trying to achieve a clear set of objectives that directly reflect the course goals. Thus, you want student energy directed toward following the assignment instructions, not guessing what the "real" instructions are.

For essays, tell students about expected minimum or maximum word count, number of expected citations, what kinds of sources are acceptable, and expected citation style so that they have clear parameters for their writing. If you are asking the students to answer a specific question, you may also include sub-questions or bullet points to highlight issues they should address. For lower division classes, you may even provide students with a sample outline showing how they should structure their answer to the question. Doing these things will help students focus their attention where it matters – on engaging with the course material – and not become distracted by questions of style and formatting. Consistency between the student responses will also make your grading easier.

When you are ready to start grading, there are several ways to help ensure that you grade students consistently. First, reread your essay instructions yourself before you start grading, and reread them during your grading to refresh your memory as often as you need to. I often leave the instructions open on a separate screen so that I can reference them easily.

Some professors then grade first the assignments of those students who seem to be the best in the class. This can give them a benchmark for what is realistic to expect in an "A" product. If you take this approach, grade several assignments because sometimes even good students can shirk and some students who have never stood out in class turn in exceptional written work. Once you have a sense for what an "A" assignment looks like, you can proceed through the rest of your stack, evaluating the submissions relative to the best work. Note that your sense of what constitutes a "good" response may shift as you work your way through the assignments. When I was starting out, I often wrote tentative grades in tiny numbers on the corner of each assignment, until I had graded half the class and had a good sense for the different levels of assignment quality. Then I would review those numbers and adjust them up or down as necessary, writing the final grade in a large hand and covering the old one with a small scribble.

Another approach is to use a grading rubric. A rubric specifies several different criteria on which the assignment is being graded (e.g., argument, structure, use of readings) and the different levels of performance possible in each category. If you make your rubric reasonably detailed, it can help students understand your grading expectations and save you grading time since you can just mark their levels in the rubric and not have to write as lengthy an explanation for their grade. By looking at the next highest level in each category, students can also intuit how to improve their grade. Sample rubrics are available online. If you use a grading rubric, it is best to share it with your students before they start the assignment. Remember, you want them to know where the goal line is so that they will work to reach it.

Regardless of how you grade, provide each student with written comments in addition to their letter grade or percentage. As you do so, focus on engaging with the student as a learner, rather than simply offering a judgment of their work product (Walvoord and Anderson 2010). It is good if you can reference one or more positive aspects of the student's work before offering critiques. This will both encourage them and help them understand what they have done well. It is also a helpful discipline for you as an instructor; looking for the positive can help you think more kindly of your students, especially when you are tired from a marathon grading session.

Next make your critical comments. If the work has many faults, I suggest limiting your feedback to the three most important ones, unless you are sure that the student will be able to accept and comprehend a larger volume of critique. I also encourage you to frame your critical comments constructively, for example, "This paper would be improved by…" or "Your argument would be more robust if…" or "In future assignments, I suggest you…" This gives students a clearer path for improvement and can convey that you are hoping for their success rather than judging their failures.

Despite your best efforts, you will still have students complain about their grades. Sometimes they will even be right to do so. For instance, I occasionally miss a place where a student has included a key citation or explained important ideas. If you write in a student's feedback, "This paper would be improved by citing at least three sources" and they can show you that they did cite three, raising their grade is appropriate. At other times, students are testing the boundaries, seeing if it is possible to improve their score even if they are not sure they merit it. Use the assignment instructions (and grading rubric) to help distinguish between students with legitimate complaints and those simply disappointed with a low grade. A student with a legitimate complain should be able to explain how their work met the assignment requirements. You can even ask students to write you a short memo explaining why they think they should have earned a higher grade (Davis 1993).

If a student lacks legitimate grounds for a grade change, try to advise them on how they can improve their grade in the future rather than raising their grade in a way that might be inconsistent with the standards you have established. Students are often persuaded by the argument that making a special allowance for them would be unfair to the rest of the class. On rare occasions, you will have students who interpret a low grade as a sign of personal animus or incompetence on the part of the instructor and push for a grade change on this sort of ad hominem basis. Again, having clear assignment instructions and, ideally, a grading rubric can help you demonstrate that the student's grade was fairly awarded. In cases like this, I also advise you to consult with the chair of the department where you are teaching. They can advise you on how to respond to the student and possibly even preview your response.

Putting Your Teaching in a Box

If I were to give students only one tip about learning how to be good teachers, it would be to limit the amount of time they spend on teaching. I suggest allocating a maximum of eight hours per class each week, inclusive of all preparation time and contact time (i.e., time spent face-to-face with students). This may seem counterintuitive, but it is actually a safeguard against two serious problems: neglecting progress on your research and overloading your students.

The impact that unbounded teaching time can have on your research should be obvious. Without boundaries, it is easy to put more and more time into teaching preparation. Teaching feels urgent and stressful and can displace important but less urgent tasks, like working on your dissertation.

The impact on teaching quality is less obvious but just as pernicious. When an instructor spends more time preparing their course, and especially reading or watching materials related to their weekly subjects, they encounter more and more great ideas and develop longer and longer lists of the things that they want to impart to students. This pushes them toward the lecture format because it is impossible to cover as large a volume of material when you allocate half your class time to interactions with or between students. Teaching becomes an exercise in "getting through the material" rather than stimulating reflection on it. As the volume of the material increases, students engage with it less deeply. Why should a student do the weekly readings when their instructor is going to provide a lecture covering all the essential points, plus lots of additional information?

In short, instructors work harder and harder on their teaching while actually weakening the quality of their pedagogy. Repeated exposure to concepts and material is a fundamental part of durable learning (Lang 2016). You should use repetition between the readings and class time to teach a smaller number of things really well, rather than a large number of things superficially and forgettably.

Limited time forces you to focus on what is important. You will do less reading, focusing on what you have assigned the students. Then you will work in class to reinforce core tenets of the material and teach students to apply it, rather than adding a lot of information to it. You will use a more interactive style because it is faster to write a series of discussion questions than it is to prepare a PowerPoint deck and detailed lecture. Your students will benefit, and you will have more time to complete your dissertation.

Conclusion

Teaching is not for everyone, but it is one of the more common career paths and sidelines for people who hold PhDs. If you think that there is a possibility that you will teach professionally in the future, it is extremely helpful to begin teaching during graduate school. Beginning as a teaching assistant will provide you with scaffolding and supervision that will make it easier to learn the trade, and teaching as an instructor of record will allow you to demonstrate to future employers your ability to teach independently.

Working as a teaching assistant or instructor of record may slow your progress toward completing your PhD, but the negative impacts on your PhD progress should be marginal if you are careful about which jobs you select and set boundaries around your teaching time. Picking courses that are aligned with your subject matter expertise will decrease your preparation time and allow you to find synergies between your teaching and your research. You can also choose to teach core courses that may involve less intensive preparation because you will be able to teach using textbooks or use others' syllabi to streamline your course preparation. These courses may be especially useful in enhancing your marketability.

Regardless of what you choose to teach, think of teaching as a skill that is learned and mastered over time. Develop a style that pushes students into active learning and decreases your own need to prepare detailed lectures. Doing so will enhance student learning outcomes and improve your teaching evaluations while saving you time, and even make teaching a more enjoyable task.

Recommended Readings

Brame, C. (2013). Flipping the classroom. Vanderbilt University Center for Teaching. Available at: http://cft.vanderbilt.edu/guides-sub-pages/flipping-the-classroom/.

Mustapha, S. M., Abd Rahman, N. S. N., & Yunus, M. M. (2010). Factors influencing classroom participation: A case study of Malaysian undergraduate students. *Procedia-Social and Behavioral Sciences*, *9*, 1079–1084.

Palmer, M. S., Wheeler, L. B., & Aneece, I. (2016). Does the document matter? The evolving role of syllabi in higher education. *Change: The Magazine of Higher Learning*, *48*(4), 36–47.

Additional Resources

Nilson, L. B. (2016). *Teaching at its Best: A Research-based Resource for College Instructors*. San Francisco: John Wiley & Sons.

OneHE. (n.d.). OneHE is an organization that "exists to support faculty and higher education institutions to improve student outcomes through effective teaching." It provides numerous resources and short lessons to help improve your teaching. Available at: https://onehe.org/.

Palmer, M. S., Gravett, E. O., & LaFleur, J. (2018). Measuring transparency: A learning-focused assignment rubric. *To Improve the Academy*, *37*(2), 173–187.

Persaud, C. (2021). Bloom's taxonomy: The ultimate guide. Available at: https://tophat .com/blog/blooms-taxonomy/.

Syllabus Rubric (n.d.). This is a tool developed by the University of Virginia Center for Teaching Excellence to "assess the degree to which a syllabus achieves a learning orientation". Avalibale at: https://cte.virginia.edu/resources/syllabus-rubric.

Walvoord, B. E., & Anderson, V. J. (2010). *Effective Grading: A Tool for Learning and Assessment in College*. San Francisco: John Wiley & Sons.

Managing Your Time and Motivation   **12**

One of the universal experiences of the PhD is that there is always more to do than there is time to do it. You would benefit from more time to polish an assignment, read the literature, conduct another interview, run a new analysis, or better prepare your teaching. If you are in a relationship or have children, you face the additional struggle of completing your work without shortchanging your significant other or your family. Even students without such obligations may wonder how they can make time for exercise, friendships, or rest.

A shortage of time can be compounded by a lack of motivation. There will be days when you know you should be working productively but just cannot seem to muster the will to do the work or the mental energy to focus on complex tasks. You may have the best of intentions when you get out of bed, but then fall until a cycle of procrastination and distraction that eats up your day.

My encouragement to you is that you are not alone. The lack of time is real, not just a product of poor time management or the demands your particular PhD program. The lack of motivation is real too, and not just a sign of personal failing. Complex, creative tasks require a particular kind of mental energy that cannot be replaced by willpower and grit. Generations of PhD students before you have faced these challenges and overcome them. You can too.

In this chapter, we will begin by outlining some of the time and motivation challenges of the PhD. Next, we will discuss priorities and values, and work to identify those relationships and habits that you want to maintain

DOI: 10.4324/9781003262831-12

during the PhD. Once you know your objectives, both in your work and outside of work, we will examine techniques for managing your time and tasks to accomplish the most important ones. Finally, we will discuss what to do when you have the time but lack motivation, examining ways to restore your motivation and to push through blockages to keep the work on track.

The Challenge

The challenges of completing your dissertation and your professional development work fall into two general categories: lack of time and lack of motivation. I will discuss each here briefly to help you reflect on your own struggles and to affirm that the challenges you are facing are real and not a signal of unique, personal failure.

Simply put, the dissertation is an enormous undertaking. You are being asked to read an enormous amount of literature, come up with an original idea, develop a research methodology, collect and/or analyze data, and then write a book-length manuscript (or perhaps a series of three high-quality articles). You will often feel like there is not enough time to do everything you would like to do and still complete the work within your planned timeframe. That lack of time only grows worse once you factor in any obligations you have as a teaching or research assistant and time away from the PhD to maintain your relationships, health, and sanity.

Preparing for the job market during the PhD can magnify your challenges. While this book emphasizes the synergies between professional development and PhD progress, there are times when the two are in a zero-sum relationship. For instance, when I was nearing the completion of the first draft of my dissertation, I started to apply for postdocs. I wanted to apply for every good position I could find, but realized that each job application delayed the completion of my draft. It felt like an impossible paradox: I could either finish the dissertation and be unemployed or win a position but not have the credential necessary (a completed PhD) to take it up!

If the lack of time is hard, lack of motivation can be even worse. There will be many moments in the PhD when you feel distracted or unmotivated. You will know that your time is scarce and that you need to make the most of it yet find yourself unable to muster the will to work. You begin the day with an ambitious to-do list, and end up spending your work time surfing the net or watching videos. If you have a significant other who is patiently waiting for you to complete your dissertation, you may come to dread that polite evening question, "So, what did you do today?"

There is abundant research indicating that resistance to doing work often has real psychological roots. When you are doing creative work, like developing new theory or searching for patterns in empirical data, your mental processes are different than when you are completing work without creative components. Sometimes creative insights require a period of unconscious thought, a sort of simmering at the back of the brain that spontaneously generates "a kind of sudden illumination" (Poincaré 1914, 58). This sort of spontaneous idea generation is so common among scholars that one of Patrick Dunleavy's (2003) tips for PhD students is to keep a pen and notepad beside their bed so that they can capture ideas that surface as they are drifting off to sleep. From this perspective, our resistance to doing at least some kinds of work can be a manifestation of incomplete processing of the necessary data. Our lack of motivation is a sort of mental "Loading..." icon, telling us that the work is in progress but not yet done.

Lack of motivation can also result from fear and self-protection. Jane Burka and Lenora Yuen (2008), for instance, suggest that when we fear that we lack the capacity to succeed in a difficult task, we may subconsciously seek to protect ourselves from the loss of self-esteem that would result from such a failure. We sabotage our own efforts through procrastination, so that when the final product fails to meet the required standard, we can tell ourselves that it was because we lacked the time needed to produce a good product, rather than that we truly lacked the ability to succeed. We can also procrastinate for a host of other reasons, including a subconscious desire to escape others' control or avoid pressure to perform, or because we persistently misjudge how much time we have available to complete the work (Burka and Yuen 2008; DeLonzor 2003).

Once you realize that your lack of time and motivation are often rooted in more than just a lack of self-discipline, you can move past the inevitable cycle of self-condemnation and attempting to "try harder." Because struggles with time and motivation are common phenomena, others have studied them and devised solutions. The remainder of this chapter will discuss some of those solutions, first for lack of time and then for lack of motivation.

Working with the End in Mind

The first step in learning how to manage your time is figuring out what you are trying to do with it. Obviously, you are trying to complete your PhD, but most students are attempting to do a lot more, whether they realize it or not. Most are seeking to maintain a relationship with their spouse, family, or friends. Many are trying to maintain their health through regular exercise. Some are working to maintain or develop their faith by making daily or weekly time to meditate or worship. Most people want some pleasure in their lives, and they pursue it through one of the above activities or through other forms of recreation, like cooking, hiking, or dancing.

It is important to acknowledge these goals and allocate time for them. Some of these goals have deep, intrinsic importance that should affect how we prioritize them in our schedule. Moreover, when students do not make time for extracurriculars, especially those that allow them to connect with other people, they become lonely and isolated. Instead of recognizing this, faculty too often cultivate a culture of overwork (Eleftheriades, Fiala, and Pasic 2020). As one student describes her experience, "I came in and was fully imprinted to believe that I was there at the expense of my work-life balance, family, hobbies to uphold the golden rule of publish or 'perish'" (Lishu 2021).

Acknowledging personal, non-PhD goals is also about recognizing reality. You can tell yourself that the PhD is the only thing you are focusing on during this week, month, or year, but for most people this is simply unrealistic. You will get the urge to call a friend, go to a café, cook a nice meal, or take a vacation. Better to acknowledge reality and account for it than to have spontaneous and unplanned breaks disrupt the flow of your work.

Acknowledging these non-PhD goals allows us to set boundaries around them. If you tell yourself that you will take a one-hour break in the midafternoon to meet friends for coffee, then after an hour you are constrained to return to work. If the break is unplanned, then the return to work is unplanned too. One cup of coffee may expand to two cups and then dinner, and work may not resume until the next day.

With that in mind, I encourage you to complete Exercise 12.1. Begin by reflecting on the essential tasks you have planned for the PhD, and then inventory your personal goals and recurring extracurricular activities.

EXERCISE 12.1: PRIORITY ACTIVITIES

Use the following questions to reflect on the tasks you want to accomplish in the current or upcoming semester.

1. What have you planned for work?
   a. What dissertation tasks have you planned (e.g., research, writing chapters)?
   b. What professional development tasks have you planned (e.g., applying to or presenting at conferences)?
   c. What additional work obligations do you have (e.g., research or teaching assistant work, adjuncting, or other professional work)?
   d. What unpaid labor are you obligated to do (e.g., childcare or cooking)?
2. What time do you need for relationships?
   a. With whom is it most important for you to interact regularly (e.g., spouse, children, close friends)?
   b. What kinds of time and attention do those core relationships require?
   c. With whom else do you desire to keep in regular contact?
   d. Do you want to make time for a spiritual relationship (e.g., through prayer, meditation, or worship)? When and how often?
   e. Do you have a mentor with whom you would like to meet regularly? How often?
3. What activities have you planned for rest and recreation?
   a. How long do you need to sleep each night to feel well-rested or wake without an alarm clock?
   b. Do you exercise? How often and for how long each week?
   c. Do you have other activities (e.g., sports, hobbies) to which you would like to devote regular time?
   d. What else do you do for fun and refreshment?

Once you have completed Exercise 12.1, I challenge you to make another list. On this one, write down everything you do in a typical day or week, highlighting those things that are not on your list of priority activities. This can include spending time on social media, reading the news, answering email, or surfing the Internet. If you are not sure, make a time diary. Set an alarm on your phone to go off every 30 minutes or every hour from the time you wake until you go to bed. Whenever the alarm beeps, write down what you are doing. Do this for several days to get a more accurate sample. You can even have some fun by doing it with a friend; text each other every hour asking, "What are you doing right now?"

This activity is not intended to shame you. Not all non-priority activities are bad: it can be good to keep up on the news, for example, and some email really does need to be answered. However, it is good to have a sense for how you are using your time currently, so that you can reflect on how you may want to change your time usage. We will use these lists of priority activities and less important activities to begin analyzing and planning your time management in the next section.

Managing the Lack of Time

To help you develop a plan to manage your time well, this section has three parts. First, we will discuss using triage to narrow the scope of your PhD and professional development work. Then we will discuss how to analyze your current activities and schedule to better understand how you are using your time and how you might want to reallocate it. Lastly, we will examine several tools to help you keep the most important elements of your PhD, professional development, and personal life from being displaced by less important tasks and activities.

A Principle of Triage

The concept of triage was developed in the late 1700s, when French army surgeons created a process to determine which injured or ill soldiers they would prioritize for treatment when medical resources were scarce (Nakao, Ukai, and Kotani 2017). In essence, it referred to a process of deciding who would be saved and who would be left to die.

While the origins of the term are grim, it continues to be used metaphorically to describe the process of sorting our various tasks. When our resources are limited, some tasks must be given priority while others must be put aside. If we attempt to do everything, nothing gets properly done.

Completing the PhD requires that you regularly and repeatedly triage your research tasks. When you first develop a research topic, it can go in many directions. You must abandon most of them to focus on one specific research question. When you review the literature for your question, you must decide which sources are most important and which ones will go unread. In deciding on your methodology, you may have many possible approaches to gathering and analyzing data. You will lack the time and resources to implement them all and must determine which methods and data are most likely to help you complete the dissertation. Without making these decisions about what to cut away or leave behind, there can be no forward motion.

It is important to recognize the continuous nature of this triage. You may have made a choice to focus on one particular research question, yet the triage is not complete. When you dig into that question, you will discover that it has many possible dimensions. Unless there are strong synergies among them, you must choose just one or two on which to focus. When you dig deeper into those one or two, your directions for research may fork yet again, in which case you will have to choose which option to pursue. This process of cutting away possibilities and options will repeat throughout the PhD.

Whenever you face a moment in your dissertation process when you feel overwhelmed, pause and triage. Often the solution to your stress is not finding more time; it is focusing your efforts within the time available. This will mean choosing to devote attention to certain aspects of your research and abandoning other potential projects and directions.

One metaphor my students have found helpful is growing a prizewinning pumpkin. In the US, fall festivals and fairs often feature competitions among gardeners for who can grow the biggest pumpkin. The winning entry can easily weigh over 1000 pounds. The way this is achieved is by forcing the pumpkin plant to put all its energy into a single fruit. Early in the growing season, the gardener picks a single, juvenile fruit that will be her or his entry. Then all the other fruit and all the flowers (which could produce more fruit) are culled from the pumpkin vine, so that all of the vine's energy goes into nourishing the chosen pumpkin.

Completing the dissertation is like growing a giant pumpkin. A deliberate process of cutting away prevents detours and distractions from consuming the time and energy you need to move to completion. Students are especially prone to getting lost in the review of the literature, reading more and more work without moving on to data collection and analysis (Dunleavy 2003). Before taking on a new task or exploring a new avenue of thought, ask whether it gets you closer to answering your research question and completing the dissertation, or whether your time would be better spent elsewhere.

You must also triage your professional development tasks. If you have followed the advice of this book, you may now have a spreadsheet featuring a dozen conferences at which you could present, and a long list of possible grants. You cannot apply for everything, because each application takes up scarce time and because that time is taken away from completing your PhD. The opportunities will multiply as your dissertation progresses. You will make new contacts at conferences or perhaps impress professors in your own institution, and these people will suggest doing collaborative work. You may develop multiple article ideas as you review the literature related to your dissertation or collect and analyze your data. There will not be time to write them all and still complete your PhD. Thus, you must decide which opportunities represent the most valuable use of your time (especially which synergize best with your PhD) and let the others go.

This process of abandoning ideas and opportunities can be made a bit less painful if you keep a file labeled "Future Research" or "Future Opportunities" where you capture the things you have had to give up. You can make outlines for future papers or lists of potential funders. When your PhD is done, you can return to this file and see what can be revived. This can be quite helpful if you are applying for academic positions. Rather than needing to dream up a post-PhD research agenda to impress your interviewers, you can build one from these collected ideas.

A Strategy for Organization

The field of time management books is a crowded one, and you can doubtless find a time management strategy that suits you well. However, a simple and intuitive approach comes from Stephen Covey, author of the classic *Seven Habits of Highly Effective People* ([1989] 2020). Covey recommends sorting one's activities using a 2×2 table. The rows of the table are labeled "Important" and "Not Important," and the columns are labeled "Urgent" and "Not Urgent." The result is a four-part matrix, wherein activities are designated "Important and Urgent" (Quadrant 1), "Important but Not Urgent" (Quadrant 2), "Urgent but Not Important" (Quadrant 3), and "Not Important or Urgent" (Quadrant 4). An example showing typical PhD tasks is provided in Table 12.1.

Our natural predilection is to work on the tasks that are the most urgent; thus, many of us spend our time addressing tasks in Quadrants 1 and 3. The challenge for doctoral students is that most of the core work of the dissertation and professional development is found in Quadrant 2. In my observation, many PhD students struggle when the coursework phase of their program ends (assuming it has one), because they no longer have the pressure of external deadlines. They are used to working in Quadrant 1 as they meet the due dates set by their course instructors. When they are faced with managing their work without the urgency created by these deadlines, their productivity slows.

Table 12.1 Typical Doctoral Student Tasks Sorted by Urgency and Importance

	Urgent	*Not Urgent*
Important	Teaching assistant work	Dissertation research
	Research assistant work	Publications
	Conference paper writing	Sleep
	(when deadline approaching)	Exercise
	Childcare or other family needs	Spiritual activities
		Relationship with spouse/ partner
Not Important	Checking email	Reading clickbait news stories
	Reading social media	Posting to social media
		Answering (some) email

Analyzing our tasks according to their urgency and importance can help us understand why some tasks are being completed while others are not, and can also help us recognize where we are wasting our time. Using the list you generated in Exercise 12.1 and your time diary, complete Exercise 12.2.

EXERCISE 12.2: ANALYZING YOUR WORK

Using the data from Exercise 12.1 and your time diary or list of non-priority tasks, complete the following tasks:

1. Plot out your current activities in a 2 × 2 Covey-style grid. Include both your professional and personal tasks.
2. Analyze your time usage:
   a. In which quadrant do you spend most of your time?
   b. Into which quadrant do your most important activities fall?
3. Triage the tasks in each quadrant (especially those in Quadrants 3 and 4) by marking for elimination those activities that do not reflect your personal or professional priorities.

Management Tools

Covey's ideal is to manage one's time and schedule so as to work as much as possible in Quadrant 2. While this is a worthy aspiration, it may not be effective for most PhD students. Instead, I suggest that you move your essential dissertation and professional development tasks into Quadrant l using commitment devices. You can also reduce the time spent in Quadrants 3 and 4 by recognizing your personal agency, using it to enforce priorities and say no to less important tasks. Lastly, you might explore using a series of daily questions to hold yourself accountable for acting on your priorities.

The easiest and most reliable strategy for getting essential work done is to make your dissertation tasks and professional development more urgent. This can be done through commitment devices: promises you make to external parties that create deadlines for specific tasks. With your dissertation, you can work with your supervisor to set deadlines for specific, incremental deliverables. For instance, you can promise to deliver a 2000-word review of a different set of sources every week or every 2 weeks, until you have reviewed all of the different parts of the literature relevant to your dissertation. You can commit to deliver a set of research tools, like an interview questionnaire or a coding framework, by a certain date, or a rough draft of a new chapter every month. The key is to pick dates that are proximate enough that they make the task feel urgent. They should produce just a little bit of stress. If you set a deadline that is four weeks away and imagine that you can produce the work in only two weeks, you may spend the first two weeks procrastinating and the last two weeks working frantically.

As noted in earlier chapters, you can use conferences as commitment devices. While you may only attend a few conferences each year, they can help motivate you to complete big sections of work, like your proposal, a case study, or one or more chapters of the dissertation.

You can also make commitments to your peers. One effective way of doing this is through writing groups. Students who are at a similar stage of their dissertation work can meet each week to discuss their progress. Another option is to make verbal commitments to some of your PhD student friends, articulating dates when you expect to complete specific tasks. Ask them to check up on you and ask you explicitly whether you have hit the promised goal.

If you need extra pressure, you can explore an option like StickK.com. StickK is an online commitment device based on the work of behavioral economist Dean Karlan, that allows users to create a Commitment Contract, in which they promise to complete certain goals (StickK 2021). Users can incentivize themselves by attaching a financial reward or penalty to their contract. For instance, you could commit $50 of your own money through StickK. If you complete your contract, you can use that money to buy yourself a present or a nice dinner out. If you do not complete your contract, the money goes somewhere you do not like, e.g., to support the reelection campaign of a politician you oppose. You can also appoint referees to verify your task completion. If you need these kinds of stakes to motivate yourself through some difficult work, StickK can be worth exploring.

While making key tasks more urgent is one important step, it is also important to reduce the amount of time spent on non-dissertation tasks and limit time spent in Quadrants 3 and 4. Fundamental to doing this is recognizing your agency. Students often use the language of "I have to do [something]," suggesting that they are powerless to constrain their schedule or choose among their various commitments. Instead, try to use the language of "I choose…" When we say something like, "I have to do my grading, so I can't work on my dissertation," we imply that external circumstances have determined our actions and absolve ourselves of responsibility. If we instead say that "I am choosing to grade papers instead of writing my dissertation chapter," we acknowledge that we have agency. We have chosen to do a Quadrant 1 activity and thus displaced a Quadrant 2 activity. We may have a legitimate reason for making that choice – perhaps we are more afraid of the displeasure of our teaching supervisor than of our dissertation advisor – but, if so, we should acknowledge it. Once we recognize that we are making choices, we can work to change them.

We can use our agency to prioritize Quadrant 2 work. One simple way to do this is to always start with Quadrant 2 work in any given day, before doing anything in another quadrant. You do not "have to" check your email or the online class you are teaching first thing in the morning; you can choose not to. Make a discipline of opening up your dissertation work, conference paper, grant application, or draft article first thing in your workday and spend an hour or two with it before opening your email, teaching work, web browser, or social media. You can go even further, setting a target output for your Quadrant 2 work (e.g., writing 500 words or coding an interview) and committing to not do your other work until after that target is met. If you are feeling the pressure to get on to Quadrant 1 work, this strategy will transfer that pressure to the Quadrant 2 task that you have decided must be completed first, speeding the Quadrant 2 work along.

Recognizing your agency also means saying "No." Taking on more commitments often means adding tasks in Quadrants 1 or 3 that compete with the work in Quadrant 2. As noted in Chapter 3 of this book, not all professional development tasks are equally valuable. Therefore, only take on new tasks when they align with your priorities. You should respond to new professional development opportunities the same way that Perlmutter (2013) suggests that you respond to questionable advice: listen carefully, investigate before agreeing, seek outside counsel, and say "No" when necessary.

A final tool bridges these strategies of making important tasks urgent and recognizing (and using) your personal agency: a list of daily questions. John Dickerson (2020) describes creating a short list of personal questions that reflect your priorities. The questions can be whatever you choose for them to be. For example, you might ask, "Did I work on my dissertation?" "Did I exercise?" and "Did I express gratitude to my spouse?" Then, at the end of each day, grade your performance in each area. If you make a habit of completing this exercise daily, the accountability it creates will help you maintain your priorities during the day, motivated by the reward of a high grade (or fear of a low one) in your daily self-evaluation. Dickerson's article is listed under Additional Resources at the end of this chapter for those who wish to experiment with this technique.

Staying Motivated

Sometimes the problem is more than time management. You may have the time and feel the urgency yet still find yourself unable to complete the work. You are unable to focus, distractions come easily, and pushing yourself to do the work feels like dragging your feet through mud. In a word, you are unmotivated.

There are many reasons why lack of motivation strikes. It is important to try to figure out why you are feeling unmotivated, so that you can choose a solution appropriate to the problem that you are facing. As noted earlier in this chapter, sometimes lack of motivation is a manifestation of an incomplete mental thought process: your brain is subconsciously rebelling against doing a piece of work because it needs to figure out how to do it well. In such a case, simply pushing harder or establishing some accountability will not overcome the blockage.

Conversely sometimes you may be pleasure seeking or undisciplined. The work seems hard and unpleasant, whereas checking social media, reading the news, or watching a movie seems light and pleasant. The distractions tempt you away from what you intend to do. Sometimes the problem runs a little deeper: you may subconsciously fear that if you commit yourself to doing the work, you are condemning yourself to an extended period of deprivation (Burka and Yuen 2008) and thus you try to claim as much fun as possible before plunging in.

Procrastination can be exacerbated by magical thinking: the underestimation of how long tasks will take or the overestimation of how much can be accomplished in a given amount of time (DeLonzor 2003). I often see it manifest in the assumption that a task will go perfectly, and so no time needs to be budgeted for revisions, changes, or unexpected problems. Many of us have experienced a special day when the traffic is light, every signal turns green as we approach, and we make it from home to work much faster than usual. A magical thinker will take this best-ever time and enshrine it as the new normal. Instead of budgeting 40 minutes for travel, they now only budget 25. People who fall into magical thinking with travel times are always late and always blaming the "unexpected" delays. Students who do it with their dissertation work and professional development consistently miss deadlines.

These are just a sampling of reasons why you may lack motivation or struggle to focus. The literature on motivation and time management is voluminous. If you struggle to complete your work even when you have time available for it, and none of these explanations resonate with you, I encourage you to dig into this literature or talk over your struggles with friends or fellow students to identify your major stumbling blocks.

Stepping Stones

Identifying the cause of your struggle can make it easier to find a potential solution, but even if you are not sure what the root problem is you can experiment with different options. As you find the techniques that work for you, they may give insight into the causes of your struggles.

Several techniques are useful if your struggle with distraction or procrastination seems unrelated to any underlying need for mental processing or a subconscious hang-up. These can be especially useful when doing non-creative tasks, like coding data or grading papers, that you simply must grind through.

- **Eliminate distractions.** If you struggle with checking social media, reading the news, or watching videos when you should be working, you can try to find a location or situation where those distractions are not available. For instance, you can go to a coffee shop, leave your phone at home or in the car, and not request the password to the local WiFi.
- **Use focus techniques and applications.** These are techniques, sometimes aided by technology, for producing a short burst of concentrated work. The popular Pomodoro Technique, for example, involves picking a single task and working on it uninterruptedly for 25 or 30 minutes before taking a break (Collins 2020). A host of applications for your computer or phone are now available that mimic this process or facilitate it, using 25-minute

timers or lock-out functions that keep you from checking email or surfing the web while you are supposed to be working.

- **Accountability.** You can work alongside peers to keep your focus. If you are all committed to doing work for a set period of time, working together can keep you from drifting off into less important tasks (Toor 2010). Some students even do this virtually, by joining live study groups online. Several of my students have also emphasized a sort of psychological accountability. When they struggle to focus on the work, they take some time to meditate on all that they or their families have sacrificed to get them to graduate school. This motivates them to work harder to make good on that effort.

- **Working to time.** Set aside a set number of hours in the day for the particular project on which you are working. Be realistic; it can be hard to be truly productive for more than four to six hours if you are working on an intellectually challenging task. Commit to work only on that task for the designated time, setting aside all of your other work. When you have completed your commitment, give yourself the freedom to rest or do other tasks, regardless of how much you have accomplished.

If you struggle because the work is unpleasant or you fear the loss of joy, you can do things to make the work more joyful or create incentives for completion.

- **Baby steps.** If you struggle to start a task because it seems daunting and overwhelming, try to break the task apart into a series of smaller deliverables. Writing a whole chapter, for example, may seem unbearably hard, but you can imagine writing the introduction or a single 1000-word section. If so, divide the big task into many smaller ones (your advisor or peers may be able to help), each of which feels like a manageable target for one week, one day, or even one hour of work.

- **Work to task.** This is one of my preferred techniques when writing, and it pairs well with the baby-steps approach. I set a target for how many words I will write in a day or what section of a chapter or article I will finish writing. If I hit that target, my workday is done. If I still feel inspired, I can keep writing. If not, I can stop working and do other things. The caveat is that the workday is not done until the target has been reached. When I was writing my dissertation, I would go into the office and not leave – not even to go home for dinner – until I had met my target.

- **Set rewards.** Tell yourself that when the work is done, you will do something fun, like watch a video or go for a walk. Keep these promises to yourself, to build a habit and expectation of reward. If necessary, give yourself rewards incrementally. When grading end-of-term papers, for instance, you might stay motivated by giving yourself a break after every three papers.

- **Dessert first.** If you really struggle to focus on your work because you want to do other, more pleasant things, try doing those things first. Give yourself the freedom to indulge in two hours of watching videos or talking with friends before you start your work. Doing this can disarm one of the drivers of your procrastination, and also set boundaries around the non-work time, so that it does not expand to take up the whole workday.

If you are struggling with a complex, creative task, things like accountability or rewards may not work. As discussed earlier, your brain may be working subconsciously, sorting ideas and finding patterns. Different techniques may be necessary.

- **Find a productive space.** James Lang (2021) – borrowing from the work of Helen Sword – suggests that some locations and spaces simply catalyze our productivity in a way that others do not. This is different for each person. Some will love a quiet office, others a noisy café. You may not be able to articulate why one place works better than others, but you will recognize it intuitively and see it in your work outputs. Finding a place that resonates with you will help trigger your creative flow.
- **Make space for subconscious thought.** Sometimes your thinking can be aided by relaxing and making space for your subconscious to work. A long walk or a hot bath can allow subconscious ideas to percolate up to the top of your mind. Once they bubble up, start making notes or head to your computer to capture them.
- **Tap into different mental processes.** For instance, if you feel stuck when trying to type text on a page, step away from your computer and try to speak your ideas aloud, as if you were explaining them to a friend. Or try visualizing your ideas, by drawing them out in diagrams or flow charts.
- **Take a break.** Alleviate frustration by giving yourself freedom to read a book or watch a movie – but stop every hour or two to try to return to your work. When doing so, use a short-term focus technique like a Pomodoro to reduce the temptation to escape back into your fun activity.
- **Productive procrastination.** If you cannot make progress on your big-think task right now, check your planner or to-do list for important tasks that require less mental energy. Clear your work email, update your conference and grant spreadsheets, check the latest job advertisements,

pay your bills, or do the laundry. At the end of the day, you will feel like you still accomplished something, even if it was not the thing you most wanted to do. Even better, tomorrow will have fewer distractions because of things you have gotten done.

There are many more self-management techniques than those I have written about here. If none of the options here resonate with you, I encourage you to find others that do. What is most important is to have a toolbox of multiple techniques. Not every blockage has the same cause, and no technique will work for you all the time. If you find a technique that works for you, use it – until it does not work anymore. Then pick a new technique and try it for a few days. If that does not solve the problem, try a third technique and then, if necessary, a fourth. Keep trying until you find something that works. Use it until it starts to fail you, and then switch again. A dynamic approach to self-management will keep you from getting stuck and feeling hopeless.

Beyond Time and Motivation

One of the goals of this chapter is to reassure you that your struggles with time and motivation are normal and manageable. Yet reading these pages, you may feel like your case still stands out. The PhD can be an extremely isolating experience that culminates in genuine mental health issues for many students (Eleftheriades, Fiala, and Pasic 2020; Levecque et al. 2017). If you feel that your stress, anxiety, or depression is not alleviated by better time and life management, I encourage you to use whatever mental health services your institution has available. There is no shame in doing so. Remember too that if the stress of the PhD feels unbearable, you can stop doing the PhD. Many students manage their stress by imagining what they will do if they do not complete their PhD; Jorge Chan, the author of PhD Comics, even devoted a strip to this topic (Chan 2012). Completing the PhD is not the only route to happiness, and the PhD is not suitable for everyone. Recognizing that the PhD is not for you and pivoting to pursue a path that suits you better is not evidence of failure. To the contrary, it shows wisdom and maturity.

Students who are the first in their families to seek a PhD or who come from minority communities are particularly likely to feel isolated and alone during the PhD. For these students, mentorship can play a key role in providing encouragement and helping navigate the unfamiliar culture of academia. Mentorship may also be particularly important for women's career success

(Center for Creative Leadership 2020). Mentors differ from advisors in that they cultivate a deeper personal understanding of you as a mentee and are invested in your long-term career aspirations, rather than just the short-term goal of completing the PhD (Montgomery 2017). You need not limit your choices to faculty who share your gender, race, or personal background (Yans n.d.; Tyree 2016; Center for Creative Leadership 2020). Someone who has completed a PhD and is interested, sympathetic, and encouraging can be enough. Meet with them regularly to get the support you need.

The PhD is supposed to be difficult. It is a test of your ability to perform a huge intellectual feat: to make a novel contribution to the body of human knowledge and do so more-or-less independently. The fact that you find it hard or unfun does not itself mean that you are not suited for a career in academia or another research profession. It certainly does not mean that you cannot complete the PhD. It is normal to struggle when learning a new skill or concept, and the PhD features many of these, one stacked atop the next. Rest assured that the research process gets easier over time. If you go on to a career as a researcher, you may well look back on your dissertation as a beginner effort that pales in comparison to your later work.

Regardless of your situation, remember that the PhD is a means to an end. Hopefully you are here not merely because you want letters after your name or to have people call you doctor. Hopefully you are here because the PhD itself (or perhaps those very letters) will open doors for you to do meaningful and important work that reflects your passions. When you struggle with the PhD or your professional development tasks, remember that all of this is in service to a bigger purpose and that, if you can push through, getting to your destination will make the journey worthwhile.

Recommended Readings

Collins, B. (2020). The pomodoro technique explained. *Forbes*, 3 May 2020.

Montgomery, B. L. (2017). Mapping a mentoring roadmap and developing a supportive network for strategic career advancement. *Sage Open*, 7(2), 1–13.

Perlmutter, D. (2008). Do you really not have the time? *The Chronicle of Higher Education*, August 2008.

Additional Resources

Burka, J., & Yuen, L. (2008). *Procrastination: Why You Do It, What to Do about It Now*. Cambridge: Da Capo Press.

Dickerson, J. (2020). The questions that will get me through the pandemic. *The Atlantic*, 22 June 2020.

Dunleavy, P. (2003). *Authoring a PhD: How to Plan, Draft, Write and Finish a Doctoral Thesis or Dissertation*. New York: Macmillan International Higher Education. Chapters 2 and 3.

Lang, J. (2021). Where do you do your best writing? A look at the connection between place and productivity. *Chronicle of Higher Education*, 26 July 2021.

Going on the Job Market   **13**

Finally, the finish line! While going on the job market may seem intimidating, if you have attended to your professional development while in graduate school, you should be well prepared. If you have written a good dissertation, presented some of your work, and published at least an article or two, your chances of getting a job are very good. Your first job may not be your ideal job, but it will have a reasonable salary and involve work you find meaningful.

With these things in mind, I encourage you to approach finding a job the way you have approached the other tasks in this book: as a challenge that can be successfully overcome with careful research, a systematic approach, and an appropriate expenditure of effort. You do not need to worry that you will never find a good job, but you should also not cavalierly assume that because you have more publications than your peers or come from a top program you will easily win the job of your dreams. Instead, work hard and approach this problem strategically, just as you have done in selecting a research topic, seeking funding, and publishing your work.

If you have perused the job search literature at all, you will know that it is voluminous. Entire books have been written on how to write a CV or cover letter and how to navigate a job interview. This chapter will not dig too deeply into the technical details covered in that literature. Job applications, including CV and cover letter formats, are very different between academic and non-academic jobs, and even between different kinds of non-academic jobs, such as corporate jobs and federal civil service jobs. Getting into the necessary minutia here would require more space than this chapter has available. Instead, a list of readings and resources at the end of this chapter will point you to some of the more technical information you will need.

DOI: 10.4324/9781003262831-13

This chapter focuses on the core skills and principles that are common to finding a job in both academic and non-academic domains. The goal is to help you connect your comparative advantage, dissertation work, and the signifiers you have acquired to maximize your attractiveness to potential employers. We will begin with a discussion of finding jobs, including when and where to look. Next, we will discuss how to identify employer needs, using both public job information and targeted inquiries. Lastly, we will discuss how to present yourself to potential employers as someone who will meet well the needs of their organization, integrating your personal characteristics and professional accomplishments into a persuasive argument for why they should hire you.

Finding Jobs

The first part of going on the job market is identifying openings in the fields in which you are interested. These may include academic positions, non-academic university posts, and research or management positions in the nonprofit, government, or corporate sectors. Finding out what is available requires understanding the timing of job postings, where jobs are posted, and the role of networking.

The first step in finding jobs is knowing when to look. If the jobs in which you are interested are only advertised during a narrow part of the year, you may be frustrated if you miss the window. With that in mind, as you monitor the job market during your PhD program, as Chapter 2 encouraged you do, note any patterns to the timing of advertisements in your field.

Non-academic jobs are typically advertised all year long and feature a fairly short wait from the time the job is posted to the time when the successful applicant is expected to begin work. For academic jobs, the timing is more cyclical and the delay before starting work is longer. Most tenure-track academic jobs in the US are advertised in the summer and fall of the year before a new hire is expected to begin work. Thus, you may need to submit an application in September 2025 for a position that will begin in August 2026. Academic jobs in Europe are often advertised in the late spring or early summer to start the following fall, although some hiring follows the US schedule. Postdoctoral fellowships may appear at almost any time in the year, although they often follow the same patterns as tenure-track jobs. Many visiting professor positions in the US are advertised in the spring, to start in the coming August, as departments look to cover the courses taught by tenure-track faculty members who are departing to take positions elsewhere. If you are planning an academic job search, especially in the US, it is advantageous to start looking for jobs (and to be ready to apply for them) about a year before you expect to finish your degree. You do not need to have a completed PhD in hand to apply for a tenure-track job or postdoctoral fellowship. Many institutions are willing to make offers to PhD candidates, contingent on them completing their PhD before the start of their contract.

You can find jobs through the websites and mailing lists you identified in Chapter 2. As described in Chapter 2, academic jobs will often be posted on a jobs board hosted by the relevant academic discipline, as well as general higher education websites. Government jobs will be posted on a government website. Some nonprofit job opportunities are aggregated by sites like Devex .com and Idealist.org. Identify multiple places to look for jobs, since no one site will capture all of the available positions. Check these sites at least twice per week while you are on the hunt.

For jobs outside of the academic and government space, you should go beyond aggregator websites to research job opportunities at individual employers. The team at Beyond Professoriate (2021a), a website dedicated to helping graduate students find non-academic careers, stresses the importance of building a LinkedIn profile, identifying employers for whom you would like to work, and then setting up a Job Alert for each employer in which you are interested.

If you are not sure which nonprofit or corporate employers would suit you best, you can do informational interviews to help you find the most suitable ones. Informational interviews are a chance to talk with someone about the work they do and how they got their job (Beyond the Professoriate 2021b). Some guidance on how to do an informational interview is referenced under Additional Resources at the end of this chapter (cf. Polk and Wood 2018).

Networking will also help you find jobs. Most academic and government jobs are advertised publicly. However, if you have contacts within the organization, you may hear about when a new job is likely to be posted. A colleague may even send you the job ad as soon as it is public, eliminating any chance that you might overlook it in your web searches. For nonprofit and corporate sector jobs, networking becomes more crucial. Employers may reach out to their networks to find likely candidates and invite them to apply. The job may still be advertised publicly, but only briefly or in a pro forma way.

If you have used your summers or spare time for interning, consulting, or volunteering, you may already have a network of contacts. You can reach out to them with tailored, individual emails letting them know that you are on the market and asking them to tell you of any opportunities of which they hear. (Do not ask them directly for a job at their organization; this can across as presumptuous and off-putting.) If you do not have a network yet or are looking to expand yours, doing informational interviews can help you build one (Beyond the Professoriate 2021b).

The scale of your search should reflect the kind of job you are seeking. Jobs in academia are scarce, and you will hamstring your search if you begin by telling yourself that you will only accept jobs in a certain region, in a major city, or at a premier research university (Perlmutter 2012). If you want an academic position, you should consider working in more teaching-oriented schools. You may even consider working at a two-year institution (i.e., a community college), especially if preferences or circumstances have led you to cultivate a substantial teaching portfolio, which is valued by these schools (Jenkins 2012). If your personal situation permits it, you should also consider jobs overseas (Kelskey 2018). Conversely, if you are looking for a non-academic job, you may need to make a more narrow, focused search. Depending on your field, there may be many more non-academic jobs available than academic jobs, but locating those jobs will require more time and networking than for an academic search. To effectively market yourself, you must understand the needs of a particular set of employers and learn how to speak their language (Denicolo, Reeves, and Duke 2014). Therefore, to maximize the efficiency and effectiveness of your search, you will want to focus on a single field (cf., Beyond the Professoriate 2021c).

EXERCISE 13.1: KNOWING WHERE TO LOOK

Use the following questions to make sure that you are ready to find appropriate jobs. Answer the questions separately for each job field in which you are interested.

1. Where are jobs in your field most commonly posted? Identify several websites that specifically cater to your field or often post jobs in your specialty.
2. When are jobs in the field most commonly advertised? If necessary, look at a jobs board that includes old postings to determine if there are peak seasons for jobs to be posted.
3. How can you set up feeds or alerts so that job advertisements are directed to your inbox?
4. Do you need contacts in the field who can help alert you to upcoming job openings? If so, how can you expand your network? At which organizations would you request an informational interview?

Understanding Employer Needs

To maximize your chances of getting an interview and being hired, you will need to identify the specific needs of prospective employers and market yourself as someone who can meet those needs well (Van Bavel, Lewis, and Cunningham 2019). Some graduate students seeking academic positions look at the state of the job market and, seeing the scarcity of jobs, assume that getting an academic job is a bit like winning the lottery (Perlmutter 2012). Their response is akin to the lottery-playing strategy of buying as many tickets as possible. They send out generic applications for every position for which they are remotely qualified, with little attention to the specifics of the job description or how it aligns with their own skills and experiences. Unfortunately, there is no such thing as a one-size-fits-all cover letter or CV. Any effort to create one generates something that is a perfect fit for almost no one. In a highly competitive job market, where employers can pick from many well-qualified candidates, you need to be a near-perfect fit to win a job. Therefore, this approach of sending out dozens of generic applications *does* turn the job search into a lottery: the student is waiting to chance across the employer that happens to be seeking exactly what is contained in the student's generic application. When I meet someone who says they applied for dozens of positions to get one interview, I do not take that as a fair indicator of the poor state of the job market or as a signal that they are underqualified. I take it as an indicator that they have not fully understood the importance of identifying employer needs and marketing themselves to meet them.

To identify employer needs, begin by dissecting the job ad. The typical job advertisement will begin by describing the sort of candidate the employer is seeking, including core competencies and subject matter expertise. Sometimes a description of the core qualifications will be followed by a discussion of optional criteria, often prefaced by the words, "The ideal candidate will have…" or "Preference will be given to applicants who have…" followed by additional qualifications. The job requirements and bonus criteria may also be formatted (or repeated) in bulleted lists of "Required Qualifications" or "Minimum Qualifications," and "Desired Qualifications." Many advertisements will also include a list of job responsibilities and a description of the employing organization.

Parse these statements carefully. First, make sure that you qualify for the position. Competition for academic positions is high, so employers rarely have to settle for candidates who do not meet their minimum qualifications. If the position is for a faculty member with expertise in US constitutional law, and you have only studied international relations, there is little reason to apply.

For non-academic positions, you may still want to make an application if you think that you can make an argument for why you could do well the job the employer needs done. If an NGO or business needs to hire someone quickly for a time-sensitive contract or is having trouble filling a role, they may be willing to be flexible about their criteria if they can be convinced that doing so will not endanger the success of their operations. You can use targeted inquiries to help you judge. For instance, if the minimum qualifications are for someone with three years of professional experience and you only have two, you may want to contact the employer to find out if they would consider your application. We will discuss making inquiries more below.

If you meet the minimum qualifications and are interested in the position, the next step is to make a list detailing exactly what the employer is seeking. When I am preparing to apply for a position, I usually open a new Word document and begin making a bulleted list of things the employer wants in a candidate, such as an ability to teach specific courses, mentor doctoral students, or teach online. I also look for language that describes how the employer sees their ideal candidate, such as someone with "a passion for teaching" or "cutting-edge research." I copy this language verbatim, in quotation marks, onto my list as well. If some items or themes repeat in different parts of the ad, I cluster the related bullet points together.

Once you have parsed the job ad, you should begin researching the organization itself. Pull up the employer's website and look for information on the organization's history, mission, projects, or distinctive features (Joy 2013b). Examine these for indicators of the organization's culture and priorities that are not communicated in the advertisement. A regional university may pride itself on serving non-traditional students or military veterans. An NGO may see itself as a voice for the voiceless or an advocate for nonpartisan, data-driven policies. For-profit corporations also have mission statements that reflect their values or long-term goals. Note whatever you find in your bullet point list, especially key phrases that are repeated in the organization's descriptions of itself or its work. You will want to signal in your application that you support (or can see yourself supporting) the mission or approach the organization favors.

In your research, you may find indications of job responsibilities that were not listed in the job ad. For instance, I was once applying for a job at a liberal arts college that prided itself on giving every student the opportunity to do research with a faculty member. While "mentoring undergraduates in research" was not a responsibility listed in the job ad, I made a note on my bulleted list to reference my experience in this area. Common unstated job responsibilities or desired abilities for faculty include things like student advising and helping students with professional networking. Non-academic jobs may focus on research but implicitly include communicating research outputs to clients or the public. You can discuss your abilities in these areas if you have space available in your application.

Many organizations also hire for "fit." Unfortunately, hiring for fit has often become an excuse for hiring people who "click" with the hiring manager or committee because they come from a similar socio-economic background or share their personality, preferences, or experiences (Spiegelman 2021; Rivera 2012). This is problematic and often unjust, particularly when it reinforces sexism or racial discrimination in hiring (cf., Ghosh 2021). However, the underlying concept is less pernicious. When used as intended, cultural fit focuses on "the likelihood that someone will reflect and/or be able to adapt to the core beliefs, attitudes, and behaviors" of an organization, not the hirers themselves (Bouton 2015). This can increase job satisfaction, decrease employee turnover, and help sustain the values or practices that have made the organizations successful (Bouton 2015; Spiegelman 2021).

Recognizing how you fit the organization can create an additional opportunity for marketing yourself. Find an organizational chart that shows who else is working in the unit where you hope to be hired. Examine any public bios they have and consider what they are communicating about their values. This can tell you something about the culture of the unit and give you ideas about how to best frame your own qualifications. For instance, if employees highlight the grants that they have won or their methodological expertise, then you may want to do the same in your application. If they all focus on their teaching and their commitment to students, it may be good to structure your cover letter to focus on your teaching approach more than your ambitious research agenda.

After you have learned all you can from the job ad and the employer website, you can make a direct inquiry to the employer to gather more details. There are often details that are lacking in the job description that can be gained through a careful inquiry. For instance, the description for an academic job may request a scholar with expertise in American government, but not mention any specific courses she or he will teach. Nonetheless the search committee may have particular courses that they know need coverage. Learning what these are can allow you to further refine your application letter. Instead of just telling the hiring committee that you are an excellent teacher or have expertise in a general area, you can tell them about how you are an excellent teacher who is enthusiastic about the particular subjects they need taught.

Inquiries are especially useful if you find a position interesting but you are not sure if you have what the employer is seeking. For instance, you may think that your year of doing doctoral fieldwork in a certain geographic area provides you with the "experience working in the region" that the job requires, but you are not sure if the employer will agree. Or you may do research on Algeria and be wondering if the employer means to include North Africa when they say they seek a candidate "specializing in the Middle East." It takes much less time to write an inquiry email than it does to prepare a whole application packet, so you will save time if you use inquiries to eliminate positions for which you are unlikely to be hired.

To gain information about an academic position, reach out to the search chair or designated contact person. Many advertisements for academic positions list a contact person whom potential candidates can contact for more information. If one is not listed (or if the listed person is in the university's human resources department), you can call or email the department conducting the search and ask for the name of the search chair. Once you have that person's name, find them and their email address on the department website. Write them a short email explaining in two or three sentences that you are interested in and enthusiastic about the position, and are hoping to gain some additional details. Then pose two or three questions to gather the details in which you are interested. I often attach my CV to the email as well, particularly if I have asked a question that relates to whether they would find me a suitable candidate. This gives them more information on which to base their reply and gets my CV in front of at least one committee member early. If they think my CV looks good, they may keep an eye out for my materials when the review of applications starts.

For non-academic positions, it may be more difficult to make targeted inquiries, particularly for larger organizations where hiring is managed through a human resources department. However, you can reach out to any contacts you have who are already employed with the organization. Be careful to frame your enquiries in a way that makes clear that you want to clarify points listed in the public job advertisement or learn about the hiring process, not gain an unfair advantage. Large organizations may have applications pre-screened by human resources before a hiring committee or manager ever sees them. Your contacts may be able to tell you about the idiosyncrasies of that process, including how to prepare your application materials so that they score well when the human resources department evaluates the applications.

EXERCISE 13.2: ASSESSING EMPLOYER NEEDS

Select one job posting in which you are genuinely interested. If you are work-ing with a friend, you may want to try both assessing the same job and then comparing your notes.

1. What specific skills and attributes does the advertisement request in a candidate?
2. What are the organization's values? What characteristics define its culture?
3. What additional job responsibilities, if any, can you identify by reviewing the organization's website?
4. Who would you contact to request additional information about the job?
5. What additional information would you request?

Telling a Story

Once you know what a prospective employer is seeking, your goal is to con-vince them that you can meet their needs well. This involves presenting your-self as someone who is not only qualified for the position, but who will also be an asset to the organization and a good colleague (Joy 2014; Neymotin 2017). You will do this through your CV or résumé and your cover letter, as well as during any subsequent interviews.

You can think about this process as akin to crafting an argument. Your goal is to convince the employer that you will meet and even exceed their needs. Review the list of points that you have assembled using the job advertisement, the organization's website, and any contacts you have with the employer. Think about what you want to tell the employer about yourself that will convince them of your ability to do the job and support the success of the organization. This should become the conclusion of your argument. To help focus your thinking, you may even want to craft a concluding statement, a few sentences long, that says, in essence, "…and because of my experiences and education, I am someone who can do [Point 1], [Point 2], and [Point 3] for your organization." These points are the "punch lines" to your story "that will make you an attractive candidate for the job" (Ratcliffe 2015).

Next, work backwards through your personal and professional history to support your claims. Validate your claims to competence or expertise by discussing your publications, awards, work experience, or conference presentations. Highlight the personal background that has given you a comparative advantage in researching certain topics. Explain how your passion for the employer's mission has driven your educational and professional choices, and prepared you to excel in the advertised role.

To organize your ideas, create a short document outlining your argument. Use your list of employer desires as a starting point, turning each one into a heading or subheading. Order them in the way that you think reflects the employer's priorities or – for points that are of equal importance – organizing them in a way that will create a narrative flow. Then note under each point the personal characteristics or signifiers that support your clam.

Whatever does not fit into this outline should be omitted. Because you are writing about yourself, it can be tempting to include everything that you value about yourself or to want the employer to see you in a certain way. Resist that temptation. Your goal here is to get a job. Therefore, you want to include the details that the employer will value most, not those that you value most. You do not want important points to be overlooked because they are embedded in information that is distracting or irrelevant to the employer.

Some students find the process of self-presentation uncomfortable, especially if they come from a culture with a strong personal-professional divide. They may want their accomplishments to stand for themselves, without having to connect those accomplishments to who they are as a person. If you share this discomfort or concern, my encouragement to you is to remember that this is still, fundamentally, a professional activity. You are doing your potential employer a service by making it easier for them to see how you would serve the needs of their organization. You do not have to bare your soul or explain who you are at a personal level. Indeed, you should tell different stories about yourself to different audiences, not as a matter of deception but as a matter of communication. Your value to different employers will be different, and you will present yourself in different ways to communicate your value to each distinct audience.

To give a personal example, I am a Christian. Following Jesus has been the core objective of my life since my freshman year of college, when some friends invited me to a Bible study and I felt, as I read the Book of Mark, like I was seeing Jesus as a real, living person with whom I wanted to be in a close relationship. The experience changed my life. I eventually led Bible studies in college myself and then went on to work for several years as an advisor and mentor to Christian college students under the auspices of a national nonprofit organization. Naturally, my faith and the activities into which it has led me are very important to me. However, if I am applying for a job teaching international relations at a secular institution I omit them entirely from my application; they simply are not relevant. If I am applying for a job teaching about nonprofits or nongovernmental organizations at a secular university, I may describe myself as a former practitioner with four years of experience working with a faith-based nonprofit, because this is the aspect of my story that is most relevant to the job. Only if I were to apply for a job at a Christian university where faculty are expected to be spiritual mentors would I describe how my own experiences in college and afterwards have given me a passion for students' spiritual development.

EXERCISE 13.3: MAKING YOUR CASE

Look again at the list of employee characteristics you developed in Exercise 13.2, and answer these questions as if you were applying for the job:

1. What is it that the employer most needs to know about you to make a decision to hire you?
2. How do you want to present yourself to the employer? What story would you tell them about the kind of employee you would be?
3. What accomplishments or characteristics would you use to back up your claims? Note specific characteristics or accomplishments that you would want to reference for each qualification or attribute the employer is seeking.

Curriculum Vitae or Résumé

The first tool you will use in communicating your argument is a curriculum vitae (CV) or a résumé. This book has mostly used the term CV, since CVs are used for academic jobs and most academics talk about adding accomplishments to their CV. However, practitioner job applications more commonly use résumés. Both documents represent an accounting of your professional experience and related accomplishments. An academic CV typically includes one's education, academic positions held, courses taught, grants and awards won, publications, and conference presentations. It may also include non-academic work experience, professional service, professional memberships, language abilities, or places you have conducted fieldwork. A résumé may omit some of these, depending on the field, and include more details about previous jobs, such as specific job responsibilities, projects completed, number of people supervised, or size of budget managed. It may also include more details about professional qualifications and certifications, or note trainings completed. Looking at the documents posted online by current employees in your field, as you did in Chapter 2, should give you an indication of which one is most appropriate for your job search and what information is commonly included.

Regardless of which type you are using, you should begin by creating a master document that includes all your relevant information and qualifications. (Because of the differences in content and format, you may want to create a separate master CV and master résumé if you are applying for both academic and non-academic positions.) Include in the master document every signifier that might be relevant to your future career. Update it regularly. If you have an article that moves from "in progress" to "accepted," for instance, update your document. If you make another conference presentation or win an award, add the information. It is far easier to keep your CV updated than to create a new one from scratch when you go on the market.

Format your CV or résumé to make it visually attractive and easy for a reader to find the most relevant information (Van Bavel, Lewis, and Cunningham 2019). How to best do this can be fairly technical; the *Chronicle of Higher Education* had a long-running column called The CV Doctor just dedicated to helping students and junior faculty create effective CVs. I encourage you to read these old columns or find similar guidance from someone working in your field. You can also model your CV or résumé on documents others in your field have posted online. Make sure to review a sample of at least six to ten documents to find the most common format rather than just using the first document you find. After you have created a draft document, you can also contact your university's office of Career Services and meet with a professional who can review your document and offer advice on how to improve it.

Once you have a master document, you will edit it for each job. Think of the story you want to tell the employer about yourself and your suitability for their position, and then revise your CV or résumé to tell this story (Joy 2013a). For instance, when applying for a job at a liberal arts college or teaching-focused university, you may arrange your CV to highlight your teaching. When applying for a postdoc or research-focused position, you may arrange it to highlight your research. For positions where the employer emphasizes preparing students for the job market, you might include any work history you have as a practitioner; for other positions, you may omit this.

Your goal is to use your CV or résumé to start making the case you outlined. Include everything that shows your suitability for the position. Omit things that might be irrelevant or distracting or do not tell the right story. Emphasize your suitability by arranging the information so that the most important pieces come early and are easy to find.

EXERCISE 13.4: THE DOCUMENTS

1. Does your preferred field of employment use a CV or a résumé?
2. How is this document typically formatted?
3. What kinds of information are included?
4. What information would you include in making your own master document?
5. Looking at your own signifiers, what information would you include/ exclude if you were applying for the job you reviewed in Exercise 13.2?
6. How would you organize your document to highlight the accomplishments or qualifications most relevant to the job you identified in Exercise 13.2?

The Cover Letter

The second document you will use to communicate your argument is a cover letter. The cover letter continues and refines the process of presenting yourself as an advantageous hire by highlighting the most important parts of your CV or résumé and adding additional details that tie them together. It provides a more complete picture of who you are as a candidate and how you would perform as an employee.

To draft your letter, refer to the draft argument you outlined in Exercise 13.3. Review what things the employer requires, what else they have indicated they desire, and what bonus features – unasked for things that nonetheless reflect their interests – might set you apart. Your goal is to present an argument for why you could do the job in question extremely well (Joy 2013b).

Write a separate paragraph for each point or cluster of points, beginning with the explicit requirements and then proceeding to the bonus features. Start each paragraph with a clear thesis statement that encapsulates how you meet the employer's requirements. This should not be a mere repetition of the language from the job ad, but rather something that is specific to you. For instance, if the requirement is for someone who can do a project assessment in Ghana, you might write, "I have extensive experience conducting research in West Africa." For a position requiring strong undergraduate teaching skills, you might write "I use robust and innovative pedagogical techniques to cultivate student engagement." Clear thesis statements will help someone quickly reviewing your letter know that you satisfy the job requirements and perhaps exceed them.

After you provide this thesis statement, you can support it by providing specific details or examples in the rest of the paragraph. You do not need to repeat everything that is in your CV or résumé, although you will want to highlight your most valuable accomplishments to ensure that they are not overlooked (Joy 2013b; Van Bavel, Lewis, and Cunningham 2019). Instead, use this space to include the sort of material that does not appear on your CV or résumé, such as details about how you teach or how your language skills complement your qualitative approach to research.

When you are done with these body paragraphs, draft an introduction that quickly and concisely previews your argument and a conclusion that summarizes it. The whole letter should generally be no more than two pages, with normal margins and a standard font.

Writing a cover letter is as much an art as a science. I encourage you to download and study several examples from your field. You will find many online. Just as listening to music is an important part of learning how to play it, reading cover letters will help you learn to write one. In general, however, the key thing to remember is that you are telling a story to the prospective employer. The conclusion of that story is not, "Hire me, I'm incredible!" but rather, "Hire me, I will make your organization very happy with how well I can do the job you need done."

EXERCISE 13.5: THE COVER LETTER

Review your answers to Exercise 13.2 and Exercise 13.3. If you were applying for the job you have been examining:

1. What would you discuss in your cover letter? In what order? Make an outline of your letter.
2. Following your outline, write a thesis statement for each paragraph in your cover letter. These statements should preview the contents of the paragraph and have an easily discernable connection to a qualification or characteristic the employer is seeking.
3. Note under each thesis statement the specific experiences, accomplishments, or personal qualities you would reference to support it.
4. If possible, have a friend review the job ad and your outline. Ask them if the links between your claims and the employee needs are clear and intuitive, and whether it is clear from your outline that you can meet or exceed all the job requirements.

Interviewing

The process of presenting yourself as an excellent future employee continues when you are invited to interview. Your goal is to project yourself as someone who will do an excellent job meeting your employer's needs and whom they can see as someone who will work well with them. This will require more preparation and a people-focused approach to the interview process.

Once you have been invited for an interview, you should reflect carefully on what a prospective employer is likely to ask you (Joy 2014). You can find common interview questions for various fields posted online (cf., Neymotin 2017). Spend some time thinking in detail about how you would answer these in a clear, concise way. If possible, include in your answer references to the signifiers that will reinforce the story you want to tell your employer.

For instance, when you go on an academic job interview, you should expect to be asked about the kinds of classes you would teach and how you would teach them. Therefore, before you go, you should review the curriculum and highlight the different courses you could teach. When you are asked about what you would be interested in teaching, you can then name specific courses in the catalog. Since a committee is likely to follow up with questions about how you would teach those courses, you should also reflect on possible readings or lessons. For non-academic jobs, the questions will look different but the process is the same: figure out what the employer is likely to ask you and prepare a careful answer that will highlight your ability to meet their needs. Practice your answers orally; you can even record yourself and listen to the recording (Joy 2014). The process will help you think through your answers and develop a smooth, concise delivery.

You also want to establish rapport with the people who are interviewing you. They are examining how you would function as a future colleague or team member, in addition to your professional competence (Neymotin 2017). American academic interviews even typically include a dinner with members of the committee. The first step in developing rapport is making sure that you know everyone's names, titles, and background. I recommend finding the biography or CV of each interviewer before you go to the interview. Review them thoroughly so that you know their names, responsibilities, and key accomplishments. You may also want to download and skim one or two recent publications from each committee member if you are applying for a research-focused job, so that you can signal that you are familiar with the committee members' work and respond well to any questions about potential collaborations.

During the interview itself, it is important to ask questions as well as answer them. You do not have to respond to every interview question with an immediate answer; you can ask questions of your own to probe the questioner's thinking and elicit more details. This can signal your interest in the question and help you craft a more specific answer. For instance, if an interviewer were to ask you how you would teach a certain class, you might ask how large the class usually is and what prerequisites, if any, students in it have taken. You could then give a response that integrates those details, for example, "With a class of 25 students who have already covered the introductory material, I would probably take a project-based learning approach, using small groups of 5 students each…"

There will also be an opportunity during an interview for you to ask questions about the position. Think of what you will ask before you go. Do not make your questions, "What is the salary range?" or "How much time off would I get?" Save these kinds of questions for the negotiation conversation that will happen after you get a job offer. Instead, ask questions that will help you envision how you would do the job or how you would integrate into the professional community. For instance, asking at a liberal arts college, "What are faculty-student interactions like outside of class?" signals that you know that such schools function as small communities and that you are interested in being a community member. Asking about research support at a large research university or a think tank signals that you are looking for the resources that will help you do your job better.

When the interview is over, make sure to write a letter to the search committee chair or lead interviewer within the next few days. Express your appreciation for their time and that of any other employees who participated. Thank them for the opportunity to learn about their organization, and note that you look forward to hearing from them soon. This will help leave a positive impression.

Conclusion

As with each skill taught in this book, succeeding on the job market requires learning, planning, and acting. You will need to research the job market for the type of work in which you are interested, learn where and when jobs are advertised, and devise a system for finding and tracking job opportunities. Once you have identified likely jobs, you will need to parse the advertisements and study the prospective employers. Finally, you will need to act, developing an appropriate CV or résumé and cover letter and, hopefully, engaging in an interview.

Cultivating these skills should not wait until the final year of your PhD. If you develop a system for tracking jobs early in your doctoral studies, you can develop a high degree of familiarity with the job market by the time you are ready to begin submitting applications. When you see particularly interesting jobs, you can practice parsing the job ad and researching the employer. You can practice inquiring about jobs by talking with faculty members in your department about searches going on at your university or discussing with mentors you cultivate elsewhere about searches in their organizations. You will develop a CV or résumé when making your applications for scholarships, grants, or summer internships. Keeping this up-to-date will streamline your job application process.

The goal of this book has been to help you prepare for the job market by building a portfolio of professional accomplishments linked to your comparative advantage and personal brand. If you have done so, you should be well prepared to find a position. You may not find your ideal position, but you should be able to find work that is meaningful and remunerative, and uses well the skills you have acquired as a doctoral student. Once you have landed that first job, you may find that it suits you better than you expected and, if not, you will be able to use the experience you have gained to seek other positions that fit you better.

Recommended Readings

Joy, S. (2013). Academic CVs: 10 irritating mistakes. *The Guardian*, 1 November 2013.

Joy, S. (2013). Academic cover letters: 10 top tips. *The Guardian*, 28 November 2013.

Neymotin, F. (2017). A short interviewing guide: Navigating the interview process in a competitive academic job market. *Academe*, September–October 2017.

Perlmutter, D. (2012). Embrace your inner North Dakotan. *The Chronicle of Higher Education*, 12 August 2012.

Van Bavel, J., Lewis, N., & Cunningham, W. (2019). In the tough academic job market, two principles can help you maximize your chances. *Science*, 10 July 2019.

Additional Resources

Beyond the Professoriate. (2021). From informational interview to job offer: 4 Proven steps. Available at: https://beyondprof.com/from-informational-interview-to-job -offer/. Accessed 28 October 2021

Jenkins, R. (2012). What graduate students want to know about community colleges, part 1. *The Chronicle of Higher Education*, 22 April 2012.

Polk, J., & Wood, L. M. (2018). Connecting on LinkedIn. *Inside Higher Ed*, 30 May 2018.

Ratcliffe, R. (2015). Applying for a postdoc job? Here are 18 tips for a successful application. *The Guardian*, 1 February 2015.

Rivera, L. A. (2012). Hiring as cultural matching: The case of elite professional service firms. *American Sociological Review*, 77(6), 999–1022.

References

24Slides (2018). The exhaustive guide to preparing conference presentations. Available at: https://24slides.com/presentbetter/preparing-conference-presentation. Accessed 16 September 2021.

AAUP (2010). *Tenure and Teaching-Intensive Appointments*. Washington, DC: American Association of University Professors.

Aldritch, J. (2016). 9 Tips to help you rock your first (or next) conference presentation. Available at: https://www.invisionapp.com/inside-design/tips-for-conference-presentations/. Accessed 16 September 2021.

Altmetric (n.d.). What are altmetrics? Available at: https://www.altmetric.com/about-altmetrics/what-are-altmetrics/. Accessed 21 September 2021.

Archibugi, D. (2021). Choosing your mentor: A letter to creative minds. *Journal of Innovation Economics & Management*, 36(3), 103–115.

ARNOVA (2021). Graduate diversity scholars and leaders professional development workshop. Available at: https://www.arnova.org/page/DiversityGradApp. Accessed 30 September 2021.

Banoo, D., & Gutmman, M. (2018). From detour to deliberate. *Inside Higher Ed*, 1 May 2018.

Bassey, A. (n.d.). Reasons why every PhD student should attend academic conferences. Taylor & Francis. Available at: https://authorservices.taylorandfrancis.com/phd-conferences/. Accessed 6 September 2021.

Belcher, W. L. (ed.) (n.d.). Journals ranking. *In Reviews of Peer-Reviewed Journals*. Available at: https://journalreviews.princeton.edu/ranking-peer-reviewed-journals/. Accessed 21 September 2021.

Belcher, W. L. (2009). Parsing the decision letter. *The Chronicle of Higher Education*, February 2009.

Beyond the Professoriate. (2021a). Launch your non-academic job search: 20 Things PhDs can do right now. Available at: https://beyondprof.com/non-academic-job-search/. Accessed 28 October 2021.

Beyond the Professoriate. (2021b). From informational interview to job offer: 4 Proven steps. Available at: https://beyondprof.com/from-informational-interview-to-job -offer/. Accessed 28 October 2021.

Beyond the Professoriate. (2021c). Nonacademic job search: The #1 mistake PhDs make. Available at: https://beyondprof.com/mistake-phds-make-nonacademic-job-search/. Accessed 28 October 2021.

Borrego, M., Choe, N. H., Nguyen, K., & Knight, D. B. (2021). STEM doctoral student agency regarding funding. *Studies in Higher Education, 46*(4), 737–749.

Bouton, K. (2015). Recruiting for cultural fit. *Harvard Business Review,* 17 July 2015.

Brabazon, T. (2013). 10 Truths a PhD supervisor will never tell you. *Times Higher Education,* 11 January 2013.

Brienza, C. (2014). Why you (yes, you!) should write book reviews. *Inside Higher Ed,* 5 December 2014.

Brill, D. (2007). Find funding fast. *New Scientist, 196*(2635–2636), 78–79.

Brown, S. A. (2019). Britain's EU referendum: How did political science rise to the challenge? An assessment of online contributions during the campaign. *European Political Science, 18*(1), 97–111.

Bryman, A. (2012). *Social Research Methods,* 4th ed. Oxford: Oxford University Press.

Burka, J., & Yuen, L. (2008). *Procrastination: Why You Do It, What to Do about It Now.* Cambridge: Da Capo Press.

Calarco, J. M. (2020). *A Field Guide to Grad School: Uncovering the Hidden Curriculum.* Princeton: Princeton University Press.

Carlin, D., & Perlmutter, D. (2006). Advising the new advisor. *The Chronicle of Higher Education,* 5 September 2006.

Carmel, R. G., & Paul, M. W. (2015). Mentoring and coaching in academia: Reflections on a mentoring/coaching relationship. *Policy Futures in Education, 13*(4), 479–491.

Cassuto, L. (2011). Changing the way we socialize doctoral students. *The Chronicle of Higher Education,* 10 January 2011.

Cassuto, L. (2016). How to fire your advisor. *The Chronicle of Higher Education,* 28 February 2016.

Center for Creative Leadership (2020). Women need a network of champions. Available at: https://www.ccl.org/articles/leading-effectively-articles/why-women-need-a -network-of-champions/. Accessed 18 November 2021.

Chaloux, K. (2016). Choosing the right journal for your manuscript: 4 Steps to finding the right fit. *The Wiley Network.* Available at: https://www.wiley.com/network/ researchers/preparing-your-article/choosing-the-right-journal-for-your-manuscript-4 -steps-to-finding-the-right-ldquo-fit-8221. Accessed 21 September 2021.

Chan, J. (2012). The plans. Available at: https://phdcomics.com/comics/archive.php ?comicid=1527. Accessed 19 October 2021.

Chapman, D. D., Wiessner, C. A., Morton, J., Fire, N., Jones, L. S., & Majekodunmi, D. (2009). Crossing scholarly divides: Barriers and bridges for doctoral students attending scholarly conferences. *New Horizons in Adult Education and Human Resource Development, 23,* 6–24.

Chasan-Taber, L. (2018). 10 Tips for successful grant-writing. *The Chronicle of Higher Education,* 14 February 2018.

Clauset, A., Arbesman, S., & Larremore, D. B. (2015). Systematic inequality and hierarchy in faculty hiring networks. *Science Advances, 1*(1), 1–6.

Collins, B. (2020). The pomodoro technique explained. *Forbes*, 3 May 2020.

Cooper, C. A. (2008). Reassessing conference goals and outcomes: a defense of presenting similar papers at multiple conferences. *PS: Political Science & Politics*, 41(2), 293–295.

Covey, S. R. ([1989] 2020). *The 7 Habits of Highly Effective People*. New York: Simon & Schuster.

Davis, B. G. (1993). *Tools for Teaching*, 1st edition. San Francisco: John Wiley & Sons.

DeLonzor, D. (2003). *Never Be Late Again: 7 Cures for the Punctually Challenged*. San Francisco: Post Madison Publishing.

Demirtaş, H. (2016). The relationship between university students' perceptions of faculty members' undesirable behaviors, their trust for faculty members and class participation. *International Online Journal of Educational Sciences*, 8(4).

Denicolo, P., Reeves, J., & Duke, D. (2014). Leaving academia? How to sell yourself to new employers. *The Guardian*, 10 Jan 2014.

Dickerson, J. (2020). The questions that will get me through the pandemic. *The Atlantic*, 22 June 2020.

Dometrius, N. C. (2008). Academic double-dipping: Professional Profit or Loss? *PS: Political Science & Politics*, 41(2), 289–292.

Dunleavy, P. (2003). *Authoring a PhD: How to plan, draft, write and finish a doctoral thesis or dissertation*. New York: Macmillan International Higher Education.

Economist. (2020). Garbage in: How to spot dodgy academic journals. *The Economist*, 30 May 2020 edition.

Eleftheriades, R., Fiala, C., & Pasic, M. D. (2020). The challenges and mental health issues of academic trainees. *F1000Research*, 9, 104.

Garland, J., & Giles, M. (2011). Ranking scholarly publishers in political science: An alternative approach, *PS*, 44(2), 375–383.

Ghosh, P. (2021). Black scientists say UK research is institutionally racist. *The Guardian*, 11 Oct 2021.

Golash-Boza, T. (2018). 6 Tips for giving a fabulous academic presentation. *The Wiley Network*. Available at: https://www.wiley.com/network/researchers/promoting-your -article/6-tips-for-giving-a-fabulous-academic-presentation. Accessed 16 September 2021.

Gupta, D., & Waismel-Manor, I. (2006). Network in progress: A conference primer for graduate students. *PS: Political Science & Politics*, 39(3), 485–490.

Haggerty, K. D. (2010). Tough love: Professional lessons for graduate students. *The American Sociologist*, 41(1), 82–96.

Hake, R. R. (1998). Interactive-engagement versus traditional methods: A six-thousand-student survey of mechanics test data for introductory physics courses. *American Journal of Physics*, 66(1), 64–74.

Harnish, R. J., & Bridges, K. R. (2011). Effect of syllabus tone: Students' perceptions of instructor and course. *Social Psychology of Education*, 14(3), 319–330.

Hoalst-Pullen, N., & Patterson, M. W. (2017). *National Geographic Atlas of Beer: A Globe-trotting Journey Through the World of Beer*. Washington, DC: National Geographic Books.

Hopwood, C. J. (2010). Finding funding: Some suggestions for graduate students. *SPA Exchange*, 22(1), 8.

Horta, H., Cattaneo, M., & Meoli, M. (2018). PhD funding as a determinant of PhD and career research performance. *Studies in Higher Education*, 43(3), 542–570.

Horta, H., Cattaneo, M., & Meoli, M. (2019). The impact of Ph.D. funding on time to Ph.D. completion. *Research Evaluation, 28*(2), 182–195.

Huerta, A. (n.d.). Advice on successfully navigating the current academic job market. Tomorrow's professor postings, Stanford University. Available at: https://tomprof.stanford.edu/posting/1368. Accessed 26 June 2021.

Hyatt, L., & Williams, P. E. (2011). 21st Century competencies for doctoral leadership faculty. *Innovative Higher Education, 36*, 53–66.

Ilieş, V. I. (2018). Strategic personal branding for students and young professionals. *Cross-Cultural Management Journal, 20*(1), 43–51.

Jenkins, R. (2012). What graduate students want to know about community colleges, part 1. *The Chronicle of Higher Education*, 22 April 2012.

Jensen, D. G. (2016). Learn to read between the lines of a job ad. *Science*, 9 March 2016.

Jerven, M. (2013). *Poor Numbers: How we are misled by African Development statistics and what to do about it.* Ithaca: Cornell University Press.

Joy, S. (2013a). Academic CVs: 10 irritating mistakes. *The Guardian*, 1 November 2013.

Joy, S. (2013b). Academic cover letters: 10 top tips. *The Guardian*, 28 November 2013.

Joy, S. (2014). How to Shine in an Academic Interview. *The Guardian*, 7 February 2014.

Kelskey, K. (2011). Why Are There No Elephants? A Common Grant-Writing Error. *The Professsor Is In.* Available at: https://theprofessorisin.com/2012/11/30/why-are-there-no-elephants-a-common-grant-writing-error/. Accessed 30 September 2021.

Kelskey, K. (2014). The top 5 traits of the worst advisors. *The Professsor Is In.* Available at: https://theprofessorisin.com/2014/02/23/the-5-top-traits-of-the-worst-advisors/. Accessed 31 August 2021.

Kelskey, K. (2018). 5 Big-picture mistakes new Ph.D.s make on the job market. *The Chronicle of Higher Education*, 21 May 2018.

Kim, S., Lebovits, H., & Shugars, S. (2022). Networking 101 for Graduate Students: Building a Bigger Table. *Political Science & Politics, 55*(2), 307–312.

Lang, J. (2016). Small changes in teaching: space it out. *The Chronicle of Higher Education*, 16 May 2016.

Lang, J. (2021). Where do you do your best writing? A look at the connection between place and productivity. *Chronicle of Higher Education*, 26 July 2021.

Larson, Z. (2020). You can't kill it with kindness. *Inside Higher Ed*, 23 June 2020.

Lei, S. A. (2009). Strategies for finding and selecting an ideal thesis or dissertation topic: A review of literature. *College Student Journal, 43*(4), 1324–1333.

Lepp, L., Remmik, M., Leijen, A., & Leijen, D. A. J. (2016). Doctoral students' research stall: Supervisors' perceptions and intervention strategies, *SAGE Open, 6*(3), 1–12.

Levecque, K., Anseel, F., De Beuckelaer, A., Van der Heyden, J., & Gisle, L. (2017). Work organization and mental health problems in PhD students. *Research Policy, 46*(4), 868–879.

Levey Friedman, H. (2020). *Here She Is: The Complicated Reign of the Beauty Pageant in America.* Boston: Beacon Press.

Lishu (2021). On grad school loneliness: A mini-rant. *Medium*, 11 June 2021.

Ludwig, M. A., Bentz, A. E., & Fynewever, H. (2011). Your Syllabus Should Set the Stage for Assessment for Learning. *Journal of College Science Teaching, 40*(4), 20–23.

Marcos, C. M. (2020). The future of conference: Will events remain virtual after lockdowns? *USA Today*, 9 May 2020.

Marx, G. T. (1997). Of methods and manners for aspiring sociologists: 37 moral imperatives. *The American Sociologist*, 28(1), 102–125.

Mata, H., Latham, T. P., & Ransome, Y. (2010). Benefits of professional organization membership and participation in national conferences: Considerations for students and new professionals. *Health Promotion Practice*, 11(4), 450–453.

Miranda, E. (2021). The leaky pipeline playbook. *Insider Higher Ed*, 13 August 2021.

Montgomery, B. L. (2017). Mapping a mentoring roadmap and developing a supportive network for strategic career advancement. *Sage Open*, 7(2), 1–13.

Musgrave, P. (2021). Against academic book reviews. *The Chronicle of Higher Education*, 8 January 2021.

Mustapha, S. M., Abd Rahman, N. S. N., & Yunus, M. M. (2010). Factors influencing classroom participation: a case study of Malaysian undergraduate students. *Procedia-Social and Behavioral Sciences*, 9, 1079–1084.

Nakao, H., Ukai, I., & Kotani, J. (2017). A review of the history of the origin of triage from a disaster medicine perspective. *Acute Medicine & Surgery*, 4(4), 379–384.

National Center for Science and Engineering Statistics, National Science Foundation (2019). *Doctorate Recipients from U.S. Universities: 2018. Special Report NSF 20-301*. Alexandria, VA: National Center for Science and Engineering Statistics, National Science Foundation.

NCSL (2017). Tips for making effective powerpoint presentation. National Conference of State Legislators. Available at: https://www.ncsl.org/legislators-staff/legislative-staff/legislative-staff-coordinating-committee/tips-for-making-effective-powerpoint-presentations.aspx. Accessed 16 September 2021.

Nelson, A. (2019). The thin line between discrimination and culture fit. Interact.com 3 May 2019.

New England Center for Investigative Reporting (2014). New Analysis Shows Problematic Boom In Higher Ed Administrators. *HuffPost* 26 February 2014.

Neymotin, F. (2017). A short interviewing guide: Navigating the interview process in a competitive academic job market. *Academe*, September–October 2017.

Nisticò, R. (2015). *The Effect of PhD Funding on Post-degree Research Career and Publication Productivity*. Working Paper 362. Naples, Italy: Centre for Studies in Economics and Finance.

Olena, A. (2020). COVID-19 ushers in the future of conferences. *The Scientist*, 28 September 2020.

Pallas, C. (2010). Good morals or good business? NGO advocacy and the world bank's 10th IDA. In A. Uhlin & E. Erman (eds.), *Legitimacy Beyond the State? Re-examining the Democratic Credentials of Transnational Actors*. Basingstoke, UK: Palgrave MacMillan.

Pallas, C. (2019). Pursing the common goods: Theorizing collective action among NGOs in transnational advocacy. *Journal of Civil Society*, 15(2), 99–122.

Pallas, C., & Guidero, A. (2016). Reforming INGO accountability and representivity: Supply vs. demand-driven models. *International Studies Review*, 18(4), 614–634.

Palmer, M. S., Bach, D. J., & Streifer, A. C. (2014). Measuring the promise: A learning-focused syllabus rubric. *To Improve the Academy: A Journal of Educational Development*, 33(1), 14–36.

Palmer, M. S., Wheeler, L. B., & Aneece, I. (2016). Does the document matter? The evolving role of syllabi in higher education. *Change: The Magazine of Higher Learning*, 48(4), 36–47.

Palmer, M. S., Gravett, E. O., & LaFleur, J. (2018). Measuring transparency: A learning-focused assignment rubric. *To Improve the Academy, 37*(2), 173–187.

Paul, J., & Criado, A. R. (2020). The art of writing literature review: What do we know and what do we need to know? *International Business Review, 29*(4), 101717.

Perlmutter, D. (2012). Embrace your inner North Dakotan. *The Chronicle of Higher Education*, 12 August 2012.

Perlmutter, D. (2013). Avoiding bad advice from your colleagues. *The Chronicle of Higher Education*, 4 March 2013.

Persaud, C. (2021). Bloom's taxonomy: The ultimate guide. Available at: https://tophat.com/blog/blooms-taxonomy/. Accessed 7 October 2021.

Plume, A. (2018). What's in your basket? Evaluating journals in the modern age. *Elsevier Connect*, 18 June 2018.

Poincaré, H. (1914). *Science and Method.* Translated by F. Maitland. London: Thomas Nelson and Sons.

Polk, J., & Wood, L. M. (2018). Connecting on LinkedIn. *Inside Higher Ed*, 30 May 2018.

Potter, C. (2009). Another year, another job market: When not perfecting your tan this summer, how can you prepare? *The Chronicle of Higher Education*, 21 June 2009.

Rackham Graduate School (2020). *How to Mentor Graduate Students: A Guide for Faculty.* Ann Arbor: University of Michigan Rackham Graduate School.

Rivera, L. A. (2012). Hiring as cultural matching: The case of elite professional service firms. *American Sociological Review, 77*(6), 999–1022.

Roberts, L. R., Tinari, C. M., & Bandlow, R. (2019). An effective doctoral student mentor wears many hats and asks many questions. *International Journal of Doctoral Studies, 14*, 133–159.

Rowe, N., & Ilic, D. (2009). What impact do posters have on academic knowledge transfer? A pilot survey on author attitudes and experiences. *BMC Medical Education, 9*, 71. https://doi.org/10.1186/1472-6920-9-71

Rubin, A. (2015). Thesis advisor horror stories. *Science*, 24 Jun 2015.

Saunders, S., & Joy, S. (2014). The game of higher education: What's the best way to play it? *The Guardian*, 27 June 2014.

Schiebinger, L., & Gilmartin, S. (2010). Housework is an academic issue. Association of American University Professors. https://www.aaup.org/article/housework-academic-issue. Accessed 31 August 2021.

Simpson, D. (n.d.). 'Mysterious, surprising, and numerous': The PhD guide to conferences. https://authorservices.taylorandfrancis.com/the-phd-guide-to-conferences/ Accessed 8 September 2021.

Spiegelman, P. (n.d.). Is hiring for culture fit perpetuating bias? *Forbes*, 1 Mar 2021.

Stahl, A. (2018). Why personal branding is key to career success: And how to create yours. *Forbes*, 30 August 2018.

StickK (2021). About StickK.com/our story. Available at: https://www.stickk.com/aboutus. Accessed 16 October 2021.

Swidler, E. (2019). A modest(y) proposal. *Academe*, Spring 2019.

Tancock, C. (2017). A new fruit in the basket: how to compare apples with pears... and now plums! *Elsevier Connect*. Available at: https://www.elsevier.com/connect/editors-update/a-new-fruit-in-the-basket-how-to-compare-apples-with-pears-and-now-plums! Accessed 21 September 2021.

Times Higher Education (2017). Of monsters and mentors: PhD disasters, and how to avoid them. *Times Higher Education*, 1 June 2017.

Tobin, T. (2021). How to make the most of an academic conference. *The Chronicle of Higher Education*, 20 September 2021.

Toor, R. (2010). A writing group of two. *The Chronicle of Higher Education*, 16 December 2010.

Tyree, T. C. M. (2016). Disregarding negative statements about the failures of race-gender mentoring pairings. In Tassie, K., & Brown Givens, S. M. (eds.), *Women of Color Navigating Mentoring Relationships: Critical Examinations*. New York: Lexington Books, 143–163.

Van Bavel, J., Lewis, N., & Cunningham, W. (2019). In the tough academic job market, two principles can help you maximize your chances. *Science*, 10 July 2019.

Walvoord, B. E., & Anderson, V. J. (2010). *Effective Grading: A Tool for Learning and Assessment in College*. San Francisco: John Wiley & Sons.

Webster, J., & Watson, R. T. (2002). Analyzing the past to prepare for the future: Writing a literature review. *MIS Quarterly*, xiii–xxiii.

Wheeler, L. B., Palmer, M., & Aneece, I. (2019). Students' perceptions of course syllabi: The role of syllabi in motivating students. *International Journal for the Scholarship of Teaching and Learning*, 13(3), 7.

White, P. (2017). *Developing Research Questions: A Guide for Social Scientists*. New York: Palgrave MacMillan.

Wisker, G. (2014). PhD students: What to do if you don't work well with your supervisor. *The Guardian*, 29 December 2014.

Wolfe, B. L., & Dilworth, P. P. (2015). Transitioning normalcy: Organizational culture, African American administrators, and diversity leadership in higher education. *Review of Educational Research*, 85(4), 667–697.

Yans, G. (n.d.). 'Rainbow Children': What grad students should know about interracial mentoring. In Brock, R. (ed.), *Higher Ed: Soup to Nuts*. Published electronically by the Chronicle of Higher Education.

Index

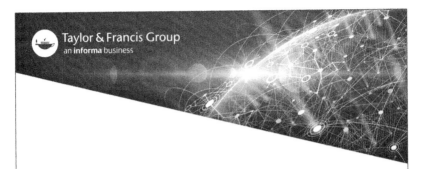

Made in the USA
Monee, IL
02 January 2025